ITCHEN COLLEGE
LRC

Please return on or before the last date stamped below

TEXTUAL EXPLORATIONS

General editors:

MICK SHORT Lancaster University
ELENA SEMINO Lancaster University

THE POETICS
OF
SCIENCE FICTION

PETER STOCKWELL

An imprint of **Pearson Education**

Harlow, England · London · New York · Reading, Massachusetts · San Francisco
Toronto · Don Mills, Ontario · Sydney · Tokyo · Singapore · Hong Kong · Seoul
Taipei · Cape Town · Madrid · Mexico City · Amsterdam · Munich · Paris · Milan

Pearson Education Limited
Edinburgh Gate
Harlow
Essex CM20 2JE
England

and Associated Companies throughout the world

Visit us on the World Wide Web at:
www.pearsoneduc.com

First published 2000

ISBN 0–582–36994–0 CSD
ISBN 0–582–36993–2 PPR

British Library Cataloguing-in-Publication Data
A catalogue record for this book is available from the British
Library.

Library of Congress Cataloging-in-Publication Data
A catalog record for this book is available from the Library of
Congress.

Set in 11/13 pt Bembo by 35
Printed and bound in Great Britain by Biddles Ltd., Guildford and King's Lynn

CONTENTS

CONTENTS

ACKNOWLEDGEMENTS

I have been reading science fiction for just a little bit less time than I have been able to use language. I have been studying both for many years, and teaching them for a few years shorter than that. In all this time, I have discussed science fiction, and language, and the linguistics of science fiction with more people than I am able to recall, so this acknowledgement is going to be shamefully brief.

Firstly, every word that appears in these pages, and all of those other words which were drafted and deleted away into unrealised parallel versions of the book, have been read by and discussed with Joanna Gavins. For reminding me that language and science fiction are supposed to be fun, and for making the universe around them a joy to live in, this book is dedicated to Joanna.

My sense of the value of stylistics was largely developed by Paul Simpson, who continues to be an inspiration and a friend. I have benefited enormously over the years from discussions and conferences within 'the village': from friends and colleagues in the Poetics and Linguistics Association (PALA), and many others involved in the academic study of science fiction, all of whom have been supportive and willing to discuss my work. I would especially like to thank Tony Bex, Teresa Bridgeman, Marilyn Burke, Michael Burke, David Cordiner, Monika Fludernik, Charles Forceville, Don Freeman, Margaret Freeman, Keith Green, Derek Littlewood, David Seed, Gerard Steen, Peter Verdonk, and Katie Wales. Cathy Emmott and Mary-Ellen Ryder were kind enough to comment on my use of their work, and I have been able to clarify my own thinking as a result.

I am grateful to the School of English at UCE, Birmingham for the study leave that enabled me to complete the book, and especially to Howard Jackson. I have had the valuable opportunity of refining my ideas by presenting my work at the Åbo Akademi, Universiteit van Amsterdam, Universität Bern, University of Birmingham, and the Universidad de Granada, and I am grateful to the staff and students at those institutions for their perceptive and testing comments. I have also learned a great deal from the many students who have taken my courses in science fiction and literary linguistics over the years, and have themselves gone on to greater things: Elliot Atkins and Louise Mullany in particular. 'No book is an island; each book rests on a library' (according to Brian Aldiss 1970: 143), and I am especially grateful to Andy Sawyer and the excellent Science Fiction Foundation archive at Liverpool University for access to the scholarship which gives this book its artificial gravity.

As an artist and a mathematician, my Mam and Dad are probably together responsible for my enjoyment of science fiction, and gave me the support over the years to enable me to think and write about it. With Sheila and Pat, and Marie-Louise and Michael, I am grateful for time and space. Parts of this book were written in Tomar, Portugal and Sykehouse in Yorkshire; I am grateful to Keith and Ute, and Deena and Gwyneth, for allowing me to invade their peaceful homes with my lap-top computer.

The general editors of this series, Elena Semino and Mick Short have ensured that the book is better than it would have been if left to its own trajectory. It is customary to end by absolving friends and colleagues from any blame. However, there must be an exception on this occasion: my exploration of the science fictional universe would never have been completed without the persistence of the general editors who must therefore bear some responsibility. In short, it's all Mick and Elena's fault, for which I am extremely grateful. I hope they think the odyssey was worth it.

P.J.S.
Nottingham

CHAPTER 1

DEPARTURES: ORIENTATION AND MAPS

COUNTDOWN: 10, 9, 8, 7, 6, 5, 4, 3, 2, 1, zero. The numerical countdown is now regarded as the symbol of century 20, representing that era's obsession with the future, 'forecasting' and the tangible passage of time. One of the common beliefs of the age was in the idea of 'progress', and human society was perceived in terms of evolution or development from primitive to sophisticated, simple to complex. The countdown was developed by rocket technicians in the former Unistates of America in order to add presentational drama to the launch of localspace vehicles (old Soviet Union rocket launches did not countdown to lift-off, but merely initiated the ignition at the appointed time). More significantly, the countdown was a sign of the measurement of the future, with the point of anticipation located by calibration in terms of seconds. It must have seemed, to the 20ers, that here was a symbol of their control of the future.

(*Encyclopedia Galactica*, 44th edition, 2099)

1.1 Preview

Time travel begins here. You are about to read the first chapter of *The Poetics of Science Fiction*. Perhaps you will read the subsequent chapters in their numerical sequence. You might jump backwards to the contents page now and again; you will in all likelihood travel forward to the references and index at the end. You might skip a chapter altogether, or dip into the stream of words at a variety of different points. Sometimes you will skim over the text; sometimes you might read each part very carefully. You might spend an hour in the book, or a few minutes scattered throughout the rest of your life. You probably won't read it through like a novel. That is not what it is. You think this first chapter was written first? You'd be wrong. Of course, you are the book's engine: when you close it, it cannot go on without you. The words require a reader. Above all, 'a book is a machine to think with' (Richards 1924: i).

In the end, the history of your reading of the book is likely to be chaotic, but if it is to be of any use, your experience of the book will need to be organised in some way. Why are you reading it in the first place? That is your business. What is it for? That is the point of this chapter.

1.2 Poetics and Science Fiction

Firstly, science fiction. This is the most singly-identifiably popular genre of literature in the Western world: 10 per cent of all fiction sold in Britain is science fiction (Davies 1990: 2); 25 per cent of all the novels published in the US are science fiction (Pohl 1989: 53). It is largely a paperback phenomenon, which puts it into the hands of the literate masses. On the basis of box-office receipts, more people go to watch science fiction at the cinema than any other sort of film. Science fiction scenarios create a psychological reality for the flashing lights and sound-effects of most computer games. Modern design and architecture over the past forty years have been informed by science fictional speculation about the future. Its influence can be seen in children's television pro-grammes, games, toys and playground culture, in the corporate imagery of large companies, and in advertising and commercials for everything from cars to jeans, chocolate bars to toothpaste. Science fiction, since overtaking poetry in the 1930s, has been the most fruitful source of any area of writing in adding new words to the Oxford English Dictionary (Delany 1977: 142), and thus to the English language.

So science fiction matters because it is popular and it is influential. It is the language of science fiction that forms the object of study of this book. By this I mean the entire system of communication that underlies the experience of reading science fiction. The organisation and pro-cessing of language is central to an understanding of science fiction, whether it is being studied as part of literary criticism, cultural history, popular culture, social psychology, or futurology. It is inconceivable to me that anyone could write about literature without knowing about language. Though the writing is an artistic enterprise, the study of it is a modern science, and the science of linguistics is the best tool for the job.

In the dim distance you might be able to hear instant objections to these statements. Listen to them, since I would not like you to read this book unquestioningly. But here are some more assertions. Science is not the discovery of truths but the search for satisfactory provisional explanations and understanding. Many literary critics are ignorant of the natural workings of language, and behave as if criticism were an art form rather than a science. Modern linguistics is the systematic study of language, with sub-disciplines dealing with, among other things, language in context, language in the mind, literary organisation, and interpretation. A scientific poetics of literature, informed by modern linguistics, can do everything that literary criticism can do, with the advantage that it is rigorously analytical, differentiates between producing interpretations and reflecting on them, and is open to informed debate. Only some literary criticism is able to do all this.

There is no space or time here for a full defence of literary linguistics or cognitive poetics. These have been elegantly constructed by, for example, Leech and Short (1981), McCarthy and Carter (1994), Carter and Simpson (1989), Short (1989, 1996), Weber (1996) and Simpson (1997). This book is concerned with the reading of science fiction. This involves many different aspects and dimensions, each of which requires different approaches. Different chapters take a theme within the overall poetics of science fiction and pursue it in the discussion. The same piece of science fiction can look quite different depending on which level of analysis is applied to it. This is because a thorough poetics is not about accounting for the text on its own and fixing a description of it; it is about finding and exercising different fruitful ways of understanding how science fiction works as a reading experience. Literary linguistics is not dissection; it is yoga (Jeffries 1993: 2).

The book is a *poetics* of science fiction (rather than, say, 'the language of science fiction') because it is also about the reading experience. This term needs some definition here. By 'poetics' I mean the linguistic and cognitive organisation of the genre. Both of these levels are inextricably linked, though in the chapters of this book the focus moves from one to the other for analytical convenience. There are some stylistic analyses of particular passages from science fiction texts. But a thorough poetics must also account for what happens when readers encounter such texts, and this involves a discussion of cognition and interpretation. The interpretations presented in the book are, of course, my own, and different readers will produce different readings. The point of a systematic account of poetics, however, is that the linguistic and cognitive patterns and processes that lead to these different readings can all be specified and discussed explicitly.

The book is concerned with the textual organisation of particular science fictional works and their effects and interpretations. In order to be a work of general poetics rather than a series of anecdotes about dozens of individual readings, the aim in every discussion is to relate the specific things science fiction does to the generic things it is able to do. I also wanted to use 'poetics' in the title in order to suggest the everyday meaning of 'poetic'. Although this is not a term which is usually found close to the words 'science fiction', poetic expression within science fictional prose is certainly a feature of the genre that I have tried to exemplify throughout the book.

1.3 How To Read This Book

In its main emphasis, this is not an introductory book to either language study or literary linguistics. There are many excellent introductions available (including Haynes 1989; Short 1996; Kuiper and Allan 1996; Jackson and Stockwell 1996; Simpson 1997; and Toolan 1998). However, I have tried to explain uses of linguistic and technical terminology as they appear in the discussion. The index can also work as a glossary: it will take you to the places a term is used, and there you will find it used in context. In my teaching of students I have found this is the best way to introduce and understand new concepts, rather than filling out a detailed but decontextualised glossary.

The chapters of the book are arranged to reflect the different levels of analysis involved in the poetics of science fiction. Analysis at the 'micro' level is sometimes required to illustrate the precise detailed workings of texts. Then analysis at the 'macro' level is needed to demonstrate connections and show how the genre works in context, in history, and as a whole. These levels are only separated for analytical convenience, and as they are mutually and interactively dependent on each other, they are threaded through each other in the course of the book. There are two macrological chapters and one micrological chapter in the first half of the book, reflecting the emphasis on history, context and sub-genres. The second half of the book focuses more on the detailed cognitive mechanics of science fictional poetics, and so there is an emphasis on the micrological. Throughout the book, however, I try to make the connections between the different levels of analysis, in order to show that the distinction is an artifice and each involves the other. Cross-referencing is included to make this even more apparent, and I have not avoided repeating myself where I think this is more useful than making you jump back to previous discussions.

Some chapters have science fiction as the focus, with linguistics as the informing background. Others are concerned to develop an argument about an aspect of language, using science fiction to do so. Science fiction is particularly useful in this respect, since it is a type of literature that stretches linguistic frameworks which are usually developed in a natural language context. However, I have tried to include an element of both of these dimensions in every chapter. I intend this both as a linguistics book and as a contribution to literary criticism.

Without trying to be all things to all readers, I have tried to provide something of interest both for established researchers in the field of science fiction study and linguistics, as well as for students interested in science fiction and language, those for whom both science fiction and linguistics are new experiences, and the general reader. As a research tool for verification of my arguments, for further study, or simply for your own intellectual entertainment, each chapter includes sections entitled *Speculations* and *Explorations*.

In the spirit of science fiction, *Speculations* take some of the ideas under discussion and suggest lines of thought away from the direct focus at hand. Some of these speculations might be highly implausible or utterly wild, or might indicate paths that linguistic investigation could take if it did not have to be so rigorous. The purpose of these sections is simply to provoke your further thought. However, you could discuss these ideas and develop them into whole different areas which I have not foreseen. Since linguistics is being treated as a science in these pages, it is only appropriate that science fictional speculation is applied to it. Practice in this sort of experimental thinking is the first step in forming new ideas and insights, which can be verified by further study.

Explorations present points for discussion or thought, and activities to do or think about doing. They represent practice in the analysis of science fictional language, and take a more practically-based view of the thought-experiments used in *Speculations*. If you are using this book as part of a course or discussion-group, these sections will be useful starting points for debate, and every one of them has been used successfully in my own explorations of science fiction with students taking my seminars. They should not be treated, though, as mechanical exercises. Some of them would take years to answer comprehensively. The

Explorations are guides to practical thinking, which you should take in whatever direction or detail you find interesting. All the bibliographical references for every text cited in the discussion or in the *Explorations* are collected together in *Further Reading*.

1.4 Prototypes of Science Fiction

Science fiction does not suffer from a lack of definitions. It is perhaps a manifestation of the scientific background of its writers, readers and critics that so many have felt the need to categorise it and pin it down with definitive statements. These have been descriptive, prescriptive, philosophical and logical, flippant and fatuous, detailed and circular. Science fiction has been called: a literary genre dealing with scientific discovery, superior or simply other than that known to exist (from the *Encyclopedia Britannica* in Jakubowski and Edwards 1983: 258); 'the search for a definition of man and his status in the universe' that is characteristically gothic (Aldiss and Wingrove 1986: 30); has been said to be based on 'cognitive estrangement' or the projection of literary defamiliarisation (Suvin 1979: 4). Writer Norman Spinrad defines it as 'anything published as science fiction' and Frederick Pohl as the 'thing that people who understand science fiction point to when they point to something and say "That's science fiction!"' (Jakubowski and Edwards 1983: 258). There are many other definitions.

The problem, of course, is that science fiction itself is very varied, and has changed over the 20th century. The more fundamental problem is that genre itself is not a thing which can be easily defined. 'A "genre definition" is a wholly imaginary object of the same ontological status as unicorns' (Delany 1989: 6, 9). Broderick (1995) has termed it a 'mode', borrowed by other genres. Recently, the discipline of cognitive linguistics has demonstrated that human categorisation itself does not seem to work on the classical pattern of discrete and uniquely identifiable groups. The notion of 'prototype effects' (Lakoff 1987; Rosch and Lloyd 1978) was developed to account for the vagueness at the edges of people's category boundaries. It seems, for example, that rather than having a mental set of 'fruit', to which certain objects belong or not, our mental representations are in the form of a radial structure, determined largely by cultural conventions and language-dependent. Central to the 'fruit' domain are objects like 'apple', 'orange', 'pear', 'banana'. Not so central are 'plums', 'nectarines', 'mangoes', for example. Peripheral fruit, for me at least, include 'star-fruit', 'tomatoes', and 'dates'.

This means that there are good and bad, better and worse, examples of fruit (or any other domain: dogs, pieces of furniture, things to drink, shades of red, literature). It also follows that objects like 'potato', or 'hazelnut', or 'rose', or 'chair', or 'spaceship' are not simply 'not-fruit', but are just very bad examples of fruit. (You can test this by putting these last few objects in order of 'fruitness'.)

This basic insight has obvious relevance for a genre definition. There are two points to note: determining the prototypical domain for a category is a matter of the perception of individuals; objects vary in their membership of categories along with differences across cultural groups. What this means for a definition of science fiction is that different readers will have different ideas of which texts count as science fiction. They will have different ideas of what criteria are more and less important in that decision. And their decisions will depend on how much experience they have of reading science fiction.

This can be demonstrated very easily by a small experiment I tried on a group of my own students. They were about to begin my science fiction course and I wanted to find out what they had been reading. I first asked them to score themselves out of 5, on a scale from reading nothing but science fiction to having read no science fiction at all. The distribution for this across the group was normal, with lots of 3s, fewer 2s and 4s, and a small number of 1s and 5s. I then gave the students a sheet with fifty names of authors and books on (including Brian Aldiss, Superman, Stephen King, George Orwell, Enid Blyton, Dracula, H.G. Wells, and so on), and asked them to indicate which they associated with science fiction, which not, and which they didn't know.

There were no 'correct' answers of course; I could have made an argument for every single one of the names on the list. What was most interesting was that a simple correlation emerged: the more science fiction the individual had read, the higher the number of items ticked as science fictional. In other words, the more you read science fiction, the more you are likely to read *as* science fiction. (Broderick (1995) claims that reading more makes you a better reader of science fiction. I would simply say that it makes the interpretations different. See Bortolussi and Dixon (1996) and Martindale and Dailey (1995) for some empirical evidence, sadly lacking in many discussions about 'readers'.) In cognitive terms, greater experience of a variety of science fiction increases the individual's prototype base for membership of the domain.

There are, for everyone, central examples of science fiction, and texts that would be considered peripheral, and this is in general a matter of cultural consensus, experience, and personal idiosyncrasy. I would prefer this approach to generic definition to attach to the texts included in this book. One of the attractions of academic work in the science fiction genre is the resistance to the idea of establishing a 'canon' of approved texts. Besides the elitism, claim to authority and authorisation, and (it must be said) nit-picking obsessive near-psychotic tidiness underlying such a tendency towards canonisation, the field of science fiction studies is simply more interesting for being so open and fluid. I hope that it remains so and that the understanding of prototype effects in generic definition helps to provide a theoretical underpinning for a rejection of the categorising syndrome.

Having come out against a canon, I must commit the sin myself in a different way. Inevitably, a book such as this, covering a whole genre, must be highly selective, and selections are never entirely random or untainted by ideological criteria. My concern with language and narrative organisation has probably foregrounded those texts that are more interesting than others from this viewpoint, though I have tried not to look only at linguistically deviant texts. Books which are also more often in print are more studied than those that are out of print, and so the field of study projects the principles of publishers and the market. I know from my own teaching that the availability of texts is a major determining factor in what is read and studied, and I must also admit the practical convenience of sometimes simply using the books I had on my shelves.

Of course, selection also involves omission. Though I certainly don't intend my selection of texts to be canonising, inevitably there are many familiar authors and texts in my study, and a book on the poetics of a genre would be strange if this were not the case. In mitigation, I have tried to look at a range of material and also discuss the parameters within which value is assigned. Nevertheless, no book such as this can be comprehensive. Though I mention them, there is not enough discussion of pre-twentieth-century science fiction, writing which is explicitly feminist, or specifically about race, not enough on the centrality of short stories to the genre, and there is a British-American bias in the range of works studied. Also, apart from a brief consideration of film, television, and electronic-based text, the focus of the book is on literary science fiction. These omissions are forced on me by the limitations of space. Where I have generalised my arguments beyond the texts directly studied, I have at least been conscious of the consequences of these restrictions.

1.5 A Very Brief History of Science Fiction

So far, I have provided a delineation of the area for study. In order to assist those readers completely new to science fiction, it would be helpful at this point to set out a very brief history of the genre. In the chapters that follow, I assume at least this much knowledge. All histories are ideological versions, of course, but what follows here is so brief as inevitably to be a caricature of the excellent histories written by Aldiss and Wingrove (1986) and James (1994). Knowledgeable science fiction readers should avert their gaze from what follows. In later chapters, I discuss some of the issues involved in the histories of the genre.

Though science fiction has precursors in ancient mythology, medieval romance, post-Renaissance fantasies and satires, and Victorian gothic, it is largely a twentieth-century phenomenon. Crudely, there is a cerebral, educated tradition from H.G. Wells, and a populist, sensational tradition from Jules Verne. The early century saw the genre polarised between philosophical speculation and pure action adventure, futurology and space opera. This was transformed by the introduction of science fiction short stories into the cheap pulp magazines in America after the First World War. Imitated in Britain, science fiction became enormously popular in the 1930s and '40s, and a new focus on rationalism and plausibility served to differentiate science fiction from fantasy. The 1940s and '50s have come to be known as the 'Golden Age' of science fiction, when many of the genre's most famous later authors were first published.

In the 1960s, beginning in Britain but involving American writers and spreading to the US, science fiction came to be interested in issues of consciousness, subjectivity, hallucination and the influence of technology on the personal life. This 'New Wave' was matched by a new self-consciousness in style, with experiments in form and content appearing in the science fiction magazines. As science fiction came out of the ghetto, the 1970s saw it being used towards new political ends. Most significantly, science fiction was adopted by the women's movement to express the desire for a more equal society, whether by reversing reality, presenting an idealised polemic, or extrapolating oppression from elements of our own world.

The 1980s continued to demonstrate the fact that science fiction is the true literature of the present. The free market experiments of monetarism and post-industrial capitalism were greeted with a return to hard-technology science fiction and 'cyberpunk'. The boundaries between the technological, the personal and the virtual were redrawn in the computer age, and this self-conscious concern with the status of reality and fiction continued into the 1990s. Simultaneously there has been a rediscovery of the icons of the science fiction tradition, with Mars, galactic exploration, invading aliens, and the rewriting of old science fictional universes appearing. The story becomes more complicated at every turn, since genre-writing carries all its baggage with it, and each decade simply adds to the repertoire rather than really displacing anything.

1.6 Review and Preview

The book is arranged in two halves, with a centrepoint providing a retrospective and prospective view. The chapters on either side of the centre mirror each other. In chapter 2, I look at the presentation of dated futures in science fiction. Different versions of the future provide another historical dimension on the genre, and the discussion offers an opportunity for examining precisely how texts anchor themselves in a created reality. I use the analysis of science fiction to demonstrate some shortcomings in the traditional linguistic approach to this area, and to suggest a revised framework.

Chapter 3 tackles the interaction of language and science fiction directly, by focusing on those texts that are concerned to manipulate style in an unusual or mimetic way. These tend to be science fictional works from the period after the New Wave. I examine the detail of the linguistic special effects used in such experimental fiction, and discuss the poetics of science fiction in relation to literary criticism, critical theory and mainstream literature. This is a point of entry into chapter 4, which is concerned with developing an account of the roots of modern science fiction in *pulpstyle*. I place the stylistic description in its historical context in order to take up the argument about science fiction and other literature. This concludes the first half of the book.

Chapter 5 reflects on the nature of the enterprise thus far and anticipates the discussion to follow. In the second half of the book, I outline in detail and at both local and global levels, how science fiction texts work within the reading process. The central importance of *neologisms* (new words) to science fictional effects is addressed in relation to their use in the language as a whole, in chapter 6. The cognitive mechanics of how these new words are incorporated into new worlds is the subject of chapter 7. A model of narrative comprehension is adapted for the peculiarities of science fiction, with a discussion of possible worlds and implications for the linguistic theory of reference. For illustration this is applied to some science fiction short stories which deal with time paradoxes and displaced worlds.

In chapter 8, I return to the everyday sense of the 'poetic' nature of much science fiction. I illustrate many of its striking images within a framework of metaphoric form. These forms are placed in relation to readerly effects, and the nature of readerly knowledge and text world accessibility is discussed. The nature of metaphor in the context of science fiction is a major theme. The final chapter takes the fundamentally metaphorical nature of knowledge manipulation, and places it into its global context using the approach of cognitive poetics. How readers understand what is going on in the science fictional world is the subject of this chapter. The representation of knowledge is discussed in relation to idealised societies, apocalyptic fiction, and the emergence of science fiction into new forms.

Throughout the book a mutually-informing balance is maintained between the analysis of a literary genre and the application of linguistic theory. This is achieved by a continual focus on the process of reading as the central issue. Reading is foregrounded as a concern at the theoretical level, in the natural language frameworks developed by linguistics and cognitive psychology, and at the empirical level, through a consideration of critical interpretations and some reader-response experiments. The poetics of science fiction is fundamentally about how readers manage new information, and can negotiate both reality and many unrealities using this most cognitively challenging of genres.

CHAPTER 2

MACROLOGICAL: OLD FUTURES

2.1 Preview

Each period in the development of science fiction has configured
its own version of the future. In particular science fiction narratives,
these are either set in the near future of the time of publication or in
a far distant future. Sometimes they are specified with a conventional
date (*1984, 2001*); sometimes the date is presented in a futuristic style
(A.F. 632 – six centuries 'After Ford' in *Brave New World*, 'Stardate
45047.2' in *Star Trek*'s captain's log); and sometimes the future time is
unspecified or more general. From the point of publication of these
narratives, of course, in reality time rolls onward and reaches each dated
future in turn. They then seem to become retrospective extrapolations,
overtaken by history, and by other, newly-conceived science fictional
futures.

This chapter examines a range of historically dated futures across
twentieth-century science fiction. A noticeable feature that emerges is
that these old futures retain a stylistic encoding of their point of origin,
and an exploration of these styles is important for a thorough understanding of how the extrapolated future works in science fiction. This
discussion is macrological in that it is concerned with the global matter
of *plausibility*. The 'world' built by the narrative must be one that
convinces the reader, at least for the duration of reading the text,
that the presented future is a reasonable and coherent scenario. Plausibility is a central feature of science fiction that this book will often
return to in the chapters that follow. In this chapter, the plausibility of
futuristic visions is explained as a product of the *deictic* and *referential*
elements in the text, as explained below (and taken up again especially
in chapter 7). The emphasis throughout is on how a plausible world is
built up by the reader from the science fiction text, and what manner
of world this is.

2.2 Future Worlds and the Framed Universe

The word **world** has many different attachments in different domains of knowledge. We live on a world, a polar-flattened sphere orbiting a star. We have recently become aware that other planets are their own worlds, with photographs from the surfaces of the Moon and Mars. We are surrounded by a world of experience, where we can encounter the natural world, the world of books, 'Disneyworld', and even 'Car-Wash World'. The word thus encompasses the concrete and the abstract, and it is the latter that has been used in linguistics and psychology to talk about the worlds generated by texts.

The notion that readers can become immersed in the world presented in a book is common. In traditional literary criticism, readers feel able to talk about events and characters in fiction, as if they existed in reality. Philosophers of language and psychologists have used the idea of the *world* of a text as a means of addressing the thorny problem of context in theories of meaning. Briefly, the meaning generated by a sentence is very often a function not only of the words and sequence involved, but also of contextual factors and knowledge such as who speaks, who hears, where they are situated, what they are talking about, and what knowledge they have and share and use in these particular circumstances to make sense of what has been said. This approach has been used to explore the idea of meaningfulness in individual utterances and sentences, in extended metaphors, and in whole texts and discourses. The notion of *world* takes on a special dimension when the status of fictional discourse is considered, and this becomes even more important and complicated in relation to science fictional discourse. Because the notion of *world* is essential to any consideration of plausibility in science fiction, at this stage we need a usable model of how the science fictional narrative is **framed** and made real during reading. (In chapter 7, a range of approaches to the notion of discoursal and possible worlds is discussed in more detail.)

The model of narrative comprehension used here is Emmott's (1997) cognitive framework which treats reading as 'the interaction of the mind with the text' (Emmott 1997: xi). This approach is useful here because it deals mainly with written textual narrative fiction, and there are even asides (discussed below) that point to how the theory can be used in a science fictional context.

Emmott (1997: 120–32) bases her approach on the notion of a **contextual frame** which is a mental store of information about the current 'context of reading'. This is constructed by the reader from the cues in the text and from inferences made from the text. Such information can be *episodic* (relevant at a particular time in the narrative, such as where two characters are located) or *non-episodic* (generally attaching to items but not immediately relevant, such as character traits or the background scenario of the whole text). There are then various ways by which the reader monitors the contextual frame. When the mind makes episodic links between people and places, they are said to be **bound into a frame**. This covers appearances (**binding in**) and exits (**binding out**) of characters into and out of a frame.

More than one frame can be in operation at once, for example when the narrative is proceeding in more than one location at a time (scientists scuttle around on Earth while the invading aliens hurtle towards them). To account for which frame is the main focus in the reader's mind, Emmott uses the term **priming**. The *primed context* is the reader's main context and the characters and setting can then be said to be both *bound* and *primed*.

Of course, the reader might be aware of many characters and other entities, but only one or a few at a time can be actually mentioned explicitly in each sentence. If a *primed* entity is explicitly referred to, it is *textually-overt*, and if it is not currently mentioned it is *textually-covert*. All of the entities discussed so far, whether *bound*, *primed*, *overt*, or not, form the **central directory** – a sort of 'cast list' of entities in the reader's awareness of the narrative world.

Emmott (1997: 129) claims that once the fictional context has been established, readers make real-world assumptions about its workings, '(unless there is some indication to the contrary)'. In other words, we apply our experiential knowledge of the world to make inferences about the sorts of things characters can and cannot plausibly do, and how the physical laws of nature restrict behaviour and events. Here, of course, there is a potential problem for an application of the framework to contexts such as science fiction, which Emmott (1997: 129) parenthetically recognises. Later, there is a brief consideration of the problem of science fictional worlds setting up different conventions:

> In science fiction, characters may sometimes appear 'from nowhere' in the middle of a context. One obvious example of this is the television programme *Star Trek* in which characters are 'beamed' from the star ship to other locations such as the surface of planets. This alters the way in which a character is bound into a frame.
>
> (Emmott 1997: 158)

In such cases, binding may need to be done retrospectively, but the example shows how readers can quickly become used to a universe in which what is physically possible is different from our own real-world knowledge. Furthermore, part of readers' accumulated experiential knowledge must include specific literary competences in understanding the generic conventions of different text-types. This connects with my assertion in 1.4 that experienced science fiction readers have less trouble processing the behaviour of alternative universes than relatively inexperienced readers.

2.2.1 Asimov's Robot World

I, Robot by Isaac Asimov (1968) is regarded as one of the classic science fiction collections of short stories from the 1940s. These are linked together to form the memoirs of Dr. Susan Calvin, charting the history of positronic-brained robots from Robbie in 1996 to the machines which run the world in 2058. Each story is a variation on the theme of Asimov's now-famous 'Three Laws of Robotics', which set out the order of priorities for robots' protection of humans and their own self-preservation. Several stories arise from contradictions between the three laws in different contexts, and they are 'fixed-up' to form an episodic 'novel'.

The novelisation is effected by a journalist narrator, interviewing robot expert Susan Calvin for a feature article for the Interplanetary Press. Each story is an episode, chronologically arranged, recalled by Calvin for the journalist. The surrounding conversations usually appear in italics, to distinguish them from the stories themselves. The characters in each story are bound into each contextual frame and primed for the duration of each individual story. At the end of each one, the story-frame is unprimed and the characters remain bound to that context. However, some characters appear in several stories, such as positronic brain pioneer Alfred Lanning, Mayor Stephen Byerley who is secretly a machine, and Susan Calvin herself. They are therefore bound to each frame period in time and appear primed in the next primed context, a few years later. This continuity assists in the sense of coherence across the universe of the novel.

Since each story frame is short, there tends to be only one or two changes in frame within each story. These are usually instantaneous 'switches' rather than slowly developed 'frame modifications' (Emmott 1997: 133). For example:

Donovan scowled [. . .] 'So we work with new-model robots. It's our job, granted. But answer me one question. Why . . . *why* does something invariably go wrong with them?'

'Because,' said Powell, somberly, 'we are accursed. Let's go!'

Far ahead through the thick velvety blackness of the corridors that reached past the illuminated circles of their flashlights, robot light twinkled.

'There they are', breathed Donovan.

(Asimov 1968: 77)

Dr. Calvin backed away. The color had not returned to her thin cheeks. She motioned the others away.

In her office, she said, 'I can't understand it. The information, as given, must involve a dilemma – probably involves death. If something has gone wrong –'

(Asimov 1968: 142)

'The ship will be back safely, *with* the men, and I want to rest. I *will* rest. Now go away'.

The ship returned to Earth as silently, as unjarringly as it had left. It dropped precisely into place and the main lock gaped open.

(Asimov 1968: 156)

In each case here, the frame is switched both temporally and spatially, signalled by the line-space in the text and usually an initial locative expression ('far ahead through . . . the corridors', 'in her office', 'to Earth'). The last of these signals a frame shift from a point 300,000 parsecs away (out of the Galaxy altogether), but the frame switches within each short story are not usually so distant. There is not the textual space in short stories for the gradual development associated with frame modification in conventional novels.

Of course, the return to 2058 and the time of narration between each story is a frame switch as well, though each repeated sequence acts as an instantaneous 'frame recall' (Emmott 1997: 150–7). Since Susan Calvin appears in many of the frames, as well as the intervening sequences, as the novel progresses the reader will hold in mind several different versions of the character through 'her' imaginary life. Each version of Susan Calvin has different traits and knowledge which are assumed to attach to 'her' (this character-entity should really be pronominalised as 'it', but I am following the intuitive sense that fictional characters are mentally managed in the same way as people in the real-world). Emmott (1989, 1992, 1997: 182) puts forward the notion of 'enactors' to cover such cases where the past and present aspects of a character are held together in the central directory. Each enacted Susan Calvin is bound to her time, but the inter-story sequences repeatedly prime the eighty-two-year-old Susan as the recalling narrator. Emmott's framework allows access to the workings of this narrative strategy of recalling a personal memoir, which is often a central means of establishing plausibility within science fiction.

As we will see in chapter 7, the idea of contextual framing has implications for the traditional way of understanding linguistic *reference*. Outlined briefly, instead of seeing expressions as referring to objects in the real world, or a possible world, reference can be seen as having the dual-aspect function of placing an entity into the mental frame and then keeping it primed or not. This perspective, at the practical level of reading texts, does away with the precise philosophical need for a distinction between reference and deixis (about which more below), since the ongoing maintenance of the world of the narrative is a matter simply between the reader and the text.

2.3 Versions of the Future

Not all science fiction is futuristic, of course – a mistake made by many people who are not familiar with the genre. Nevertheless, futuristic scenarios can be said to be the prototypical version of science fiction, and there is an enormous variety of futures to be found across the range of science fiction narratives. In general, these futures can be arranged along two dimensions: firstly, those that are set along the future time line of our real world; secondly, those that deal with futures in alternative universes. The former are *serial* versions of the future and the latter are *parallel* versions of the future. This means that serial science fiction is extrapolative and parallel science fiction is speculative.

For example, *2001: A Space Odyssey* (Clarke 1968) is a serial vision of the future, with the detail of the world presented (pictured in the film attached to the novel (Kubrick 1968)) in as extrapolative a 'realistic' way as possible. As Clarke (1982, 1988, 1997) has subsequently pointed out in the three sequels to the novel, some of the detail turned out to match reality, such as the image of the astronaut Frank Poole exercising by running around the storage cabinets like a hamster on a wheel, just as the astronauts in Skylab did in the 1980s. However, these sequels themselves represent parallel visions. *2010: Odyssey Two* is a sequel to the universe of the film (Kubrick 1968) rather than the novel (Clarke 1968). Writing at the end of *3001: The Final Odyssey*, Clarke – unusually for a writer – acknowledges the inconsistencies of his universes, and then cunningly employs a science fictional conceit to 'explain' them:

> As I wrote in the introduction to *2061* [Clarke 1988: 11]: 'Just as *2010* was not a direct sequel to *2001*, so this book is not a linear sequel to *2010*. They must all be considered as variations on the same theme, involving many of the same characters and situations, but not necessarily happening in the same universe.'

> (Clarke 1997: 272)

This distinction between serial and parallel versions of the future, of course, is dependent on seeing the projected universe from the point of view of the original date of writing and publication. They are thus historicised notions, relative to a point in time. Serial versions of the future also include works of futurology, astrology, weather forecasting, TV listings, almanacks, tide tables, train times, and horse-racing odds, with various degrees of commitment and certainty. These predictive genres share with serially futuristic extrapolated science fiction the capacity for being judged 'wrong', on a literal level, once the cited date of setting has been reached in real time and the scenario does not occur.

However, such extrapolative science fiction possesses more dimensions than this. People still read Orwell's (1948) *1984* and Wells's (1901) *The First Men in the Moon* even though Big Brother and Ingsoc didn't materialise and Neil Armstrong didn't travel on a rocket powered by cavorite. These novels are still valued and enjoyed after their 'target' settings. Such texts are often interpreted additionally as being satirical of their own time or possessing a generically applicable relevance. Viewed ahistorically then, or after their 'target' settings, such texts tend to lose their extrapolative function and only retain a readership by being valued as historically interesting or canonical literature. This is what distinguishes literary futuristic science fiction from future predictions that have become merely antique curiosities. Furthermore, in terms of the *serial/parallel* distinction established so far, such science fictions become parallel versions of a history not our own. It is the ultimate fate of all science fiction eventually to become *alternative history*, and I will return to this idea at the end of the chapter.

To illustrate the points made so far, and for discussion later in the chapter, I have selected a set of futuristic science fiction novels from across the twentieth century. The basis for selection was that they all have the early twenty-first century as their 'target' settings. Since the universes they present are dissimilar, they present parallel versions of an alternative future in relation to each other. The texts are as follows:

Text	Date of Writing	Target setting
Last and First Men (Olaf Stapledon)	1930	Cosmic span, 2000 to p.75
The Shape of Things to Come (H.G. Wells)	1933	1930–2105
I, Robot (Isaac Asimov)	1940s	1996–2058
The Martian Chronicles (Ray Bradbury)	1951	1999–2026
2001, A Space Odyssey (Arthur C. Clarke)	1968	2001–2006
The Shockwave Rider (John Brunner)	1975	2010–2020
Neuromancer (William Gibson)	1984	Early 21st century
Vurt (Jeff Noon)	1993	Early 21st century

Each of these novels pictures human society in the first part of the twenty-first century, but the universe they construct is different in each case. These texts thus represent 8 parallel futures at roughly the same moment in time. I will briefly outline the scenarios of these novels.

Olaf Stapledon's (1972) *Last and First Men* is a novel written at the end of the 1920s, and deals with the most cosmic timescale treated in science fiction. In the form of a history or encyclopedic documentary description, it details the evolution of humanity until the 'last men' two-thousand million years from now. Each chapter covers exponentially greater periods of time with the early twenty-first century treated up to p. 75. The serial world of this text is a political history of wars, culminating in the annihilation of Europe by American chemical and biological weapons. The characters are the leaders and physicists who meet in a series of crisis talks at each stage, but the main actors are nations and armed forces.

H.G. Wells's (1993) *The Shape of Things to Come*, published in 1933, is the closest of all the selected texts to futurology – the social prediction that increasingly characterised Wells's later work, though it is still cast in the form of a novel. It too takes the form of a serial history, 'edited' by Wells from a manuscript mysteriously originating in the future, left by 'Dr. Philip Raven' after his death in 1930. Like Stapledon's text, it describes world events, though there is less explicit evaluation and more of an attempt to simply 'report' history. The early twenty-first century is dominated by the rule of the 'Air Dictatorship', a technocracy acting as the Second World Council (which lasted from the Treaty of Basra in 1978 to its reconstitution at Mégève in 2059).

Asimov's (1968) *I, Robot*, as we saw in 2.2.1 above, is a collection of short stories inhabiting the same universe from 1996 to 2058, written between 1940 and 1950. Later in his career, Asimov created a parallel universe of the far-future Galactic Empire, in his *Foundation* trilogy (Asimov 1960, 1962, 1964). The two universes were united as a serial universe when Asimov amalgamated the Robot and Foundation narratives, by placing the Galactic Empire as the distant future consequence of a robot plan (Asimov 1982, 1983, 1985, 1986, 1988). Incidentally, Asimov's universe has been taken up by other authors in *Foundation's Fear* (Benford 1998) and *Foundation of Chaos* (Bear 1998). Asimov's original 'Three Laws of Robotics' have since crossed over to robot stories in other serial science fiction universes, from the namesake Robby the robot in the film *Forbidden Planet* (Wilcox 1956) to the android Data in *Star Trek: The Next Generation*, where a serial history is also maintained with in-joke references to science fictional characters such as Susan Calvin.

Similarly, Ray Bradbury's (1977a) *The Martian Chronicles* is a 'fixup' of stories published in magazines at the end of the 1940s, and originally grouped together as *The Silver Locusts* (in 1951). Of the many dozens of Martian stories written by the prolific Bradbury, only those which clearly belong in the same universe form this collection. Other stories set on a parallel Mars are scattered throughout his other anthologies. *The Martian Chronicles* chart events from the first human landing on the planet in January 1999 to the annihilation of humanity on Earth, leaving the last human family on Mars in October 2026.

Arthur C. Clarke's (1968) *2001: A Space Odyssey* is the novelised form of the screenplay he wrote with Stanley Kubrick (1968). A black monolith appears to prehistoric humans and alters our evolution. At the beginning of the twenty-first century, another monolith is discovered on the Moon, sending out an electromagnetic signal towards Saturn, and five years later a ship, the *Discovery*, is sent to investigate. The novel is a serial extrapolation, in as realistic a form as possible, from the technological position of the late 1960s.

John Brunner's (1988) *The Shockwave Rider* can be seen as a 1970s precursor to the concerns of later cyberpunk science fiction, dealing with a maverick computer hacker who escapes from a centre where elite children are bred to run the USA. The novel acknowledges its debt to Alvin Toffler's (1970) *Future Shock*, a work of sociological futurology, and so *The Shockwave Rider* presents a serial future (2010–2020) in which a technological data-net is the site of much of the communication of the world.

Neuromancer is the novel which is largely (incorrectly) credited with inventing the sub-genre of cyberpunk. Written in the early 1980s, Gibson (1984) creates an urban twenty-first century dystopia in the Sprawl, a sleazy extrapolation of techno-capitalism. Here, and in the conceptual world of cyberspace and virtual reality, the computer cowboy Case is an instrument of an artificial intelligence named Wintermute. This serial extrapolation is further developed in Gibson's (1986, 1988, 1993, 1996) novels *Count Zero, Mona Lisa Overdrive, Virtual Light* and *Idoru*, all set in the same universe.

Finally, Jeff Noon's (1993) *Vurt* is a serial extrapolation of a Britain of the near future, told through the perceptions of the character Scribble, searching for his sister lost in the drug-hallucination 'vurtuality' accessed through vurt feathers. Its style is a similar sort of futuristic vernacular used by Gibson. Run-down landmarks of present-day Manchester are extrapolated into a dystopian setting where the world of vurt encroaches on the real world.

These novels represent different versions of the same point in the future, seen from different decades in the twentieth century. I am not claiming here that they are idealised versions of the decades to which they belong. There are many texts contemporary with these which present radically different versions of the future, and there are many points of connection in both style and presented universes between early and late science fiction. However, there is, intuitively at least, something that is archetypally 1930s, 1960s or 1980s (and so on) about these selected texts, and part of the purpose of this analysis is to investigate precisely what this is.

With early science fiction, for example, it is often easy to identify the precise dates at which the novels are set, since these are given explicitly in the text. Stapledon even has a diagram showing the timescale of his novel, and Bradbury presents the text as a chronicle, with date headings for chapters. In more recent science fiction, however, the precise target setting is more vague, and can only be discovered by closely reading the text. Explicit dates are rare here; time is set in relation to the death of a real celebrity, or reference to characters' childhoods in the 1990s, for example. The extrapolations of the 1970s, '80s and '90s seem to narrow the distance between the present (of writing) and the future, which makes the extrapolation more closely a caricature of the present than a predictive warning or prophecy.

In the discussion so far, the main issues have centred around spatio-temporal relationships between past and future, time of writing and target time of setting, time of writing and time of reading, characters as past and present narrating enactors, future narrators and present readers, and readers existing in the future of writers. These relationships are further complicated by the internal relationships within the fictional universe, in which manuscripts from the distant future are delivered to present-day editors and purport to deal with the more recent past – which is, of course, in our future. Such temporal complexity means that we cannot even strictly say that the characters and events are fictional because they never happened, since (from the reality-point of the text) they have not had a chance to happen yet. This is a strange sort of reverse history. We are dealing with the archaeology of the future, whose only trace in the present is in the universes set up by futuristic literary texts. The only way to un-earth the workings of the future is to examine closely the structure of these artificial artefacts, and this is the matter of the rest of this chapter.

Explorations

■ A definition of science fiction that was based only on non-existent technology would exclude the whole tradition of alternative history narratives. These are usually set in a past that is not our past, and often take a pivotal point in history as the catalyst for the story: Napoleon was not defeated, Hitler was assassinated, the atomic bomb was not dropped, the Axis powers won the Second World War, and so on. However, thinking about this narrow definition of science fiction, for the sake of argument, can be illuminating.

■ Imagine a few technological advances, either real (such as the moon landing, personal computers, fax machines, mobile phones) or yet to come (the Mars landing, final proof of the impossibility of faster-than-light travel, alien first contact). With these in mind, which science fiction texts would cease to be science fictional as soon as the techno-logy was actually invented? Out of these, what other elements remain that still make the story science fictional? Answering this question takes you some way to deciding what other aspects of science fiction are central and peripheral to the genre.

2.4 Exploring the Universe

Emmott's (1997) cognitive model of narrative comprehension has been used so far in a general way to account for the perception of science fictional universes. She says of science fiction:

> It seems, from this brief examination, that in science fiction and stories about the supernatural, readers and viewers will still attempt to build and maintain frames. Indeed in some cases, monitoring of contexts and characters may be a more complex task than for other types of text. 'Contextual frame theory' is not, therefore, invalid for these stories, although it may need to be developed further. Without contextual monitoring by means of frames, the reader of a story would be disorientated.
>
> (Emmott 1997: 159–60)

This section addresses the further development of the framework by looking at the precise detail of the ways language can be used to indicate objects and relationships within a frame: this is the area associated with **deixis**, explored below. The whole discussion is illustrated at each stage with examples of science fictional reading (from the sample texts introduced above), in order to arrive at a thorough understanding of the workings of the science fictional literary universe. (Chapter 7 returns to consider these issues further.)

2.4.1 An Overview of Deixis

Deixis, derived from the Greek for 'pointing', relates to those aspects of language which anchor the utterance or discourse in a particular situation or contextual world.

> Deixis is the name given to uses of items and categories of lexicon and grammar that are controlled by certain details of the interactional situation in which the utterances are produced. These details include especially the identity of the participants in the communicating situation, their locations and orientations in space, whatever on-going indexing acts the participants may be performing, and the time at which the utterance containing the items is produced.
>
> (Fillmore 1982: 35)

Prototypical deictic expressions would be contrasting words like 'this' and 'that', 'come' and 'go', 'now' and 'then', 'I' and 'you', for example. Those aspects of language that constitute deixis are generally agreed amongst writers who have discussed the area, from the seminal work in the 1930s by Bühler (translated extracts, 1982), through the work of semanticists such as Lyons (1977) and pragmaticists such as Levinson (1983), to the collections edited by Jarvella and Klein (1982), Rauh (1983a) and Green (1995a). A particularly clear exposition in terms of poetry is outlined by Semino (1997: 31–54), after Levinson (1983: 54–96), and the basic deictic categories which follow are mainly adapted from there.

There is an initial problem, however, in that deixis is primarily a feature of spoken, face-to-face conversation, a situation quite different from literary reading, and most of the linguistic work on deixis concerns this primary context. Green (1992, 1995b) argues that deictic usage in literature should be treated in essentially the same way as primary examples of deixis, with the generic context taken into account. In relation to literature, Bex (1995) argues that the particular genre which is under consideration can affect the deictic usage quite significantly. It seems to me even more likely that science fiction, with its bizarre characters and universes quite explicitly distinct from our own, requires some 'tweaking' of the categories of deixis, as follows. (The traditional terms are also rather inelegantly collocated and are imprecise, I think.)

Basic Deictic Categories	Correspondences in Literary Fictional Context
Person deixis	Perceptual deixis
Place deixis	Spatial deixis
Time deixis	Temporal deixis
Social deixis	Relational deixis
Discourse deixis	Textual deixis
Syntactic deixis	Compositional deixis

These categories will be explained and discussed in the rest of the chapter. My intention throughout the following discussion is to use the categories of deixis as a means of examining some historical developments in science fictional writing. Though the exploration focuses on science fiction, clearly other literary genres also use deixis in particular characteristic ways. I recommend my relabelled categories for their study too, though a comparative analysis of deixis in science fiction and other literature is beyond the scope of this chapter.

The literary fictional deictic categories are correspondences rather than equivalents, because they are internal to the world of the text. In other words, at the general level of author-reader interaction in *The Shape of Things to Come*, the text can encode 'I' and 'me' as the long-dead author H.G. Wells and 'you' as one of many thousands of possible readers (person deixis); the 'coding time' can be 1932–3 and the 'receiving time' 1996 when I first read it (time deixis); and the introduction written by 'H.G.W.' refers to the manuscript of Philip Raven which constitutes the main part of the novel that follows (discourse deixis). All of these aspects are expressed in the lexical and grammatical choices of the text. However, I am fairly certain that the novel itself is fictional, that Philip Raven is a figment of Wells's imagination, that no manuscript ever existed other than the one Wells submitted to his publisher Hutchinson in early 1933; and the divergence between Wells's anticipations and the history after the Second World War that I learnt at school prove to me that Wells had no precise idea of the real future in which his book would be actually read.

To handle these difficulties with fictional reading, it is necessary to conceive of another level or frame in which the deictic elements encode a world of pretence. Person deixis then attaches to the narrator 'Wells' as constructed by this novel, characters with counterparts in reality ('Napoleon', 'Stalin', 'Ramsay MacDonald') and imaginary characters ('Ariston Theotocopulos', 'Philip Raven'). The fictional coding time which determines temporal deictic expressions is not 1933 but 2106, when the book was (tense problems, discussed below, here suggest 'is' or 'will be') written as a history. The text itself pretends to address a contemporary (twenty-second century) student reader as the 'narratee', though the introduction by 'H.G.W.' also provides a frame addressing the contemporary (1930s) reader. Syntactic deictics encoded as interrogatives and imperatives (uttered by a speaking voice located in a specific place) are also compositional rhetorical features in science fiction, all designed to increase the plausibility of the text. These special features of deixis in the context of literary fictional reading require a brief discussion of deictic projection in terms of *cognitive frames*.

2.4.2 Frames and Deictic Projection

In traditional deictic theory, the *deictic centre* or *zero-point* is 'egocentric' (Bühler's 'origo' 1982: 13, Lyons 1977: 638, Levinson 1983: 63–4), based on the speaker ('I'), time of utterance ('now'), and place of utterance ('here'). This is perhaps all right for face-to-face conversation. However, as the discussion of Wells's text demonstrates above, this sense of the deictic centre is too simplistic for such science fiction. Lyons (1977: 579) allows derivative uses of deixis so that deictic expressions can be seen to be used by characters in different *contextual frames*. This is **deictic projection**, and it applies to every *framed* context in science fiction (and fictional literature generally). (Fillmore (1975) regards this as a shift in point of view. If by this he means *focalisation*, then this is a matter of *perceptual deixis* (2.4.3), but relational point of view is better handled within the arena of *social deixis*, 2.4.6.) In another attempt to account for this effect, Tracy (1983) asserts

> In order to ensure that the 'journeys' through deictic spaces (Lyons 1977: 72) need not be lonesome endeavours, speaker and listener must share a conventionalized system of instructions, in other words, deictic egocentrism but be essentially intersubjective in order to work.

> (Tracy 1983: 138)

These neat but unconvincing sidesteps around the problems which fictional narratives bring to traditional accounts of deixis require that deixis is placed within a cognitive theory of narrative comprehension such as Emmott's. This is because deixis depends on different *framed levels*, and any sense of *projection* involves differentiating the point of projection from the image projected and viewed, and the viewer. In short, the traditional account of deixis is too producer-oriented and too egocentrically focused. This is most evident with science fiction which foregrounds notions of temporality and the relative authorities and contextual knowledge of writer, narrator, addressee and reader.

My desire for a holistic view of deixis in the context of fiction is supported by Jones (1995), in a critique of the traditional account. He berates its asocial and utterer-centred focus, and points out that very often what speakers say is 'addressee-centred' at the deictic level (Jones 1995: 47). It should be noted that science fiction texts often acknowledge the relatively uninformed position of the reader, by encoding those elements of the unshared context that are absolutely necessary for the reader to figure out the primed frame of the science fictional universe (clumsily done in the case of *pulpstyle*: see chapter 4).

2.4.3 Perceptual Deixis

In science fiction, **perceptual deixis** corresponds with 'person' deixis, since in science fictional (and other fantastic) universes humans, aliens, robots, computers, animals, and inanimate objects can have consciousness and so are able to use deictic expressions: in short, any entity with perceptual capabilities is open to speak using perceptual deictic expressions. In Bradbury's (1977a) *The Martian Chronicles*, for example, blue fire spheres address Father Peregrine:

> And a voice touched his mind, and the voice said:
> 'We have come for a little while.'
> 'You may stay,' said Father Peregrine.
> 'For a little while only,' said the voice quietly. 'We have come to tell you certain things. We should have spoken sooner. But we had hoped that you might go on your way if left alone.'
> Father Peregrine started to speak, but the voice hushed him.
> 'We are the Old Ones,' the voice said, and it entered him like a blue gaseous flare and burned in the chambers of his head.
>
> (Bradbury 1977a: 129)

Here the telepathic voice is inside Father Peregrine's head, and the two are mainly differentiated by the shifting deictic expressions 'we' and 'you'. The spheres turn out to be ancient Martians who have escaped sin by evolving beyond their physical bodies, but for the sake of the science fiction reader and Father Peregrine, they are still able to communicate using the conventional English pronoun system.

The traditional view of person deixis (Lyons 1977: 638–9) allows first and second person pronouns into the category, since 'I,' 'we' and 'you', and their verb forms, encode the participants in a discourse. Third person forms are excluded as being non-participatory.

This distinction cannot hold in relation to fictional discourse. Strictly, there are no participants in literature other than the reader. The author is putatively a participant through the reader's mental reconstruction of the universe of the text and its likely creator. First, second and third person deictics must all be included in perceptual deixis since they are aspects of the contextual framing managed during reading. They all operate at an embedded discoursal level, and so they all have a status different from the reader.

Furthermore, authors often have narrators describe the apparently internal thoughts or spoken words of a character in the third person, such as in *indirect discourse* and *free indirect discourse* (Leech and Short 1981). In this way the third person form attracts a deictic dimension, as far as the reader is concerned, just as much as other characters who are presented similarly indirectly by the author through a narrator. Changing direct thought (She wondered, 'Why do these types always pick out me to ask?') into indirect thought (She wondered why those types always picked her out to ask), for example, 'shifts any deictic items from the direct thinker's orientation to that of the framing narrator (here, *me* – *her, these types* – *those types*)' (Toolan 1998: 107).

Levinson (1983: 68) indicates the importance of *participant roles* within person deixis, noting that *speaker* can be separate from *source*, *recipient* distinct from *target*, and *hearers* different from *addressees*. In face-to-face interaction, usually within 'I' and 'you' there is no differentiation between these roles, but there certainly is in fictional written discourse. Indeed, the ways in which readers negotiate differences between authors, implied authors, narrators, the host of speaking characters in the narrative, narratee, implied reader and themselves as real readers are through perceptual deictic markers distinguishing each of these entities.

All three of the earliest texts selected for this chapter (Stapledon, Wells, Asimov) have a complicated narrative structure which requires that the reader negotiates perceptual deictic elements. This structure presents the narrative frame as a set of embedded documents, which serve to assert plausibility by authorising the text through several witnessing narrators. At the same time, the core narrative itself is distanced from the reader, and its circumstance of production can then reasonably be presented as being vague and mysterious. Wells's (1993) narrative has the future historian referring to himself as 'we' and the future student as 'he'; the manuscript is passed on by Philip Raven, whose conversation ('I') is reported directly in the introduction, which itself is written in the first person by 'H.G.W.'. He appears in editorial interjections in the text, signed 'ED'. The complex narrative structure of Stapledon's (1972) text is apparent from the opening perceptual deictics:

Introduction
By One of the Last Men

This book has two authors, one contemporary with its readers, the other an inhabitant of an age which they would call the distant future. The brain that conceives and writes these sentences lives in the time of Einstein. Yet I, the true inspirer of this book, I who have begotten it upon that brain, I who influence that primitive being's conception, inhabit an age which, for Einstein, lies in the very remote future.

The actual writer thinks he is merely contriving a work of fiction. Though he seeks to tell a plausible story, he neither believes it himself, nor expects others to believe it. Yet the story is true. A being who you would call a future man has seized the docile but scarcely adequate brain of your contemporary, and is trying to direct its familiar processes for an alien purpose. Thus a future epoch makes contact with your age.

(Stapledon 1972: 15)

The novel could have been written simply without the introduction, but the mediation of the narrative frame through another narrator adds an extra level of authorisation (apparent authenticity). And this pre-emptive admission that the story is so fantastic it is implausible, is a traditional 'double-bluff' strategy of claiming plausibility.

As detailed above (2.2.1), Asimov's (1968) text also has an embedded narrative structure. For a novel entitled *I, Robot*, this manipulation of perceptual deixis is hardly surprising. Within each primed story frame, the unnamed journalist (*speaker*) recounts the story told to him by Susan Calvin (*source*). The *target* of his narrative is the galactic readership of the Interplanetary Press. He is the *addressee* of each story, and the galactic readership the *addressee* of the whole text of the novel. At the highest level, of course, the *speaker* is the narrating journalist and the 'overhearing' audience is me, the real-world reader (*hearer*), knowing that the actual *source* of the text is Asimov. All of this is encoded in the shifts of perceptual deictic expressions across the novel. Here is the very end of the final story, in which Susan Calvin realises that the robot Machines have taken away humanity's freewill for our own good, in accordance with the First Law of Robotics:

[Stephen Byerley:] 'But you are telling me, Susan, that [. . .] Mankind *has* lost its own say in its future.'

'It never had any, really. It was always at the mercy of economic and sociological forces it did not understand – at the whims of climate, and the fortunes of war. Now the Machines understand them; and no one can stop them, since the Machines will deal with them as they are dealing with the Society [for Humanity], – having, as they do, the greatest of weapons at their disposal, the absolute control of our economy.'

'How horrible!'

'Perhaps how wonderful! Think, that for all time, all conflicts are finally evitable. Only the Machines, from now on, are inevitable!'

And the fire behind the quartz went out and only a curl of smoke was left to indicate its place.

'And that is all,' said Dr. Calvin, rising. 'I saw it from the beginning, when the poor robots couldn't speak, to the end, when they stand between mankind and destruction. I will see no more. My life is over. You will see what comes next.'

I never saw Susan Calvin again. She died last month at the age of eighty-two.

(Asimov 1968: 205–6)

Here the conversation between Byerley and Calvin, without any reporting clauses (such as 'he said . . .'), is largely negotiated by the reader through the perceptual deixis of the personal pronouns 'you' and 'me'. Since the reader has Byerley and Calvin bound and primed in this frame, and Byerley is the locally primed and overt character currently speaking, the reader is able to understand that, in the first sentence above, 'you' means Calvin and 'me' means Byerley. At the end, after a frame recall back to an inter-story frame (marked by the ellipted line and italics), Byerley and the enacted younger Calvin are bound to the previous story frame which is now unprimed. The newly primed frame contains the primed enactor older Calvin, and the journalist; and the shift from the locally primed speaking Calvin to the subsequent locally primed narrating journalist is marked by the shift of deictic centre across the last two paragraphs. This is how the reader is able to understand that 'I', 'my' and 'you' are from Calvin's view, while the 'I' of the last paragraph refers to the journalist. Of course, there is a further frame switch in the last paragraph, with the journalist speaking a month or so later, modifying the frame by binding Calvin out ('She died').

It should be clear from this brief analysis how Emmott's (1997) framework can be augmented at a detailed level by a further consideration of deixis (she also discusses the issue directly: Emmott 1997: 210–12). This gives detail to the framework for the purposes of science fiction, and also adds a cognitive dimension to the theory of deixis.

2.4.4 Spatial Deixis

In Green's (1995b: 21–2) typology of deixis, the 'spatio-temporal' category conflates the two aspects of time and place, and it is true that we seem to conceive of time and express it linguistically largely in terms of physical space (Lakoff and Johnson 1980, Lakoff 1987). However, it is clear that in science fiction the aspects of spatial location and temporal location are more important than in many other contexts, so it is useful in my framework to treat temporal and spatial deixis separately.

I do not believe there has been alien contact with our planet in recent history, so I am fairly certain that all science fiction has been written on the planet Earth. However, much of that material sets the narrative extra-terrestrially. One of the first cues that a science fictional universe is about to be primed is thus when 'here' of the 'coding location' of the narrator does not correspond with my home planet.

Space is symbolically important in science fiction, though of course almost all narrative genres involve the action being set in a particular place, and most of them include movement to different locations through the narrative. Emmott (1997: 147–54) handles these with the notions of frame switching and recall, mentioned above (2.2). As she says, 'frame switch [. . .] is signalled by a reference to the location of the new frame [. . .] often accompanied by an orthographic break in the text created by starting a new chapter or section [. . .] or by simply leaving a gap of a few lines' (Emmott 1997: 148). This last pattern was seen being used by Asimov (1968), in 2.2 and 2.4.3 above.

The spatial location of a new frame is typically signalled by a locative adverbial phrase such as 'on the planet Mars' (Bradbury 1977a: 14), 'in the Sense/Net lobby' (Gibson 1984: 82), 'inside of a dream' (Noon 1993: 96). Since these are always uttered by a narrating speaker, about a primed frame, and in effect set up the 'here and now' of the discourse, they can be treated as deictic expressions relative to that speaker. Traditionally, the usual features of spatial deixis are: the demonstratives 'this' and 'that', verbs of motion such as 'come' and 'go', 'bring' and 'take', and adverbs such as 'here' and 'there', 'nearby' and 'far away', and so on (see Levinson 1983: 79–85).

Of course, it matters whether the narrating speaker is inside the frame (participating in the action) or is external to it. The latter is a more complicated deictic situation and will be discussed below. First, though, an example of the former case is the opening of *Vurt*, after the participating narrator has set up a scene outside 'the all-night Vurt-U-Want' with a robo-crusty beggar and his thin dog on the pavement:

> I was watching all this in the halo of the night lights. We
> stuck to the dark hours in those days. The Thing was on
> board and that was a major crime; possession of live drugs, a
> five-year stretch guaranteed.

(Noon 1993: 6)

This passage locates the narrative deictically in a number of ways. 'All this' points to the physical scene just set up, supported by the locative expression 'in the halo of the night lights' (*spatial deixis*). 'I' and 'we' encode the *perceptual deixis* of the narrator, Scribble, and his gang, the Stash Riders. 'In those days' is *temporal deixis*, and 'that' refers to the Thing being on board and is an example of *textual deixis*. *Temporal deixis* is also carried by the tense and aspect choices of 'was watching', 'stuck' and 'was'. All of these will be discussed below (2.4.5 and 2.4.6).

In the case of a narrator who does not participate in the action (such as in Clarke's (1968) *2001: A Space Odyssey*, with its omniscient third person narrator), it should first be noted that all the usual features of spatial deixis are found routinely within the reported speech of characters in science fiction, specifying their local position, in relation to points which have already been set up by the surrounding narrator. However, the speaker him/her/itself can also exhibit deictic aspects of language use, if we extend the notion that readers reconstruct literary characters – including non-participating narrators – in the same way as in face-to-face discourse. This narrator then stands as a poetically constructed 'persona' (Green 1992). Fillmore (1982: 43) suggests that locating expressions work 'through reference to something else whose location can be taken for granted'. Following Talmy (1980), this referent is termed the 'Ground', and the speaker is then cognitively treated by the reader as the 'Figure' against that background setting. In other words, even non-participating speakers in narrative are treated by readers as personas having a spatial location in relation to the narrative. All narrators use deictic expressions.

Clarke's (1968) omniscient narrator moves the spatial setting of the narrative around using locating expressions:

> The drought had lasted now for ten million years, and the
> reign of the terrible lizards had long since ended. Here on
> the Equator, in the continent which would one day be known
> as Africa, the battle for existence had reached a new climax

of ferocity, and the victor was not yet in sight. In this barren and desiccated land only the small or the swift or the fierce could flourish, or even hope to survive.

[. . .]

No matter how many times you left Earth, Dr. Heywood Floyd told himself, the excitement never really palled. He had been to Mars once, to the Moon three times, and to the various space-stations more often than he could remember. [. . .] The jet that had rushed him here from Washington, after that midnight briefing with the President, was now dropping down towards one of the most familiar, yet most exciting landscapes in all the world.

[. . .]

Between Planets

The ship was still only thirty days from Earth.

[. . .]

There was no sense of motion, but he was falling towards those impossible stars, shining there in the dark heart of a moon. No – *that* was not where they really were, he felt certain. He wished, now that it was far too late, that he had paid more attention to those theories of hyperspace, of trans-dimensional ducts. To Dave Bowman, they were theories no longer.

Perhaps that monolith on Japetus was hollow.

(Clarke 1968: 11, 43, 97–9, 225)

Clearly, besides the usual spatial deictic forms such as 'here', 'there', 'that' and 'those,' there are many other locating expressions that operate here as spatial deixis. In fact, even though I have brought these four excerpts together from different parts of the novel, the deictic expressions make it easy for a reader to locate each setting in relation to an assumed speaker. In the first excerpt, the narrating voice is omniscient and disembodied. However, there is still a strong sense of a narrating persona here, and this is largely a product of the deixis in the passage. The centring of the persona is effected by locatives including 'now' and 'here', spatial deictics such as 'in this barren and desiccated land', and temporal deictics such as 'had lasted now', 'had long since ended', 'which would one day', 'had reached' and 'was not yet in sight'. All of these create a tangible persona, who is able to take the reader to the Equator, and call it 'here'.

When the narrative is focused through one of the characters, as in the second excerpt, it is even easier to see the workings of deixis to create a character in a setting. Floyd's internal perceptual thoughts serve to signal to the reader that this narrative point is about another time 'you left Earth'. Similarly, the demonstratives in the final excerpt help to locate Dave Bowman's perception in relation to 'those imposs-ible stars', 'shining there', '*that* was not where they really were', 'those theories'.

Also apparent from these extracts is how closely tied spatial deixis is to temporal deixis, as two aspects of the locating function of narrative deixis generally. In the third excerpt, the spatial locating expression ('Between Planets') is followed by a measurement of space (distance to Earth) in terms of time ('only thirty days'). Science fictional space is measured in light years; and temporal deixis is discussed next.

2.4.5 Temporal Deixis

Science fiction prototypically deals with events in the future, and the notion of time travel is closely associated with science fictional narrat-ives. Locating the narrative temporally is obviously, then, an important feature for the genre. In English, only the past and present are fully grammaticalised; English has developed a means of expressing prospect-ive time modally. Science fictional narrative has been bound by this system too, but the conceptual shift towards measuring the future and seeing it as a prospective history is an idea that has found its main expression in science fiction, and the tense and aspect system of English has been stretched to the limit in the process.

> Speculating, one may argue that, in the history of mankind, it has not been for long that the future has been schedulable and scheduled, that the need or even the mere desire arose to differentiate temporal sections of the undifferentiated uncertain future. However, how this is done deserves atten-tion. What is to be observed here I am inclined to call an application of the 'deictic principle'.
>
> (Rauh 1983b: 238)

This links in with my argument so far that the existing deictic system is adapted for literary reading. Though temporal locating expressions such as 'in your day' (Stapledon 1972: 16) and 'after three million years of darkness' (Clarke 1968: 92) pinpoint time relative to a projected point, the main indication of temporal deixis in narrative is situated in verb forms.

Fleischman's (1982, 1990) study of tense in narrative, though mainly concerned with medieval romance, is useful here. In her earlier work (1982: 17–20), she lists the possible ways in which narratives can refer to the future. These are: **future tense**, which does not exist morphologically in English but is often regarded as the WILL + VERB form; **adverbials**, such as *tomorrow, next week*; **modals** and **auxiliary forms**, such as *I have to leave* and *he is to leave*; and **go-futures** such as I AM GOING TO + VERB.

Go-futures have several meanings: they invoke the immediate or proximal future; the inceptive present (beginning now and prolonged into the future); the intentive present (a declaration of intention to do something); and the notion of imminence. Of course, any text using these forms inevitably foregrounds the fact that the future is not an area of knowledge but one of belief, and the observation that these forms occur most commonly in personal face-to-face interaction further serves to underline their subjectivity.

Such forms are potentially a threat to plausibility, and for these reasons science fiction is not written in the modalised future. Instead, it is usually written in the various past forms. Fleischman (1990: 5, 56) notes that, in everyday conversation, the present tense forms are those that are unmarked; but in narrative it is the *past* that is unmarked and normative. She asserts, furthermore, that this is a *defining characteristic* of narrative, since it is 'a verbal icon of experience viewed from a *retrospective* vantage; the experience is by definition "past," whether it occurred in some real world or not. Hypothetical or future experiences are also commonly narrated as if they were past, for this, I submit, is the only way one can *narrate*' (Fleischman 1990: 23–4).

Science fiction thus borrows the normative form of recounting real experience to present its unreal universe plausibly:

> In predictive genres, although events are assumed to have future time reference, they are nonetheless reported in the PAST. In other words, they are *narrated*. All narratives, even those that refer to the future, speak of the unreal as if it were past, as if the events had actually occurred.
>
> (Fleischman 1990: 104)

This normative status of the past in narrative means that past forms in science fiction are unmarked, and variations mainly then take on an expressive function, marking the fictional narrative as possessing verisimilitude. Where there is any temporal deixis involved, it is relative to the narrator's past experience (Fleischman 1990: 112), and we have noticed several times in this chapter how futuristic science fiction has a future-based narrator, whether mediated through a present-day editor or not.

Tense and aspect variation in science fiction, then, can be used to differentiate 'speaker-now' from 'story-now' (Fleischman 1990: 125), can indicate foreground and background in a text, can seem to speed up or slow down the narrative, and can mark out separate contextual frames (as noted by Emmott 1997: 150). It is in these expressive functions of tense and aspect style that there is the widest divergence between the earlier and later texts selected for this chapter.

The early science fiction novels (Wells, Stapledon, Asimov) present an authoritative and chronologically ordered history of the future. The shifts from the core narrative in each case to the editorial interludes are marked by tense and aspect shifts, but within the core narrative the style of temporal deixis is consistently in the prototypical forms of past narration: simple past and progressive past. For example:

> There was no further change in essential political structure between 1978 and 2059, but there was a great change in the spirit and method of that supreme government, the World Council. A new type of administrator grew up, harder, more devoted and more resolute than the extremely various men of the two Basra Conferences. These younger men consti-tuted what our historian calls here the Second Council, though it was continuous with the first. There was a struggle for power involving the deaths of several of the earlier coun-cillors, but no formal change of régime; there continued to be a World Council constituting the supreme government of the world.

> (Wells 1993: 344)

The only move to a non-past form here is attached to the editor's current comment on the historian's manuscript ('here'). Such a style is generally typical of the earlier texts, and is a consequence of the monologic authoritative narrator. Only with the Asimov, Bradbury and Clarke

texts is there any significant introduction of the direct speech of characters, which of course allows for simple present forms relating to the
characters' situations.

In the later texts (Brunner, Gibson, Noon), the narrative becomes
focalised through several characters' minds, which offers possibilities for
presenting their thoughts, and projections to unrealised or comparable
situations. For example:

> Must MUST learn to control my temper even in face of
> an insult to humanity like –
> *What the hell?*
> He emerged with a gasp from coma-like sleep. Last night
> he had lain awake for hours with Fluckner's threat reverber-
> ating in memory, and ultimately resorted to a pill. It took a
> long time for an all-important fact to penetrate his muzzy
> mind.
> The hum of the air compressor had stopped.
> Rolling over, he checked the self-powered illuminated
> clock at the head of his bed. It showed 7:45 A.M. But the
> windows of his trailer were solidly dark, although by now
> the sun must be high in the sky, the forecast had been for
> more fine weather, and when it was stretched taut the plastic
> membrane of his roof was quite translucent.
> Therefore the power had been cut off and the dome had
> collapsed. All twenty-two and a half tons of it.
>
> (Brunner 1988: 22–3)

There is a far greater variety of verb forms even in this short passage
than in whole chapters of the earlier texts. These include, for example,
the traditional simple past and progressive past, as well as a range of
modalised auxiliary forms ('must learn to control'), present participles
('reverberating', 'rolling'), past perfective ('had lain awake', 'had been
cut off') and even forms with the verb ellipted ('all twenty-two and a
half tons of it'). These accompany the narrative focus moving into the
character's mind, where past and future events are considered, where
subjective attitude is expressed, and where the comparisons and speculations of logical reasoning occur.

Finally, there is a general difference between early and late science
fiction in the way past perfective ('had lain awake', 'had stopped',
'had been cut off', above) is used. As the Brunner passage shows, in

more recent science fiction this 'past in the past' form is used alongside other forms, and is subject to the focalised consciousness of the character. In earlier science fiction, however, this form often marks out whole paragraphs in which the reader is brought up to date with the pre-narrative events. This rather clumsy feature of early science fiction writing is especially apparent in short stories and pulp science fiction (see chapter 4).

Exploration

■ What would a science fiction story written in the future aspect in English look like? You might try to write a few paragraphs of one. Your options within Standard English, remember, are limited to auxiliary verb forms such as WILL + VERB, modals, go-futures, and *deictic adverbials* (see the beginning of 2.4.5), since English does not have a proper future tense. Would the story still read as a piece of science fiction, or even count as a narrative at all?

For illustration, here is an extract from Michael Frayn's (1981) *A Very Private Life*:

> Once upon a time there will be a little girl called Uncumber.
>
> Uncumber will have a younger brother called Sulpice, and they will live with their parents in a house in the middle of the woods. There will be no windows in the house, because there will be nothing to see outside except the forest. While inside there will be all kinds of interesting things – strange animals, processions, jewels, battles, mazes, convolutions of pure shapes and pure colours, which materialize in the air at will, solid and brilliant and almost touchable. For this will be in the good new days a long, long while ahead, and it will be like that in people's houses then.
>
> (Frayn 1981: 1)

This book does not usually count as science fiction, and the fantastic elements inside the house would seem to confirm this. However, there is something about the assertiveness of the 'will' form here, and the authority of the third person narration, that seems to suggest prediction rather than wishfulness. Are the effects of your narrative like those in this text? Can you imagine a whole science fiction story written like this?

2.4.6 Relational, Textual and Compositional Deixis

The final three forms of deictic expression all reveal differences between the early science fiction and the more recent texts. **Relational** expressions encode the social viewpoint of the narrator and characters (Levinson (1983: 89) calls this 'social' deixis; Green (1995b: 22) terms it 'subjective' deixis). This is most easily apparent in the forms of naming and address used by narrators for other characters, with more familiar terms and nicknames used in the more recent vernacular narratives. Compare Wells's (1993: 335) Prince Manfred and Rin Kay with Gibson's (1984: 199) Case, Wintermute, Dixie and Noon's (1993: 15) Scribble and The Beetle.

These relations between characters are also expressed in a variety of modal expressions which stylistically encode characters' point of view (see Fowler 1986 and Simpson 1993). As we noticed in the discussion of modal auxiliaries (2.4.5), the shifting focalisation and direct speech of characters in the later texts give more opportunities for a wider range of modality to be expressed. There tends to be a correspondingly greater range of viewpoints presented as well. And where early science fiction predominantly features declarative assertions, the later narratives feature comparatives, conditionals and forms with varied speaker-commitment to the truth of the utterance. For example, notice the variety of such forms in these extracts from *Neuromancer*, and compare the different types with any passage from the earlier science fiction quoted in this chapter:

> Their room might have been the one in Chiba where he'd first seen Armitage. He went to the window, in the morning, almost expecting to see Tokyo Bay. There was another hotel across the street.
> [. . .]
> She closed her eyes and there was a click that Case felt rather than heard. It made him remember the magnetic locks on the door of her cubicle in the puppet place. The door had opened for him, even though he'd had the wrong chip. That was Wintermute, manipulating the lock the way it had manipulated the drone micro and the robot gardener. The lock system in the puppet place had been a subunit of Freeside's security system. The simple mechanical lock here would pose a real problem for the AI, requiring either a drone of some kind or a human agent.
>
> (Gibson 1984: 108, 213)

Correspondingly, there are chronological differences in the use of **textual** (or 'discourse' – Levinson 1983: 85) deixis. This describes the expressions that are used when narrators refer directly and explicitly to their own narration. It is a technique that foregrounds the textuality of the narrative, but it can also increase the plausibility of the narrative rather than draw the reader's attention to the literary fiction. In *Last and First Men* and *The Shape of Things to Come*, for example, the texts are presented as organised documentaries, and the editorial textual deixis is a reminder of this:

> I have remarked already how impersonal is this school history of the year 2006 in comparison with the histories of our own time. [. . .] Then suddenly this history lapses into something like melodrama. [. . .] I think some explanatory links must be missing here, some comments that might have pointed to the value of this episode in illuminating the play of motive that led to the Air Dictatorship. But let me give it as it came to me.

> (Wells 1993: 326)

Textual deixis is manifested here by the lexical choices ('history', 'explanatory links', 'episode') that refer directly to the text in hand. The first-person narration and demonstratives ('this school history . . . this history . . . this episode'), the directionality of the verbs ('give it as it came to me'), and the use of spatial and temporal pointers ('our own time', 'here') are all devices used in the Wells fiction to point reflexively to the textuality of the future history.

In *Vurt*, too, there is textual deixis, as you might expect from a narrator called Scribble. As in the Wells passage above, the frame recall is accompanied by personal deictic expressions and a temporal switch into the present tense (the narrating time rather than the event time of the narrative). However, here the reflexive reference to the narrative text is marked by a more uncertain and hesitant modality. This is a narrator not authoritatively recounting events but rehearsing an ongoing act of piecing them together:

> I'm not telling this very well. I'm asking for your trust on this one. Here I am, surrounded by wine bottles. [. . .] I'm trying to get this down with a cracked-up genuine antique word processor, the kind they just don't make any more, trying to find the words.

Sometimes we get the words wrong.
Sometimes we get the words wrong!
Believe me on this one. And trust me, if you can. I'm doing
my best to tell it true. It just gets real hard sometimes . . . This
is how we lost Desdemona.
No. No, not yet.

(Noon 1993: 153–4)

Lastly, this impression of the relative unreliability or intersubjectivity
of the narrators of the later texts is generally encoded in the **compositional** choices these narrating personas seem to make. (This deictic
category, termed 'syntactic deixis', is pointed out by Green 1995b: 22.)
The syntactic arrangement within the selected texts tends to conform
to the generic text-type which they mimic. In the *Vurt* passage just
quoted, for example, the compositional deixis marks out a 'confessional'
mode. There are similar deictic commitments by the other narrators in
the global forms of documentary, history, memoir, autobiography,
stream-of-consciousness, and journalistic reportage, all of which are
complexly stylistically encoded.

Exploration

■ The frameworks used in this chapter have set out a means of thinking
about deixis in literature, and an understanding of tracking episodes and
characters (this is more fully developed in chapter 7). These are scientific frameworks which a science fiction story could use as the basis for
alteration. Can you imagine characters or events in a science fictional
context that could subvert any of the frameworks introduced in this
chapter, or at least stretch them to their limits?

For example, how would the notion of enactors and primed frames
be used to describe shape-changing aliens or simulacra of real people
(Campbell 1975), or serial multiple reincarnation (Farmer 1974)? What
about dead characters whose voices are still around to be heard by other
selected characters (as in Ben Kenobi's voice in *Star Wars* (Lucas 1977))?
Or a dead character as narrator's focaliser (Dick 1973)? What if a person-
ality could be downloaded into a computer memory and replayed
(Bear 1985, 1996) or uploaded again into a newly created body to live
again (Banks 1997)? You might think of other science fiction scenarios
to test the model further.

2.5 Review

This chapter has been concerned with identifying the *mechanics* of plausibility in a selection of science fiction texts over time. I have focused on the deictic elements of the texts, as these are the ways in which the narratives are anchored to an apparent reality. But it is important to see this aspect of the textual organisation of science fiction as being subject to the cognitive processes and interpretative position of the reader. Similar arrangements of deictic patterns, with only quite subtle variation across texts, can produce quite different global effects.

For example, in each of the sections on different deictic categories (2.4.3 to 2.4.6), it was apparent that the early texts (Wells, Stapledon, Asimov) share with the later texts (Brunner, Gibson, Noon) a fragmentation of speakers and a multiplicity of narrative viewpoints, each of which can be identified through their characteristic personal deictic expressions. However, the set of speakers in the early texts serves to create a documentary embedding of witnessed accounts (see 3.4.1 for more on this). In the later texts, the 'narrator' is more of an organising principle or system of narration (even the first person narration of Scribble in *Vurt* organises the other viewpoints). Both sets of texts thus share a fragmentation, but the early texts achieve authority by it and the later texts a confused and breathless chaos. This difference is mainly an effect of small differences within the *spatial deixis* of each. Later narratives tend to use the proximal and distal demonstratives ('these – those', 'this – that') to mimic the co-present pragmatic context of everyday face-to-face conversation. This means that they come across as being more colloquial and vernacular in style, and this makes them apparently more subjective and idiosyncratic.

The texts of the middle period (Asimov's core narrative, Bradbury and Clarke) differ further from the later texts in that they tend to have a single omniscient narrator, manifest in the personal deictic choices and the handling of tense as simple and conventional past narrative. In addition, they lack the metalinguistic and reflexive patterns of *textual* and *compositional deixis* apparent in the later texts.

Such differences in readerly affect are only discernible at the theoretical level if it is recognised that readers impute speaker-generation to all texts. Narrative texts allow a narrating persona to be constructed by the reader, working backwards up the anchor chain, as it were. Since the unreal science fictional universe is constructed in parallel with this, deictic anchoring points function as links between textual expressions and their indicated referents. And since the science fictional context raises doubts about the logical status of the objective referent-world of referring expressions and deictic expressions equally, a cognitive dimension would seem to remove the need for a deixis/reference distinction altogether (see chapter 7 for a development of this).

It is important to notice that, even with this cognitive revision of deixis, the basic categories used in this chapter have nevertheless allowed me to talk about science fiction. The universes of science fiction may be radically different, but they use generally conventional narrative patterns as one strategy of maintaining plausibility. Science fiction, though, allows one further, unique twist to narrative theory: the deictically-indexed fictional universes of science fiction texts are real.

Gibson and Sterling's (1990) *The Difference Engine* presents London in 1855. But this is an Industrial Revolution in which Babbage managed to perfect his Analytic Engine, and information technology, cinema and pneumatic trains arrive a century early, where Byron is prime minister, Disraeli a disreputable hack journalist, and there is a Marxist commune in Manhattan. In short, this is a parallel science fiction narrative, but of the past rather than the future. Despite this, it is anchored in the reader's mind in the conventional way, using deictic expressions, framed episodes, past tense narration, and so on. Stylistically it is identical to the narrative patterns of futuristic science fiction.

As mentioned above (section 2.3), such narratives are termed *alternative histories* in science fiction, but past and future are treated fundamentally in the same narrative way. Each science fiction narrative creates a *plausible* universe (that is, one that is coherent and internally consistent), which could have come into being at some decisive point in the past at which that universe diverged from our own. There cannot be an infinite and endless set of possible outcomes, though. Since the universe is made up of a finite set of particles, the number of possible parallel universes might be very large but it is also finite. In other words, plausible universes exist in parallel with our own, branching out from our own past 'timeline'. This is why, in theory, time-travel into the past is possible, but the travellers' existence there creates a branch into a different universe that diverges from their own future. They can never return 'sideways' to their own parallel reality, nor get back to their own future.

Let us conclude with a bit of mischievousness. Some of the plausible universes are indexed by science fiction narratives. Of the totality of possible universes in existence, the ones most similar to our own (those we would be able to understand) are very likely to be the plausible universes of science fiction. It follows that any science fiction universe that is plausible is somewhere real. This would mean that it is physically, mathematically and existentially real.

The future is not yet determined, but the past is. There are just a lot of different versions of the past, inaccessible to us at the moment other than vicariously through reading narratives. Our sense of history is simply our reasonably unified view of the trail of past actions and events. The future has not yet happened, but any possible future *will* really happen. Science fiction, then, in both the idiomatic and the literal senses, will always have a future.

Explorations

■ This chapter has considered the status in science fiction of characters, entities, frames and reference. Consider these in relation to non-science fictional serial futures: futurology, astrology, weather forecasting, TV listings, almanacks, tide tables, train times, and horse-racing odds. Are there examples of fictional projection and enactors here? How does each of these sorts of text anchor its projected realities deictically? Take an example of each text-type and identify the enactors involved. How is the commitment to a future reality stylistically expressed?

■ There is a tradition in science fiction in which writers create sequels building on their own or even others' fictional universes. For example, Asimov (1986, 1988) developed his earlier *Foundation* universe (Asimov 1960, 1962, 1964), and later both Benford (1998) and Bear (1998) have taken the same universe into new narratives. Select an existing science fiction universe and sketch out a possible sequel. Would your narrative take place in a different part of the universe, later or earlier, or woven into the existing fabric? What would you introduce or change? Would you revise any parts of the original universe? Would you develop the same characters, introduce new ones, kill any off? In making these decisions, what are your objectives for the narrative? Would you write it in the same style as the original? Why? If not, how would your style be different, and would it in itself reflect a different universe?

Speculations

■ It seems that cognitively we treat the internal organisation of framing, tracking and reference in both reality and fiction in the same way. Most well-adjusted people can tell the difference between fiction and reality by identifying certain contextual markers: buying the book, holding the magazine, being in a cinema, sitting in an amusement arcade, knowing that the product is marketed as fiction, for example. However, in relation to the film industry and computer games, reality is increasingly too low-budget to seem real. The development of virtuality technology, such as in theme-park rides, is gradually removing the markers we use to differentiate fiction from base-reality; indeed, this is the design-objective of such projects. Consider what the logical status of fiction would be if the technology ever became good enough such that these markers were entirely removed. Would the fiction become the reality, in a very real sense? Would this be an undesirable development, given that, in any case, people structure their view of the world in accordance with their own ideology? Is this sort of absolute plausibility by immersion the goal of art, or is artifice and the awareness of artifice part of the pleasure of the fictional experience?

■ Those languages that have a true future tense still tend to present science fiction in the past (or have a special 'literary' or 'narrative' tense that is nevertheless a past tense). This seems to support Fleischman's (1990) assertion that the past is prototypical for narrative, and is even a defining characteristic. Can you imagine a true future tense for English (in a parallel science fiction universe, of course)? This could be simply a matter of a morpheme added to verbs, such as 'el', as a development of 'will': 'I walkel' (will walk), 'the aliens arrivel' (will arrive), 'the Earth bel destroyed' (will be destroyed), perhaps. You might think of an alternative form, or invent different personal pronouns to account for future hypothetical enactors ('Il', 'yul', 'heel', 'theil'?). What if Middle English had borrowed the future tense from French after the Norman Conquest, along with the thousands of words which were actually borrowed? In that case, would futuristic fiction written in the future tense retain the concrete sense of accomplished realism that the past tense gives current science fiction? Or would science fiction be more philosophically analytical and lyrically descriptive than it is? Would science fiction be a non-narrative genre, in the light of Fleischman's position? Might science fiction not exist at all in this speculative universe? If not, does this mean that the past tense is not only central to narrative but is especially important for science fiction?

Further reading

For any research in science fiction, Clute and Nicholls (1993) is the essential encyclopedia. The standard histories of the genre are Aldiss and Wingrove (1986) and James (1994), while Aldiss and Harrison (1975) and Jakubowski and James (1992) are biographical histories. Bibliographical material appears in Barron (1987). The main work on deixis is in Levinson (1983), and the collected essays edited by Jarvella and Klein (1982), Rauh (1983a), and Green (1995a). Cognitive views of deixis appear in Duchan, Bruder and Hewitt (1995), and the psychology of narrative reading in Gerrig (1993). Point of view in fiction is discussed by Fowler (1986) and Simpson (1993). Hacker and Chamberlain (1981) contains a bibliography of alternate history science fiction. The discussion of other real universes relies on the 'many-worlds' interpretation of quantum wave mechanics (see DeWitt and Graham 1973; Rogers 1968), which resolves the paradox of 'Schrödinger's Cat' (Schrödinger 1935, 1978). The 'many-worlds' interpretation (originally suggested by Hugh Everett in 1957) asserts that in resolving an uncertainty, all an observer does is see the particular outcome which leads to his or her own reality, and the other unrealised reality carries on as another universe. Philosophically, the notion that all possible worlds are real is the 'principle of plenitude', argued by Lovejoy (1930).

CHAPTER 3

MICROLOGICAL: FUTUREPLAY

3.1 Preview

This book is primarily concerned with the language in which science fiction is written, and how it is arranged and read as a genre. However, the relationship between language and science fiction has also been addressed directly, both by researchers and by science fiction writers in their stories. In some science fiction, there is a consciousness not just of language and style but of linguistic theory as well. This has led, in turn, to conscious effects being built in to the stylistic surface and narrative organisation.

The development of linguistic input into science fiction seems to be different from the use of other sciences in the genre. It is perhaps not surprising, given the background of many science fiction writers, that speculations on atomic and cosmic physics, biology and genetics, chemistry, and materials engineering have tended to be plausible and knowledgeable projections. There are many cases in which the science in the fiction is only a few steps ahead of reality, and there has been some fruitful interaction between real science and fictional science. An early example of science and art imitating each other is the case of H.G. Wells, who was reading about Professor Soddy's nuclear experiments before the First World War, and wanted 'to know quite the latest about the atomic theory and sources of energy [. . .] My idea is taken from Soddy' (letter quoted in West 1930: 199). In the subsequent novel, *The World Set Free*, Wells (1914) speculated on the discovery of radium and its consequences, and was accurate even to the year of its isolation by Marie and Pierre Curie in 1933. Then, when the physicist Leo Szilard read the book in German in 1932, he applied for a patent to cover his method of setting up a chain-reaction: 'Knowing what this would mean – and I knew it because I had studied H.G. Wells – I did not want this patent to become public' (quoted in Mackenzie and Mackenzie 1973: 299). Later, Szilard (1961) even had a foray into science fiction writing.

When it comes to projections of the science of linguistics, however, science fiction writers seem not to be so well informed. The next section briefly discusses the ignorance or backwardness of linguistic understanding in science fiction. The results of this for explicit fictional treatments of language issues are discussed in 3.3, though even poor linguistic knowledge is no bar to producing interesting and poetic writing (see 3.4). The chapter ends with an outline of literary critical arguments that follow from certain theoretical approaches to language.

3.2 Linguistics on Another Planet

With a few honourable exceptions mentioned later in the chapter, the history of linguistic understanding in science fiction is not a distinguished one. Meyers (1980), in the best discussion of the use of linguistics in science fiction, points out several howlers committed in the genre. He reserves special sardonic comment for accounts of language change (or no change at all!) over many centuries:

> In general the treatment of linguistic change in science fiction is like the sky on a hazy night: a few bright spots seen through an obfuscating fog. When we look more specifically at the treatment of the future development of English, the fog does not lift.

> (Meyers 1980: 18)

In futuristic science fiction, the language of the future is either seen as 'degenerate' and the population illiterate, or everyone speaks a form of English as a *lingua franca* (a common language), perhaps with some Russian (before the end of the Cold War), Japanese or Chinese mixed in. Such science fiction ignores the dialectal variation that is a central characteristic of most languages, especially one as geographically dispersed as English, preferring to believe in a universal 'Standard Future English' (Meyers 1980: 33).

Where language issues are directly addressed, there is likely to be a confusion between written and spoken forms. Perhaps unsurprisingly for a written mode of art, science fiction indicates alienness or futurity by inserting a few aberrant spellings. Often it is obvious that these simply represent modern pronunciations, as in Kornbluth's (1953: 77) story 'v thi Taim Polis' and their 'Twenti-Fifth Sentch'ri ekzistens' (quoted by Meyers 1980: 29). Of course, Meyers examines the linguistics in science fiction in the same way as discussions of the 'science in science fiction' proceed: he measures it against the authorised version and treats its use in science fiction as having the status of prediction. This is reading science fiction as futurology. Reading science fiction as art allows a more charitable view of linguistic 'mistakes' to be taken: a fictional adjustment to the representation of language is an index of the future rather than a hard prediction of its actuality. The form itself is symbolically important.

This is evident in Ray Bradbury's (1977b: 88–99) story, 'A Sound of Thunder', which begins with a group of men travelling back in time on safari to shoot a dinosaur. Leaving the approved path, one of them accidentally kills a butterfly, and the effect on the time line is exponential, affecting politics, society and language. The sign outside the time machine now reads:

TYME SEFARI INC.
SEFARIS TU ANY YEER EN THE PAST.
YU NAIM THE ANIMALL.
WEE TAEK YOU THAIR.
YU SHOOT ITT.

(Bradbury 1977b: 98)

Here, the aberrant spelling is indexical of the altered future, rather than being a fully-worked out piece of parallel-universe orthography. It would be possible to make some comment on the mixture of Middle English, Dutch, and Noah Webster-ish variation here, or note the subtle difference between 'yu' in subject position and 'you' in object position, but this just looks like a plain typographical mistake, and in any case such an analysis would sacrifice the main point of the story for a linguist's interest.

Alien languages themselves are also usually indexes of alienness rather than fully worked-out linguistic systems. Friend (1973) lists the means that science fiction deploys to avoid the tedious business of imagining an alien language:

1. Telepathy and automatic translators.
2. 'He spoke faultless Anglic'.
3. 'We call it Amer-English. I happen to be a student of dead languages'.

4. 'It was in a curious slurred English that I could barely understand'.
5. 'The whole galaxy operated on an English basis. It's the court language of the Mother Planet, you see'.

(Friend 1973: 998–9)

To these, Meyers (1980: 218–19) adds the 'Men of Earth, we have learned your language from radio broadcasts' ploy. As he points out,

> Writers of science fiction seldom spare their characters: they may slam their heroes' ships into planets or send their heroines to kill tigers with knives; they may freeze them into statues on Pluto or shoot them through exploding suns. Hardly any degradation or suffering is spared – with the exception of exposing them to the rigors of learning a foreign language.

(Meyers 1980: 117)

Such ridicule is certainly justified in general, though perhaps we should not be too harsh when poetic licence is extended into 'scientific licence', in the interests of a fluent narrative. There are often many liberties also taken with the laws of physics in science fiction, and the point is not that these are 'accurate' but that they are believable and plausible. This is a matter of readerly judgement, and the fact is that most readers are neither trained physicists nor professional linguists.

3.3 Linguistic Science in Science Fiction

A curious feature of science fiction emerges if you compare the texts of chapters 2 and 4. Though science fiction is the most conceptually experimental of genres, breaking and rewriting the laws of physics, moving planets, travelling through time and questioning the nature of matter and existence, the style of its language has traditionally been very pedestrian, conservative, unimaginative and unspectacular. Science fictional prose is stereotypically blandly descriptive to the point of banality. It moves beyond that only to the hyperbole of 'Gosh-wow!' awe and wonder. It is writing that is about conceptual alternativity, rather than an exemplification in its style of fantasy and unrealism.

Of course, across the range of science fiction, this stylistic pedestrianism can easily be explained as a necessary antidote to the wildness of the conceptual content. It could also be seen as a rhetorical ploy to assist in establishing the verisimilitude of the extrapolated world. Prosaic delivery realises the fantastic content, reifies it and makes it more plausible. It borrows the apparently neutral, objective and reporting register from the natural sciences to keep the reader's disbelief safely suspended (see especially chapter 4 for a detailed account of this).

Modern linguistics views using language in the same way as taking a photograph: the photographer has to stand somewhere in relation to the object through the lens, and this involves a choice, whether conscious or not. In other words, however 'objective' or 'truthful' it seems, there is no such thing as a neutral photograph nor a piece of language that expresses a neutral or objective viewpoint or ideology (see Fairclough 1989, Simpson 1993, Caldas-Coulthard and Coulthard 1996). Some stylistic forms (such as scientific reports and journalistic accounts) have popularly come to be regarded as objective, but in fact the view that language can be used neutrally is a 'folk-theory' of linguistics which does not bear up to analytical scrutiny.

Nevertheless, this view is one that is apparently widely held in science fictional practice. Coming out of the magazines from the 1920s to the '50s, there is an implicit poetics which sees form and content as being separate. This 'folk-poetics' is inescapable in the lurid content expressed through journalistic reportage (see chapter 4 on *pulpstyle*). The view seems to be accompanied by a similarly traditional conception of the natural sciences as rational and objective systems. In this scheme, the universe is filled with objects and phenomena that are to be explored, named and explained. Mysticism tends to be explained within the framework of physics or chemistry; intuition through biological or clinical psychological terminology. It is a view of science that is pre-quantum in its underlying philosophy, though it might use aspects of contemporary physics for their narrative potential. For example, it treats faster-than-light travel as merely an extension of conventional travel, rather than a fundamentally different category of experience, not strictly 'travel' at all. Starships look just like flashy cruise-ships or warships. Science, in this perspective, is the discovery of truths, and its success is measured out in categories and invented terminology, a new label for a newly discovered object (see chapter 6).

The folk-theory of language, together with this traditional objectivist view of science, produces a folk-theory of linguistics. This is rational and objective, and also dualistic: meaning is immanent in words, such that language and communication is simply the sum of word-meaning, and the conceptual content of words can be expressed in a variety of styles without any change to the meaning. There is a perception of an abstract meaning, a pre-linguistic deep structure which is merely encoded differently by different languages. This origin-meaning is a reductive essence. In this view, linguistic form is simply a code, a representation system that provides our handle on given reality.

Such a view, for example, is what enabled *Star Trek* creator Gene Roddenberry to use the 'universal translator' to explain why the new life and new civilisation encountered where '*no one has gone before*' all appear to speak English. It is parodied by Douglas Adams's (1979) 'Babel fish'. This creature, when inserted into the ear, creates a telepathic feedback loop that converts incoming alien/foreign words into the hearer's language. The fish itself does not understand either code that it ingests and excretes, but the implicit assumption in both the universal translator and the Babel fish is that meaning is a pre-linguistic essence that is simply coated in a carrying language.

As Meyers (1980: 118) points out, where both source and target languages are known, such a machine is conceivable. There are current computer software packages that can translate passages from one language into another, though the results are sometimes comical. It is easy to imagine advances in these programs improving the performance to near-fluency. The fact which helps such systems, of course, is that the two languages will both be human, and might share cross-cultural norms or known differences that can be built into the machine's capability. When it works perfectly, it will certainly not rely simply on word-for-word exchange, but will have an algorithm to generate coherent syntactical sequences, recognise idiomatic expressions, match proverbial and metaphoric utterances, and translate pragmatic markers such as tone of voice, politeness forms, degrees of formality and genre, and so on. Advanced features such as recognising irony and humour would be nice additions.

All of this awaits considerable advances in both cross-cultural discourse theory and computer programming, but it is at least plausible. Meyers (1980: 118–30) uses the fact of the sheer absurdity of the alien-language automatic translator to discuss the notion of plausibility. He points out that relying too heavily on plausibility as a defining feature of science fiction means that much of the genre must be judged poor, because it includes such implausibilities as the automatic translator. This is clearly unsatisfactory, and Meyers moves to a weak form of the plausibility issue, so that 'artistic licence' is allowable. However, Meyers's position is based on a very writerly and authoritative notion of plausibility, very different from the readerly notion I developed in chapter 2. For him, plausibility is judged against the current state of real science, rather than against readers' beliefs. His view leads him to adopt a distinction between real authorised science and literary conventions (time travel, faster-than-light travel, universal translators) that are allowable if implausible. The outcome of this, as he implies, is not very satisfactory either (Meyers 1980: 130).

Basing plausibility in readerly beliefs allows folk-theory and authorised scientific theory to co-exist, and for experienced science fiction readers it encompasses literary genre conventions as well. This approach also avoids the problem (recognised by Meyers 1980: 125) of defining science fiction against whatever scientific progress has been made when the text is written. Otherwise the definition of what counts as science fiction alters with every scientific innovation, which is clearly absurd.

However, returning to the alien-language automatic translator, there is obviously a difference between this and other conventions. The scientific jury is still out on time-travel (especially forwards or sideways), and there are ways of cheating on the faster-than-light problem (space warps, wormholes, instantaneous changes in information attaching to each atom, see Bear (1994) for example). Einstein's theory restricting this might even be supplanted some day. However, these are philosophical and scientific problems; the automatic translator is of a different order in that it is a piece of technology. Since language is a closed system of arbitrary meanings, and without any data on the target language, it is absolutely impossible that an alien-language automatic translator could ever work in a first contact situation. A Babel fish, on the other hand . . .

. . . could only work if telepathic thought were pre-linguistic. Here we are back to the question of whether thought and language are identical, and whether content and style can be separated.

There are some science fiction texts, however, which deal less reductively with the issue of language. Jonathan Swift's (1967) *Gulliver's Travels* ridicules literal mindedness in the description of the academicians who carry around the actual items they want to refer to in their speech. Here is a theory of reference that operates entirely at the level of direct assertion, literally by producing the thing itself. Swift parodies this literal-mindedness.

In the last voyage made by Gulliver, what appears to be a utopian environment for the horse-creature Houyhnhnms is based on a similar sort of literal-mindedness in language. The Houyhnhnms are incapable of 'saying the thing which was not' (Swift 1967: 286): that is, lying. Of course, this would also include not being able to use conditionals like this sentence, metaphors or any other figurative expression, not being able to learn any new concepts, and not being able to hypothesise, speculate, tell stories or write science fiction. Both Meyers (1980: 197–200) and Philmus (1973) point out that absolute social orders such as **utopias** and **dystopias** (which I discuss in chapter 9) depend for their maintenance on a suppression of linguistic innovation. They make a strong connection between language and thought. Language must not allow creativity, because that would create new concepts that would upset the social order; and new concepts cannot be allowed, because that would cause linguistic chaos and ambivalence of meaning. The strong form of the idea that concepts are limited by the availability of words to describe them has come to be known as the Sapir–Whorf hypothesis, after its two main proponents (Sapir 1949; Whorf 1957).

Language constraining thought is evident in Aldous Huxley's (1955) *Brave New World*, in which genetically engineered babies are environmentally conditioned through language. Their social roles and rules are inculcated by recorded repetition. It is language which structures the reality that they see, and Huxley shows how the different orders or classes of society, from Alphas to Epsilons, regard that reality differently. Each class is conditioned to appreciate and desire its predetermined lot.

Another book that was heavily derived from Yevgeny Zamiatin's (1972) *We* is George Orwell's (1948) *1984*, perhaps the most famous science fictional treatment of the issue of language and reality. The future totalitarian state is engaged in establishing and promoting the language of 'Newspeak', an extrapolated caricature of what Orwell saw as the linguistic degeneracy of his own 1940s. In the novel, the Party aims to reduce the total number of words to reduce the availability of meaning (again, this is a very reductive view of how language works). The lexicographer Symes tells the character Winston Smith:

> 'Don't you see that the whole aim of Newspeak is to narrow the range of thought? In the end we shall make thoughtcrime literally impossible because there will be no words in which to express it. Every concept that can ever be needed, will be expressed by exactly *one* word, with its meaning rigidly defined and all its subsidiary meanings rubbed out and forgotten [. . .] It's merely a question of [. . .] reality-control'.

> (Orwell 1948: 49)

Orwell elaborates his Sapir-Whorfian view of language in the fictional essay attached to the end of the novel: 'Appendix: The Principles of Newspeak'. He imagines the synthetic language to be governed by the aim of reducing the number of words by 'destroying' them. This is done by removing them from the Newspeak dictionary, the 11th edition of which is being compiled in 1984, so that no one will speak anything other than the approved language by 2050. There is no indication how people are to be made to forget words and meanings simply because they have been expunged from the dictionary, but given the brutal measures to enforce 'doublethink' later in the novel, we can perhaps guess.

Much of the destruction of words is effected by the removal of separate antonymic, comparative and superlative lexical items to leave a regular system of root word and affixes: 'good', 'ungood', 'gooder', 'goodest', 'plusgood', and 'doubleplusgood', for example. The dictionary also aims towards a non-differentiation between nouns and verbs, and Orwell cites 'knife' as a noun used for the verb 'to cut' as an example (and one which is now in common usage in our reality). All inflections apart from past '-ed' and plural '-es, -s' are eliminated.

Most of the essay, however, is concerned with the reduction of nouns. Newspeak divides the language up into three lexical fields. The 'A Vocabulary' consists of words used in everyday life, and it is the largest class. The 'B Vocabulary' is made up of political words, or words with some sort of ideological basis. The 'C Vocabulary' covers all scientific or technical words. There are problems with this system, of course. The essay has already equated science, in its Newspeak sense, with correct ideology (that of Big Brother and the Party), so that, on inspection, the distinction between the B and C vocabularies collapses. There is also a perception, in Orwell's thinking, of language, and its ideological basis, as being primarily in lexis (words) rather than in grammar – specifically, rather than in syntactic relations or pragmatic force. There is no sense of the modern critical linguistic position that even both everyday words and technical words have an ideological basis. Nevertheless, in spite of its folk-linguistic view of how language works, its lexicocentric approach and extreme Sapir-Whorfianism, Newspeak remains a prime example of science fictional commentary on language. (It has also been the motivation for critical linguistic work on the discourse strategies, or 'Nukespeak', used by politicians during the Cold War. See Aubrey 1982; Chilton 1985; Stockwell 1990.)

Exploration

■ Consider whether Newspeak could work on sound linguistic princi-ples: that is, without the reliance on the strong version of the Sapir-Whorf hypothesis. Meyers (1980: 200) gives the conditions that would be necessary for the restriction of words: prevent borrowing from another language; prevent the metaphorical extension of word-meaning; prevent new words being coined (see chapter 6 for all these processes at work in science fiction). Can you imagine a state, community or society in which this could happen? Can you think of other ways to restrict the ability of people to think? Can you imagine a science fiction novel being written in a version of Newspeak? In considering this, you will have to decide for yourself the extent to which language constrains thought. You will also have to decide whether science fiction is fundamentally concerned with new ideas expressed in propositions, or whether it could be a purely lyrical mode of writing. Can science fiction only be a narrative genre?

3.4 Linguistic Special Effects

1984 was written around 1948 (the reversal of the last two date digits to give the novel's temporal location indicates it is a caricature of its written present rather than an outright prediction), and *Brave New World* appeared in the 1920s, dates which encompass the era of pulp magazine science fiction (see chapter 4). In spite of the fact that science fiction ought to be highly experimental in this era, science fictional comment-ary on the soft science of linguistics and its object, language, is rare, and the stylistics of science fiction in general was mundane.

The 1960s saw a new science fictional interest in the concept of inner space and in the capacities of language both as medium and as subject of science fiction. This so-called 'New Wave' in Britain was led by Michael Moorcock, J.G. Ballard and Brian Aldiss, and exhibited a

> heavy emphasis upon the manner in which a story is told, sometimes almost to the exclusion of its matter, with an accompanying borrowing of devices old in the mainstream but new to science fiction, such as stream of consciousness, dadaism, typographical tricks, on-stage sex, Yellow Book horror, and naughty words.
>
> (James Blish, quoted in Taylor 1990: 612)

These linguistic special effects were new to science fiction, and have since been used by a variety of writers to thematise the linguistic surface of texts in ways which were appropriate to the subject-matter. Science fiction, in other words, discovered a mimetic style which at last moved it away from the pedestrian reportage of the tradition.

3.4.1 Collage and Documentary Fragmentation

One special effect employed widely is the technique of **documentary fragmentation**. The text is presented as a **collage** of texts as if from several different sources, assembled as if by a historian or archivist, from which the story emerges. (Several of the texts mentioned in chapter 2 exhibited this feature of narrative organisation.) The single narrative voice is thus broken up and the science fictional world appears as a readerly construction from evidence.

Margaret Atwood's (1987) *The Handmaid's Tale* is presented in this way, as part of a university seminar from the novel's distant future. However, the reader does not realise this until the end. The narrative of the handmaid, Offred, is followed by 'Historical Notes on The Handmaid's Tale', thus textualising the personal account. These are presented as

> *Being a partial transcript of the proceedings of the Twelfth Symposium on Gileadean Studies, held as part of the International Historical Association Convention, which took place at the University of Denay, Nunavit, on June 25, 2195.*
>
> Chair: *Professor Maryann Crescent Moon, Department of Caucasian Anthropology, University of Denay, Nunavit.*
>
> (Atwood 1987: 311, original italics)

This is followed by a historical talk on the authenticity of Offred's account and the characters involved. Connections are made between the Christian fundamentalist misogyny of the Gilead regime, other state systems in Iran, Romania, India, and comments on pollution and militarism in the twentieth century. The end-frame provides a distancing effect from the core narrative that precedes it, and also encourages a particular interpretation of the novel. The world of 2195 is significantly different from the world of Gilead: Professor Crescent Moon and (later) Professor Johnny Running Dog indicate an ascendancy of native Americans over white ethnic Europeans, who are now the object of study of a university department; the Professor's female 'Christian' name is so emphatically different from the male-derived 'Of-fred' that it is doubled ('Maryann') and combines the names of the mother and grandmother of Jesus.

However, the status of cues to an interpretation in the talk that follows is as ambivalent as this name, in relation to the core narrative. The speaker tells his audience that 'we must be cautious about passing moral judgement upon the Gileadeans. Surely we have learned by now that such judgements are of necessity culture-specific [. . .] Our job is not to censure but to understand. (Applause)' (Atwood 1987: 314–15). However, the terrors of the core-narrative make this sound very hollow, and cast doubt on the 'objective' practices of academic analysis. The pre-talk announcements about missing lunch and the 'Outdoor Period Costume Sing-Song' serve to make the academic meeting seem concerned with trivialities. And there is a subversive sub-text available to the reader: the speaker is almost a male apologist for the Gileadean regime, down-playing its inhumanity in the context of other similar common historical movements; the talk ends with 'Are there any questions?', inviting disagreement; and the opening quoted above twice tells us to 'Denay, Nunavit', deny none of it.

Atwood uses this documentary style to conflate two sets of values, inviting the reader to re-read history and not accept a narrative simply because it is authorised (biblically or academically). In general, the practice is obviously a rhetorical frame-up to establish the verisimilitude of the text-world, comprising letters, reports, diary entries, messages from the future, and so on, but it is noticeable that these are all techniques from the early evolution of the novel form, prior to the predominant realist mode. The title page of Doris Lessing's (1981a) novel which has come to be known simply as *Shikasta*, actually comprises the following:

CANOPUS IN ARGOS: ARCHIVES

Re: Colonised Planet 5
SHIKASTA
Personal, Psychological, Historical Documents
Relating to Visit by **Johor** (George Sherban)

EMISSARY (Grade 9)
87th of the Period of the Last Days

In my edition, this is followed further by: 'GRAFTON BOOKS. A division of the Collins Publishing Group.' The text of the novel is made up of a variety of typefaces, with *italics*, SMALL CAPITALS, standard font, sans serif and **bold formats** all used to mark out sections of text from different sources (Lessing 1981a).

Such an epistolary technique removes the apparent reliance on a single and possibly unreliable narrator, and simply presents documentary evidence. It also calls up the foregrounded textuality of the novel, as exemplified by Lessing's title-page. The range of graphological and typographical tricks is accompanied by the register of report-writing. In the title-page above, the list of noun-phrases, the colons, identifying authors and dates, abbreviations such as 'Re:' and the omission of articles from most of the noun-phrases indicate this register. The text that follows displays its status as apparently collected fragments, undermined only by the single name 'DORIS LESSING' with her smiling photograph on the cover, to indicate that this is a novel. Of course, all this only further serves to emphasise the texture of the text. Similarly, Lessing's (1983) later book in the series, *The Making of the Representative for Planet 8*, about the death of a species caused by an ice age, is followed by her essay on Shackleton's Antarctic expedition.

Such textual embedding can be extrapolated to an extreme using hypertext technology. At a 1989 conference at Leeds university (collected by Slusser and Shippey 1992), a discussion about HyperCard novels, in which the reader has options over plot development and the novel is genuinely non-linear, led science fiction writer Greg Bear to speak of 'the death of individual artistry' (see 9.6). His novel *Queen of Angels* (1991) is a riot of graphological variation. The fictional poet/murderer Emanuel Goldsmith (recalling the hate figure Emanuel Goldstein in *1984*) is quoted in the epigraphs to chapters. Typographical tricks abound, with a standard font used for the main narrative, italics for the musings of Goldsmith, and sans serif font in the 'telegraphese' of computer messages for the 'LitVid' (internet) texts and the 'thoughts' of the advanced computer, Jill. At the end of the novel, as Jill becomes the first machine to develop self-awareness, this is dramatised by her/its thoughts being presented with a gradual increase in the use of the first person pronoun:

```
!Jill (Personal Notebook)> [Deep crypto: Do I know
how to lie? Can I I refuse a direct order? Am I
I I capable of defending myself?
[...] I I I I I I I I I I think I I I I I I I
lack experience and understanding in all of those
areas. But I I I I I I I I I I I I I I I I will act
to protect myself from dissolution. I I I I I I
I I I I I I I I I am without sin for the moment.
```

(Bear 1991: 470–1, original font)

This is followed by the final page of the novel taken up with a half-page sized 'I' made up of hundreds of little 'I's, as the computer/thinker Jill achieves self-consciousness.

3.4.2 The Vernacular of the Future

Another linguistic special effect used in science fiction is the use of dialectal variation to express the language of the future. Social change, or change brought about by some political or environmental catastrophe, is reflected by linguistic changes. Philip K. Dick (1965), in *The Man in the High Castle*, subtly signals the Japanese victory over the USA in the Second World War by deleting the articles and prepositions from American English to produce a Japanese-sounding language that is still English. Barry Hines (1990), in the teleplay *Threads*, has the second generation survivors of a nuclear war in the north of England lose their language ability altogether. *Threads* ends with the silence that is the last thread of civilisation, language, being cut.

Similarly, Russell Hoban's *Riddley Walker* figures a post-holocaust south-east of England in the first person narration of the eponymous character, 'written not even in proper English but in a broken-up and worn-down vernacular of it' (Hoban 1982: flyleaf):

> On my naming day when I come 12 I gone front spear and kilt a wyld boar he parbly ben the las wyld pig on the Bundel Downs any how there hadnt ben none for a long time befor him nor I aint looking to see none agen. He dint make the groun shake nor nothing like that when he come on to my spear he wernt all that big plus he lookit poorly. He done the reqwyrt he ternt and stood and clattert his teef and made his rush and ther we wer then. Him on 1 end of the spear kicking his life out and me on the other end watching him dy. I said, 'Your tern now my tern later.' The other spears gone in then and he wer dead and the steam coming up off him in the rain and we all yelt, 'Offert!'
>
> (Hoban 1982: 1)

The non-standard future English used here is based on a range of features from traditional rural southern vernacular, such as 'dint' for 'didn't' and 'He done' for 'He did'. The minimal use of written conventions such as punctuation, the high use of conjunctions ('and'), and sentences that are not fully realised clauses ('Him on 1 end of the spear . . .') all serve to suggest a spoken monologue. The many simplified spellings ('ther', 'wer', 'agen') are usually indexes of a lack of education in the writer; here in this futuristic context they signal a simple-minded perception. The writing is full of conversational tags ('any how'), and spelling pronunciations ('teef,' 'kilt,' 'parbly') which possibly indicate a return in the southern accent to rhoticity (r-pronouncing, as Irish, Scottish and most American accents). In English accents at least, such rhoticity is associated with rural areas, and there is unfortunately still a widespread common stereotype of speakers with such accents as being simple in outlook and uncivilised.

The opening passage quoted above is accompanied by a hand-drawn map of what is now Kent, with place-names that reflect both the catastrophic disjunction in language and the brutalised society that now exists: 'Do It Over' (Dover), 'Sams Itch' (Sandwich), 'River Sour' (Stour), 'Bernt Arse' (Ashford). 'Bollock Stoans' (Birchington), 'Horny Boy' (Herne Bay), 'Widders Bel' (Whitstable), 'Fathers Ham' (Faversham), and so on. These forms reflect the predominance of spoken forms over written conventions, such as the elimination throughout the novel of the possessive apostrophe (-'s). They also reflect current stigmatised pronunciations, towards the current local vernacular, but extrapolated further. Thus 'Canterbury,' often now pronounced with a glottal stop for the medial /t/ in casual speech (/kaʔəbri/), is in the novel further ellipted to a sustained nasal: 'Cambry'.

In a detailed piece of stylistic analysis, Schwetman (1985) points out further historical changes such as the simplification of voiced dental [d] to a general unvoiced [t] to indicate past tense ('kilt', 'ternt', 'clattert'). Terminal consonant clusters are simplified ('ben', 'groun'), and folk-etymologies reflected in spellings (later 'tack ticks'). Schwetman calls this 'Post Modern English', and suggests that it has the flavour, if not the precise specifics, of medieval English, evoking a peasant people and asserting the regressive effect of the nuclear apocalypse.

Here is the familiar science fictional pattern of a partial recognition of our reality, but with sufficient alternativity to render the effect of defamiliarisation, or what Darko Suvin (1979) with specific reference to science fiction calls 'cognitive estrangement'. The experience of reading the whole novel is of a difficult struggle for meaning, as the character Riddley Walker himself tries to piece together what happened from confused myths of 'the 1 big 1' (nuclear war), the 'Master Chaynjis' (social breakdown), engineered by the 'Eusa folk' (USA) splitting 'the littl shining man the addom', all phrases that Walker uses totemically without really understanding their meaning at all. This is an example of language being used iconically as well as to indicate a predictive account.

3.4.3 Affective Thematising of Language

The use of a thorough dialectal variation in Atwood, Lessing and Hoban serves to foreground the language to the extent that the reader is likely to thematise the stylistic form itself, in a way that would not happen in traditional science fiction. This 'affective thematising' can be seen in Brian Aldiss's (1973: 35–61) short story, 'Orgy of the Living and the Dying'. The story opens by describing in detail the stages by which a televisual connection is made from Britain to a refugee camp in a famine-stricken Indian village. Communication is thus foregrounded for the reader as a theme from the beginning, and the story itself is concerned with personal miscommunication. This is thematised by the graphological structure of the text, which intersperses the narrative with disjointed lines, like radio interference:

> as he took off the towel, so she turned back the sheet. Because she was a modest Muslim woman, the gesture was curiously <u>modest, a confidence between them. Her body, the flesh built on</u> <u>O Babi Babi will the children remember me their mother like</u> to fine Asiatic bones, was an oasis compared with the deserts of starved bodies outside, the famine-clad mothers who walked a <u>hundred miles to find water for their children. Tancred tried to</u> <u>and in the well only a smell of old bones the rotted carcases of</u> dismiss the tiresome voices and images that punctuated his be- ing, and climbed beside that beautiful creature, prepared even <u>before he touched her to possess her again. Kissing her belly, he</u> <u>whose sorrows lay more siege unto my soul that all my some-</u> could almost ignore his disruptive and fragmentary thoughts.

> (Aldiss 1973: 37, layout as original)

These lines can be quotations from elsewhere (future or past) in the narrative, or literary allusions from outside the text. The latter is evid- ent by the shift in register ('O Babi', 'unto my soul'), as well as by the separating lines and the syntactic mis-sequencing from the previous few words ('Tancred tried to // and in the well . . . the rotted carcases of // dismiss the tiresome voices'). This foregrounds the texture of the text, and emphasises the function of narrative as communication. In the disruptive lines, the style reflects the theme of miscommunication in the story, which comes to a climax at the end. Low-air vibrations, generated by an air-conditioning unit, are used to make a group of bandits sick, but they also cause Tancred to hear voices, just like the interpolations of text from mythic Indian fragments, past and future. Western values and technology and Indian history and culture are blended, both thematically and stylistically, in this complexly layered story.

Aldiss's technique of affective thematising is exploited to its full potential in his novel *Barefoot in the Head* (Aldiss 1990), written for the magazine *New Worlds* and assembled as a novel in 1969. It presents a Europe saturated with psychochemicals from bombing in a war with the Middle East. The novel begins fairly conventionally, with a description of the focalising character, Colin Charteris, driving across Europe. However, as the hallucinogens which permeate the food chain gradually work into his brain, the narrative becomes more and more deviant at every level of textual organisation.

There is typographical and graphological fragmentation, with the narrative prose interrupted with poems and song lyrics (such as 'Fragment of a Much Longer Poem'), palindromes, anagrams and other concrete poems, many ostensibly written by characters in the novel. Most remarkable of all is the technique of lexical blending and deviant syntax, which increases in deviance and complexity as the narrative progresses and Charteris leads a Messianic convoy of acid-heads through a series of massive motorway pile-ups and riots. The following quotation is typical of the last fifty pages of the novel:

OUSPENSKI'S ASTRABAHN

Sparkily flinging up stones from the tired wheels the gravelcade towed darkness. Headlights beams of granite bars battering the eternal nowhere signposting the dark. The cuspidaughters of darkness somebody sang play toe with the spittoons of noon the cuspidaughters of darkness play toe with the spittoons of noon. Only some of the blind white eyes of joyride was yellow or others but altirely because the bashing the cars the jostling in the autocayed. And hob with the gobs of season.

In these primitive jalopsides herding their way like shampeding cattletrap across the last ranges of Frankreich that square squeezing country sang the drivniks. Cluttering through stick-it-up-your-assberg its nasal neutral squares its window-bankage to where the Rhine oiled its gunmottal under the northstar-barrels and a wide bridge warned zoll. Break lights a flutter red I'd ride the rifled engines ricochetting off the tracered flow below.

Cryogenetic winds bourning another spring croaking forth on the tundragged land doing it all over and bloodcounts low at a small hour with the weep of dream-pressure in the cyclic rebirth-redeath calling for a fast doss all round or heads will roll beyond the tidal rave. RECHTS FAHREN big yellow arrows splitting the roadcrown. Writhing bellies upward large painted arrows letters meaningless distant burriers seducing him to a sighfer in a diaphram.

Clobwebbed Charteris stopped the Banshee. He and Angeline climb out and he wonders if he sees himself lie there annulled, looks up into the blind white cliffs of night cloud to smell the clap of spring break its alternature. About him grind all the autodisciples flipping from their pillions and all shout and yawn make jacketed gestures through their fogstacks.

They all talk and Gloria comes over says to Angeline, 'Feels to me I have bound the hound across this country before'.

(Aldiss 1990: 183)

The richness of this passage is as dense and rewarding of close analysis as some poetry. At every linguistic level, deviant patterns create a dizzying synaesthesia in the reading experience. Beginning with syntax, sentences that are not fully realised are very common throughout the novel. Main verbs are often replaced with a collection of present participles ('Headlights beams of granite bars battering the eternal nowhere signposting the dark'), which is a form most common in the titles of paintings. Where main verbs do occur, they often do not agree for number with the noun-phrases nearest them ('Only some of the blind white eyes of joyride was yellow'), which suggests that collections of things are being perceived as single unities, and entities as collections, in reverse. There is an enormous range of verbal tense and aspect forms. Syntactic variation enables register to be mixed, from the formal-sounding construction of, 'In these primitive jalopsides [. . .] sang the drivniks', to the colloquial 'stick-it-up-your-assberg' and 'heads will roll'.

There are several metaphorical forms, including verb metaphor, puns and lexical *blends* (see chapter 8 for a typology of these). Like the forms of syntactic deviance, these mismatch different conceptual domains through unusual collocations. 'The gravelcade towed darkness' is a verb-metaphor that solidifies the darkness and makes the convoy of vehicles sinister and magical. Puns such as 'tired' (tired / with tyres), half-puns such as 'altirely', and homophones such as 'break lights' (brake lights), bring together concepts that are salient in the local text. Together with these are lexical blends, such as 'gravelcade' (road gravel / cavalcade), which are also locally salient. Other lexical blends are more generally suggestive, as in 'autocayed' (automobile / cavalcade / decayed) and 'jalopsides' (jalopy / lopsided). Some are very connotatively complex, such as 'tundragged'. This combines the cold and bleakness of 'tundra' with the chaos of 'ragged', but the word can be divided into other, chance roots, such as 'tun-dragged', suggesting a more active violence.

Such lexical blends within a syntactically deviant sentence seem to create a grammar in which syntactic agreement is based on the connotative connections between words rather than on their denotational or simply functional value. For example, 'these primitive jalopsides herding their way like shampeding cattletrap', conflates the notions of decrepit vehicles and cattle, so the participles 'herding' and 'stampeding' are used, but blended into a 'sham' 'trap'. The mixing of phrases from different registers also supports this sense. Besides blends of formal and colloquial mentioned above, the passage contains blends of stereotypically 'literary' poeticisms and technological terms ('Cryogenetic winds bourning another spring'), conversational idiom and medical terminology ('doing it all over and bloodcounts low'), and even switching into foreign languages ('Frankreich', 'zoll', 'RECHTS FAHREN').

Sound-effects (rhyme, alliteration and repetition) are a particularly noticeable feature, and they similarly blend meanings: in 'Break lights a flutter red I'd ride the rifled engines ricochetting off the tracered flow below', broken brake lights aflutter sound like a red-eyed ride. Extended alliterative phrases dominate the passage. There are other sound-parallelisms throughout, such as in the phrase 'the cuspidaughters of darkness play toe with the spittoons of noon', in which almost all the consonants are produced by the tip of the tongue against the teeth or at the front of the mouth (/n/, /s/, and voiced and unvoiced versions of the same place of articulation, /d/, /t/, /θ/, /ð/). The rhyming of 'spittoons' and 'noon', repeated in the passage, reinforces the awareness of other rhymes ('blind white eyes of joyride', 'hob with the gobs'). Unlike the regular Post Modern English of Hoban (1982), the grammatical patterns in *Barefoot in the Head* continually shift as the novel progresses.

I have quoted the above passage at length to give an example of the range of effects generated by the disjunction at different linguistic levels. You might also have felt the effect of 'tuning in' to the style, so that it becomes easier to read the more time is spent on it. This intuitive effect has been reported to me by various readers of the book. The aim and effect of over 200 pages of this is to immerse the reader in synaesthetic overload. Informally, readers have reported feeling dizzy, not being able to form normal English utterances, and experience short-term spatial confusion after reading the novel for extended periods. Ketterer (1974: 255–60) criticises the novel for reversing the usual science fictional pattern: instead of extraordinary content presented in a pedestrian style, it privileges style over a circular and pointless content. Of course, this is the point. At least Ketterer recognises that

> In adapting these experiments [of Joyce, Burroughs and Robbe-Grillet] to his own dimensional speculation as to the nature of reality, Aldiss is attempting that appropriate combination of style and content that may truly liberate science fiction from the ghetto of its own clichés.
>
> (Ketterer 1974: 260)

It seems to me that the intuitive sense of the disorientating effect of the prose style has some justification in the brief stylistic analysis outlined above. If so, this would make a strong case for the value of matching deviant style with a deviant reality possible in science fiction, as Ketterer recognises. A properly controlled experiment to test this would have begun with three groups: the first administered with a hallucinogenic such as LSD, the second 'doped up' on a passage from the novel, and a final group who had been prepared by reading a less deviant prose style prior to the experiment. However, for obvious ethical and practical reasons, I was not able to conduct such an experiment.

It seems that a major part of the immersion into the universe of *Barefoot in the Head* is effected by the deviant stylistic texture of the novel. The report of readers that they became better and quicker at reading the book with prolonged exposure suggests that this particular style in conjunction with this particular theme primes a sub-conscious level of reading that is an extreme example of the common experience of 'tuning-in' to a writer's idiosyncratic style.

Such an immersion into the science fictional universe is an effect inherited from the early neologising habit of pulp magazine science fiction. Aldiss's stylistic universe is an extreme extrapolation of the creation of individual neologisms in science fiction. (Chapter 6 deals directly with *neologisms*, and chapter 4 explores *pulpstyle*.) More recently, cyberpunk science fiction has extrapolated this impulse for technical-sounding neologisms to create a projected futuristic techno-vernacular. Cyberpunk science fiction writer William Gibson (1984: 12) famously described cyberspace as 'consensual hallucination', which might equally apply to the texture of Aldiss's novel. The problem with an immersion in the language of the future, if it is to be understandable and readable, is one of contextual knowledge and contextualisation. Future fiction of various types always poses a tension between unknowable contexts and the textual provision of a sufficiently familiar context to be readable. (This difficulty is directly addressed in chapter 9.)

Exploration

■ Both Aldiss's and Hoban's experiments with language are presented as the result of catastrophic environmental damage. Hoban's socio-linguistics of the future is based on a generalised accent and dialect of south-eastern England, with existing features exaggerated and developed. Take your own part of the world and plot the particular effects for your own accent and dialect. In deciding which features are extrapolated, you will have to consider questions such as which groups will survive, how will the social organisation be reflected in linguistic usage, how will landscape terms alter, and so on. For example, the initial survivors of a nuclear blast are likely to be those living in sturdy houses in rural areas. What sort of people are they? How do they talk? Alternatively, rising sea-levels from global warming would flood many low-lying areas, causing refugees to migrate to higher ground, with possible overcrowding and conflict. Imagine how different people might express their group-solidarity in these circumstances.

3.5 Science Fiction and Non-Science Fiction

The central part of this chapter (3.4) has been concerned with texts which are stylistically experimental. Within the tradition of science fiction writing, the passages cited above are linguistically on another planet, but (as Ketterer (1974) recognises) that planet had already been colonised by the modernist stylists of mainstream fiction. It is tempting to see the innovations of the 1960s New Wave as science fiction 'catching up' with modernism, and then to see 1980s cyberpunk as a point of contact with post-modernism. McCaffery (1991: 11), introducing a collection of articles on the theme, says that this equation is too simplistic. Since much of the argument concerns the use of language in science fiction, this last section will explore the debate, and outline another position.

3.5.1 Modern Science Fiction as Post-Modern Literature

Most debates about post-modernism are defined by Jameson's (1984, 1991) statements equating the artistic form with a cultural movement embedded in post-industrial capitalism. To summarise, post-modernism in the arts is generally agreed to have arisen in the late 1950s, claiming a populist break with the elitism of previous forms (though how popular it ever was is a matter of debate). It involved a breaking down of the boundaries between high and low art, and between art and non-art. It was rich in layers of social meaning, which rendered it anti-authoritative and readerly in its orientation. It tended to be playful, ironic and self-ironising, using pastiche and intertextual sampling and allusion to be self-reflexive.

Certainly this sounds very like Aldiss's (1990) *Barefoot in the Head*. According to Delany (1990), the science fiction writer Kim Stanley Robinson, in a series of lectures, has declared the view that much post-'60s science fiction can be equated with post-modernism. The general consensus among other writers is more narrow than this, restricting the notion of post-modernist science fiction to post-'80s *cyberpunk*, with some notable precursors such as Philip K. Dick, William Burroughs, J.G. Ballard, and Brian Aldiss, among others (see Butler 1996; and James 1994: 100).

The strongest and most sustained argument along these lines is that of Csicsery-Ronay (1991: 182), who asserts that, 'As a label, "cyberpunk" is perfection. It suggests the apotheosis of postmodernism'. McHale (1991), in the same volume (McCaffery 1991), also argues for this intersection. He charts the historical development of the genre: ghettoized from the 1920s to the 1940s; followed by a 'levelling up' to the stylistic norms of the mainstream bestseller, in the work of Heinlein, Asimov, Clarke and Sturgeon; leading to an interaction in the '60s and '70s of science fiction and progressive or state-of-the-art mainstream fiction. McHale claims that the generic borrowing of this latest period was mutually regressive: science fiction borrowed from modernism, and the mainstream borrowed from pulp science fiction. By the 1980s, a genuine feedback loop had developed, manifesting as cyberpunk. Jameson (1991) claims that cyberpunk is the supreme expression of late capitalism.

A variation on this view can be seen in the work of Tabbi (1995), in a book that partly deals with cyberpunk as 'the technological sublime' (p. 219). Here, cyberpunk is seen as applied post-modernism:

> The difference between cyberpunk and its postmodern textualist predecessors is the difference, in the aesthetic sphere, between paper science and lab science, ideal and practical reason, the material advance of current computer technologies and the previous generation's heady theory.
> [. . .] Cyberpunk levels distinctions between the technical and the literary, fiction and history, 'high' and 'popular' cultures [. . .] This generic flexibility [. . .] is also a feature of the sublime moment in both modernist and romantic literature.

> (Tabbi 1995: 210–11)

Much of the work on cyberpunk focuses on William Gibson. (Suvin (1991) even claims that Gibson is the only genuine cyberpunk and all the other authors are just expert publicity men!). Csicsery-Ronay (1992), for example, suggests that *Neuromancer* (Gibson 1984)

> stands as a masterpiece of cyberpunk because it exemplifies the poetry of the retrofuture, the linguistic texture that dazzles the host consciousness, inspiring it with a dizzying sense of power – derived from the illusion that it is fluent in the dialects of the future before they have even emerged.

> (Csicsery-Ronay 1992: 37)

He goes on to draw a contrast between Gibson's style and a more 'symbolist' style in which the density of the futuristic dialect is 'excessive', reconstructing its own context 'in opposition to the codes of critical realism' (Csicsery-Ronay 1992: 37). Hoban's (1982) *Riddley Walker* is cited as an example of this. Gibson's style, more spare, extrapolated from 1980s drug and computer slang, alluding to a pretended common culture, is seen as just 'sufficient' to be convincing and realistic. Hollinger (1991: 205) also discusses Gibson's 'rhetoric of technology'. She is revisionist in that cyberpunk and post-modernism do not seem to be identical; rather cyberpunk is 'post-humanist' (see also Atkins 1996). For Hollinger (1991: 218), this is not a nihilistic term, but represents in cyberpunk 'the *reinsertion* of the human into the new reality which its technology is in the process of shaping'.

All of these views represent a use of science fiction from the perspective of mainstream critical theory and literary history. McCaffery (1991) develops a more science fiction-based evolution, discerning an early 'expansionist' phase and a later 'implosive' phase:

> Beginning in the 1950s science fiction writers began to abandon the conventions of expansionist SF: heroic planetary exploration, space travel without boredom, the dignity of aliens, small groups of harmonious researchers, and in style, lucid, utilitarian prose emphasizing the no-nonsense attitudes of adventurer-scientists in command and control. [. . .] In the 1960s this vector was reversed.

> (McCaffery 1991: 186–7)

In the post-1960s concern with inner space, 'more and more science fiction treats hallucination as an object in the world' (McCaffery 1991: 190). This is the view of science fiction as *dramatisation*, a theme which I will return to several times in this book, and which is central to an understanding of science fictional poetics.

3.5.2 A Poetics From Science Fiction: Samuel Delany

In order to question many of the arguments outlined in the section above, I will end this chapter by discussing the work of science fiction writer and academic Samuel Delany, who has himself even been classed as a post-modernist science fiction writer (in Clute and Nicholls 1993: 950). In these various roles, Delany is certainly linguistically knowledgeable. His novels, especially *Babel-17*, *Nova*, *Dhalgren*, and *Triton* (Delany 1966, 1968, 1974, 1976), deal directly with linguistic issues. The first of these creates a new language, the second deals with syntactic innovations in dialect, but (as Meyers (1980: 178–84) points out) they are based on the Sapir-Whorf hypothesis in a way that the last two novels supersede.

It is in his critical work that Delany contributes most to the poetics of science fiction, however. He has argued against the easy identification of science fiction and post-modernism outlined in the previous section. This is partly a result of his suspicion of simply importing critical terms and literary history from the mainstream of fiction. Science fiction arises from a different tradition and responds to different social phenomena and a different readership. Delany (1989), in a long article introducing critical theory to science fiction readers, insists that the genre should be read and treated critically in its own terms (though he spoils this a little by using terms from French post-structuralism and psychoanalysis to discuss it himself).

Similarly, mainstream literary history cannot simply be overlaid onto the evolution of science fiction in the ways suggested in the previous section. The problem with this, or in distinguishing different movements within the compass of only one century, is that science fiction is not a microcosm of the mainstream literature of the last four hundred years. In any case, while general literary movements can be said to shift whole-sale across centuries (Augustanism to Romanticism to Modernism, very crudely), science fiction has been around for such a short time that it has tended to carry along all its traditions cumulatively. So (as I will argue in chapter 4), the style of early pulp science fiction, or the reportage of the 1940s, or the innovations of the New Wave, and so on, can all still be found being written today. New styles might appear within science fiction, but the older ones tend not to be utterly displaced. This makes the equation with the literary mainstream structurally problematic.

The final difficulty I have with the identification of science fiction with post-modernism is that criticism focusing on the former is gener-ally clear and analytical, whereas the worst sort of criticism of the latter descends into poetic though impressionistic nonsense. Tabbi (1995: xi), for example, asserts that 'these writers share an exemplary willingness to push beyond the limits of the literary, to bring their writing into con-tact with a nonverbal technological reality'. Besides the confusion here between reality and unreality and the inconceivability of anything which is nonverbal or written 'beyond' the literary, the concretising metaphor evades responsibility for analysis of the sense in which any of these terms are being used. Science fiction, with its traditions in science and entertainment, does not need this sort of gobbledygook.

In relation to 'mainstream' literature, Delany goes further by ques-tioning the validity of that term. He claims that science fictional poetics encompasses the mainstream:

> I can think of no series of words that could appear in a piece
> of naturalistic fiction that could not also appear in the same

order in a piece of speculative fiction. I can, however, think
of many series of words that, while fine for speculative fiction,
would be meaningless as naturalism. Which then is the major
and which the sub-category?

Consider: naturalistic fictions are parallel-world stories in
which the divergence from the real is too slight for historical
verification.

(Delany 1977: 49)

Therefore he suggests that science fiction should be distinguished from
non-science fiction by calling the latter *mundane* fiction. He feels that:

The science fictional enterprise is richer than the enterprise of
mundane fiction. It is richer through its extended repertoire
of sentences, its consequent greater range of possible incident,
and through its more varied field of rhetorical and syntagmatic
organisation.

(Delany 1977: 95)

The claim here is that since science fiction deals conceptually with a
wider range of *possible worlds* (see 7.2), it makes available to itself a
potentially greater range of as yet unrealised sentences. It must be said
that we are talking about the capacity of the genre, rather than what it
mainly achieves, but a poetics of science fiction must account for what
the genre is capable of as well as what it has already produced in practice. (Perhaps 'mundane' is too disparaging of other fiction here, and a
better term would be 'prosaic', referring both to the everyday, natural-
istic content of prose fiction, in relation to science fictional themes.)

All the possibilities that a poetics of science fiction would include,
constitute what Delany (1977: 95–6) calls the *textus*: the web of possible
sentences, unrealised worlds and existing intertextual connections. Science
fiction, rather than being a mystical contact with the nonverbal, is seen
as 'casting a language shadow over coherent areas of imaginative space'
(Delany 1977: 133–4). Its method is not mystical but 'Symbolist':

Science fiction is the only area of literature outside poetry
that is symbolistic in its basic conception. Its stated aim is
to represent the world without reproducing it. That is what
dealing with worlds of possibilities and probabilities means.

(Delany 1977: 197)

3.6 Review

Delany's views inform many of my discussions in later chapters. The second half of the book specifies how science fiction achieves its evocation of the *textus*, from individual acts of world-building to the global negotiation of imaginative space. I also discuss the *symbolist* strategies of surface and conceptual metaphor. Providing a description of the differences between science fiction and prosaic fiction underlies the motivation for the whole book.

This chapter has been about consciousness of language from within science fiction. This was discussed in terms of uses of language issues in specific texts, as well as the thematisation and foregrounding of stylistic innovation. For a stylistician, deviant or unusual language is easy to write about. It offers the opportunity for using a linguistic model or framework, developed in the context of natural language data, in the literary context. Stylistics is very good at accounting for non-natural uses of language, and this information makes a discussion of the effects of such innovations operate on a firmer foundation.

However, I have tried to restrict science fiction texts that are most obviously stylistically experimental to this chapter. Although they are disproportionately interesting within a poetics of the genre, they are by no means the whole story. It is to the mainstream tradition within science fiction that I turn in the next chapter.

Explorations

■ In Asimov's (1960) *Foundation* universe, the science of 'psychohistory' is proposed: a general extrapolation of social biology, sociology, cultural psychology and technological progress that predicts the social trends of the future. On a more limited basis, it is possible to develop a reasonable guess at the sociolinguistic situation of the future (as Hoban (1982) attempts). Try the following scenarios as starting points and consider their effect on language. You should base your projection on firm principles of language change (see chapter 6 for introductory reading on this).

- a *lingua franca* (common working language) develops on the Moon or Mars, combining English syntax with Russian and Chinese vocabulary. Over 100 years this develops into a fully-fledged language (becomes *creolised*). Using a Russian/English translating dictionary (or a Chinese/English one) try to imagine a few sentences in this future lunar language. For example, you might just replace a few English words, or all the 'content' words but leave the articles, prepositions, conjunctions and so on in English. Imagine how this new language would fit into the political relationship with old Earth.

- a computer model of psychology replaces current 'psychobabble' (which is largely based on concrete metaphors of 'layers' of consciousness, 'depth' of feelings, involving 'barriers', and 'self-discovery'). What might the following mean: 'download your anger'; 'access and randomise your boot-up routine'; 'learn to initialise your command environment'; 'modem that thought, disc it!'; 'they're only software friends'. Imagine others. Does the fact of using these different metaphors change our understanding of psychology and relationships?

- brain augmentation implants allow conversations to be recalled in precise recorded detail. How might this affect the structure of conversation? Consider how people take turns in conversation, and how they interrupt each other. How would such an innovation affect the length of time people talk in each turn? How might instant questions and answers be affected? Could people keep many more topics 'in the air' as a result? It might be useful to adapt a real transcribed conversation as a basis for revision.

■ What is the relationship between scientific hypothesising and the imaginative motivation in science fictional invention? In other words, is forming a hypothesis (before actually testing it) the same process as imagining a science fictional innovation? You might consider whether teaching creative writing to scientists might be worthwhile!

Speculations

■ In Bear's (1985, 1989a, 1996) *Eon* universe, humans 'pict' images to each other's implant-enhanced perceptions. This symbolic extension of Swift's academicians is similar to a sign-language system, in which some items are iconic but many are arbitrary. That human language is basically a sound-system is one of its design features (Hockett 1963). What would be the effects of shifting the medium altogether? What would be the equivalent of an accent? Would art-form categories shift? Consider dance, poetry, graphic art, sculpture, architecture, reading literature, football chants.

■ Is it possible to isolate the literature of alternativity from its divergence from the post-Romantic mainstream? Which works would be reclaimed in a revisionist historical line from mythology, medieval fantasy and gothic, through Renaissance unrealities, utopias and satires, through the mock-heroic, Romantic hallucination and dreams, Victorian gothic and the range of twentieth-century science fiction, fantasy and magical realism? How would this version of literary history relate to the authorised version? Would new labels for movements ('opium literature', 'Victorian Baroque', 'novels of social mechanisation', and so on) be useful?

Further reading

On the use of language and linguistics by science fiction, Meyers (1980) is the most comprehensive account, though Le Guin (1982, 1989), Barnes (1974), Friend (1973), Krueger (1968), Doherty (1964), Watson (1975), Hockett (1955), and de Camp (1938) are all interesting comments by critics and writers on the issue. The history of the New Wave is covered by Greenland (1983). Science fiction in the 1980s and the postmodernist debate is discussed in Malzberg (1982), McHale (1987, 1991), McCaffery (1991), and Broderick (1995), and criticised especially for its ignorance of the feminist heritage by Wolmark (1994). Csicsery-Ronay's (1991, 1995a, 1995b) trilogy of essays on Gibson are an illuminating balance. Delany's essays on language are collected in Delany (1977, 1984), and a gloss on his work, with a comprehensive bibliography, is in Samuelson (1994).

CHAPTER 4

MACROLOGICAL: OUTER SPACE

4.1 Preview

The stylistic experimentalism explored in the previous chapter represents the avant-garde of science fiction. However, these edges circumscribe the universe of the centre, and critics and linguists tend to seek out the unusual, eccentric, unique and deviant in the intriguing stellar peripheries, rather than explore this planetary mass close at hand. Of course, a proper consideration of the genre must include some description and analysis of what is mainstream within science fiction. Such an examination can reveal that assumptions and expectations about traditional science fiction do not always tell the whole story. This is the mission of this chapter.

The vast majority of science fictional writing is not syntactically deviant or semantically challenging. It does not present jaw-droppingly startling poetic metaphors (see, though, chapter 8), nor play tricks with graphology, typography, morphology or narrative structure. Mostly, science fictional texture is about reporting a story, in a fairly plain manner. While no style can be said to be 'neutral', most students' reactions to the mass of science fiction style seems to be that it is so pedestrian and unremarkable that they do not even notice it much. This is the case where the writing is merely competent; sometimes the writing is just plain bad, and the incompetence of the writer is noticed.

General invisible competence and some in-your-face ineptitude, then, mark out the central range of science fiction style. In this chapter, the origins of these conventions are examined and tracked into what has become the default style for mainstream science fiction writing. The description of the conventions is largely a matter of the *register* of the text, and this is explored in detail (see specifically 4.2.6). The register of what was to become the conventional generic style was born in pulp science fiction.

4.2 Pulpstyle

The science fiction writer Theodore Sturgeon is famously (and possibly apocryphally) supposed to have declared that '90 per cent of science fiction is crap' (with various synonyms of the last word appearing in different accounts). His qualification, '. . . but 90 per cent of anything is crap', is less widely cited. The general perception that most science fiction is not great literature, that it is trashy and 'crap', is largely attributable to its connection with the pulp magazines of the first quarter of the twentieth century.

Aldiss and Wingrove (1986) describe two early traditions in the development of science fiction: an intelligent middle-class audience reading Edgar Allan Poe and H.G. Wells; and a more sensationalist tradition in the serials and dime novels of the late nineteenth century. The former can be seen to have successors in Aldous Huxley, Olaf Stapledon, George Orwell, and, more loosely, Kurt Vonnegut, Thomas Pynchon, Mervyn Peake and Doris Lessing. However, in terms of sheer volume of wordage it is the magazine tradition that has been most influential in shaping the prototypical template of the genre. Prototypes of science fictional form include the single-issue short story with the spectacular twist in the tale, serialised episodes which can be gathered together into a 'fixup' novel of sorts, or extended narratives set in the same universe manifest as a collection of fat-paged sequels. All of these have their origins in the short stories and serialisations of the pulps.

From the 1890s to the 1940s, the pulps were produced on the cheapest low-quality paper, from pulped-up chemically-treated sawdust waste, old paper and rags. The pages, 7 × 10 inches (25cm × 18cm, super royal octavo), could be rough and mottled, and the edges uneven and untrimmed. Even the better quality productions were able to keep their cover prices down, but the literal texture soon lent its name to the literary texture, so that the contemporaneous 'slicks' and later 'glossies', produced with lithographic prints and quality colour pictures, nevertheless retained a 'pulp' content. They were a development in America of the nineteenth-century 'dime novels', the equivalent of the British Victorian 'penny-dreadfuls'. Science fiction was a latecomer to the pulp format, with writers happily crossing genres from detective, horror, cowboy western and fantasy fiction, often with dire results.

The symbolic father of the science fiction magazine tradition is usually seen to be Hugo Gernsback, a Luxembourgian immigrant radio salesman who launched his magazine *Modern Electrics* just before the

First World War. The serialised stories proved more popular than the circuit diagrams, and the magazine eventually became *Amazing Stories* in 1926 (though Aldiss and Wingrove (1986: 251–2) point to many science fiction magazines in Europe and America that predate this, and the first science fiction magazine was probably *Mirprik[u]sheniya* – 'World of Adventures' – in Russia from 1903 to the mid-1920s). Gernsback's American 'scientifiction' magazines spawned dozens of imitators: *Argosy, Astonishing Stories, Astounding Stories of Super-Science, Comet Stories, Cosmic Science Fiction, Dynamic Science Stories, Fantastic Adventures, Future Fiction, Galaxy SF, Modern Wonder, Planet Stories, Science Wonder Stories, Startling Stories, Stirring Science Stories, Strange Stories, Unknown Fantasy Fiction, Weird Tales,* and many others. The quality of these, and the writing they contained, varied enormously, but the pulp conventions of the 'neutral' narration of a clearly explained and plausible science fictional scenario were established. This central concern with scientific rigour and plausibility was retained even after the demise of the pulps due to the paper shortages of the Second World War. The most famous example, John Campbell's *Astounding* (launched in 1937, later becoming *Analog*) set the standard for logic and rationalism into the 1950s.

Though most later science fiction is written in a derivation of pulpstyle, the original material from the 1920s and '30s is quite difficult to find: pulp paper does not last very well, and often the writing is of such poor quality that no one has thought it fit to re-print. Later anthologies (such as those edited by Bensen 1963, Moskowitz 1970, Asimov 1974, Boardman 1979, Greenberg, Waugh and Waugh 1992) thus tend to be nostalgic and rosy-tinted collections of the best stories, and so are not truly representative. Fortunately, Asimov's (1975) three-volume anthology of early science fiction from the 1920s and '30s contains several examples of pulpstyle in all its glory. The illustrations which follow are taken from there, focusing on a story entitled, 'The Brain Stealers of Mars', by the same John Campbell (1975) who was later to become the architect of the rational 'Golden Age'. The story was the first in a series of 'Penton and Blake' tales, appearing in the December 1936 issue of *Astounding Science Fiction* under Campbell's usual pseudonym 'Don A. Stuart', the maiden name of his wife Donna. Mention will also be made of Murray Leinster's (1979) 'First Contact', a classic short story published in May 1945, also in *Astounding Science Fiction,* and which was used by Taylor (1990) in his brief typology of pulpstyle. The following description of the linguistic features of pulpstyle is based on Taylor (1990).

4.2.1 The Conditions of Pulp Production

Pulpstyle is circumscribed by its conditions of production, as most writing is, but the economics specifically of pulp writing are highly salient to a stylistic description. Pulp writers were often hack journalists or relatively inexperienced technical professionals writing to tight deadlines for short shelf-life magazines that needed a high turnover. Many of them, such as Murray Leinster (real name Will F. Jenkins), wrote in several different genres, including westerns. The main publishers, Frank A. Munsey, William Clayton, Street & Smith, and the Popular Fiction Company of Chicago, set the payment level for writers. Most pulps, such as Gernsback's *Wonder Stories* and Thomas O'Conor Sloane's *Amazing Stories* (taken over from Gernsback), paid poorly per word, usually between a quarter of a cent to a cent. Street & Smith's *Astounding Stories* paid two cents. Writers had to put down several stories across several different genres in different magazines to survive financially. Only those who were judged to be any good, and who developed a base of enthusiastic fans, were able to progress onto the higher-paying, larger-format ($8\frac{1}{2} \times 11$ inches), slimmer (96 pages with trimmed edges) glossy magazines, such as *Argosy*, at anything up to six cents per word through the 1930s. Sloane also tended to hold on to manuscripts for a long time, and payment was only on publication.

The readership of the pulps is equally important. Generally sold alongside newspapers and other magazines from news-stands in American towns and cities, a science fiction magazine such as *Unknown* cost twenty-five cents at the end of the 1930s. In the 1935–6 price-cutting war, *Wonder Stories* went down from twenty to fifteen cents. In his March–April editorial, Gernsback exposed how unscrupulous distributors were removing the covers and selling the contents as damaged issues, keeping the money themselves and tightening the revenue margins for the magazines even further. All this put the pulps within the buying power of adolescent boys with pocket-money, and the poor immigrant population of cities like New York and Chicago.

Published usually monthly, every issue could be collected relatively cheaply, and the magazines often serialised stories to ensure continued sales. Such an arrangement of stories in instalments meant that the word-limit for writers was much more flexible, and there was scope to pad the story out with dramatic incident. It also encouraged the evolution of a 'cliffhanger' end to each issue, which served to break the overall text up into exciting episodes with a succession of mini-climaxes or conundrums. With increased sales came increased size. In March 1934

Frederick Tremaine (editor before Campbell) raised the number of pages of *Astounding Stories* from the pulp standard 144 to 160. In the following August the print size was reduced to allow a further increase in the number of words, though the price remained at twenty cents and the payment to writers did not change.

Pulp content was enormously sensitive to the opinions of its market. *Wonder Stories'* 'The Reader Speaks' pages, with vociferous fan letters on every aspect of style, character and plot, were copied by most of the science fiction pulps. Editors vied with each other to introduce innovations, which were immediately copied by other magazines. Tremaine introduced his commissioning policy of the 'thought variant' story in 1933 – each scenario had to be completely original in idea and scope, rather than a re-hash of old concepts – and this was instantly imitated by Charles Hornig, the seventeen-year old editor of *Wonder Stories*, as his '*new*' policy'. All of these factors can help to explain the presence of the features of pulpstyle that follow.

4.2.2 Pulp Titles

The titles of pulp stories tend to be plainly descriptive of the content, like an abstract or digest of the story that follows. They are most commonly proper names or simple noun-phrases, often with definite articles: the plainest form of title. For illustration, here is the complete contents page of titles from Asimov's (1975) anthology:

The Man Who Evolved	*by Edmond Hamilton*
The Jameson Satellite	by Neil R. Jones
Submicroscopic	*by Capt. S.P. Meek*
Awlo of Ulm	*by Capt. S.P. Meek*
Tetrahedra of Space	*by P. Schuyler Miller*
The World of the Red Sun	*by Clifford D. Simak*
Tumithak of the Corridors	*by Charles R. Tanner*
The Moon Era	*by Jack Williamson*
The Man Who Awoke	*by Laurence Manning*
Tumithak in Shawm	*by Charles R. tanner*
Colossus	*by Donald Wandrei*
Born of the Sun	*by Jack Williamson*
Sidewise in Time	*by Murray Leinster*
Old Faithful	*by Raymond Z. Gallun*
The Parasite Planet	*by Stanley G. Weinbaum*
Proxima Centauri	*by Murray Leinster*

The Accursed Galaxy	*by Edmond Hamilton*
He Who Shrank	*by Henry Hasse*
The Human Pets of Mars	*by Leslie Frances Stone*
The Brain Stealers of Mars	*by John W. Campbell Jr.*
Devolution	*by Edmond Hamilton*
Big Game	*by Isaac Asimov*
Other Eyes Watching	*by John W. Campbell Jr.*
Minus Planet	*by John D. Clark*

(Asimov 1975: 5–6, typographical errors retained)

Though a recent anthology, the two typographical errors (unitalicised 'Neil R. Jones' and uncapitalised '*tanner*') echo the spirit of the poor speedy proof-reading of the original magazines. The names in titles tend to be exotic, futuristic or alien (Awlo, Tumithak). Otherwise the titles are prosaic and everyday, disguising science fictional referents ('Old Faithful', a Martian, and 'Big Game', in which intelligent dinosaurs hunt the rest to extinction). The phrase structure is often very simple, with nouns tending to take only a simple modifier (The Moon Era, Parasite Planet, Minus Planet) or a simple prepositional phrase as a qualifier (Tumithak in Shawm, The Brain Stealers of Mars). Even those titles with verbal elements tend to subordinate the verb (The Man Who Evolved, The Man Who Awoke, He Who Shrank), and without a subsequent main verb the subordinate clause acts as a qualifier within the whole single noun-phrase.

For comparison, here are some later, non-pulp science fiction titles: *Flow My Tears, The Policeman Said* (Philip K. Dick 1974), *To Your Scattered Bodies Go* (Philip Jose Farmer 1974), ' "Repent, Harlequin!" said the Ticktockman' (Harlan Ellison 1989). The syntactic form here is more complex. Pulp titles are unambiguously related to the content of the story, having a similar function (though a different form) to the sort of newspaper headline which would be most familiar to the typical pulp writer. They are prosaic and non-evocative, compared with later, non-pulp poetic examples: 'The Golden Apples of the Sun' (Ray Bradbury 1977b, after W.B. Yeats), 'The Compass Rose' (Ursula Le Guin 1983), or 'The Doors of his Face, the Lamps of his Mouth' (Roger Zelazny 1971).

4.2.3 Pulp Names

In general, pulp science fiction was written by young white men with an interest in science and technology, and most densely published and read in the American cities of the east coast. It is not surprising then that many pulp characters have very white, Anglo-Saxon Protestant (WASPy) names, which are as prototypically all-American and down-to-earth as possible: Professor Jameson from 'The Jameson Satellite', Courtney Edwards from 'Submicroscopic', Ham Hammond from 'The Parasite Planet', Brett Rand and George Worth from 'The Human Pets of Mars', Ted Penton and Rod Blake from 'The Brain Stealers of Mars'. These characters are almost always male. When the stories are Earth-bound, as well, they tend to be set on the eastern side of the US. This seems to be both a fictional projection of the author's situation, as well as a realisation of the landscape with which the readers are likely to be familiar; either way, it roots the implausible action in a plausible, mundane, and everyday environment.

By contrast, aliens take names with consonant clusters that tend not to occur in the English phonological system, as an index of their alienness: Fasthun Loshthu from 'The Brain Stealers of Mars'. Non-WASPy words, even if they could be from other human languages, are also given to extra-terrestrial aliens: Tholura, Zar-Emo, Hakh-Klotta, Luramo, Nikadur and Datto from 'Tumithak in Shawm', for example. Foreignness and exoticness are also the indexes of alienness. Even the Russian-named Asimov (1975: 567) acknowledges the easy racism in this depiction of aliens and the short conceptual step to un-American aliens and foreigners. The strategy is a simple one of differentiating goodies from potential baddies, but it also emphasises the homeliness of the American heroes in contrast with the downright all-round weirdness of the aliens.

4.2.4 Neologism in Pulp Science Fiction

Pulp science fiction often disguises gaps in scientific knowledge by patching a technically-sounding invented word over a phenomenon. In pulpstyle, such new words (*neologisms*) tend to be fairly simple in construction, and their sources are almost always in the hard sciences of physics, chemistry, biology and materials engineering: 'over-drive', 'visiplate', 'ion-gun', 'receptor', 'decapods', 'radiogram', for example. Later science fiction sometimes takes its neologisms from the soft sciences of psychology, linguistics, sociology and cultural studies ('archaeopsychic', 'cyberspace', 'neuromancer'), but this is rare in pulpstyle. Neologisms in pulp tend to have referents which are material and technical: physical objects rather than abstract concepts (see chapter 6).

4.2.5 Narrative Focalisation in Pulpstyle

Like newspaper journalism and scientific reports, pulp writing is almost always in the third person with an apparently objective and often omniscient narrator. Occasionally it is in the first person, but it is always the WASPy human character through whom the action is focalised (see Rimmon-Kenan 1983). Similarly, in third person narratives, the external narrator tends to follow the action through one or two WASPy male humans. Here is the opening to 'The Brain Stealers of Mars':

> Rod Blake looked up with a deep chuckle. The sky of Mars was almost black, despite the small, brilliant sun, and the brighter stars and planets that shone visibly, Earth most brilliant of all, scarcely sixty million miles away.
>
> 'They'll have a fine time chasing us, back there, Ted'. He nodded toward the brilliant planet.
>
> Ted Penton smiled beatifically.
>
> 'They're probably investigating all our known haunts. It's their own fault if they can't find us – outlawing research on atomic power.'
>
> 'They had some provocation, you must admit. Koelenberg should have been more careful. When a man takes off some three hundred square miles of territory bang in the center of Europe in an atomic explosion, you can't blame the rest of the world for being a bit skittish about atomic power research.'
>
> 'But they might have had the wit to see that anybody that did get the secret would not wait around for the Atomic Power Research Death Penalty, but would light out for parts and planets quite unknown and leave the mess in the hands of a lawyer till the fireworks quieted down. It was obvious that when we developed atomic power we'd be the first men to reach Mars, and nobody could follow to bring us back unless they accepted the hated atomic power and used it', argued Blake.
>
> (Campbell 1975: 764)

The focalisation through Penton and Blake in this story is effected in large part through a high density of direct speech. The characters are apparently allowed to express their own thoughts in reported conversation, as in the example above. As Leech and Short (1981: 324) point out, this form of speech presentation has the effect of seeming to minimise the apparent narrator's control over the narrative. The story seems to unfold itself, with the characters negotiating the action, rather than with the narrator being seen to manipulate events. This makes the science fictional universe seem much more like a narrative unfolding in the real world than an artificial fictional story.

Similarly, where the thoughts and perceptions of the characters are presented, the omniscient narrator focalises the scene through whichever character is primed at that point in the text. In the opening passage above, the sentence, 'Rod Blake looked up with a deep chuckle', binds him to the scene and primes his perceptions for the reader, so that the following description of the Martian sky is apparently what Blake sees. Shortly after the extract, the reader is taken into Blake's focus again: 'He tried a rope on one leaf, but the leaf neither stabbed, grabbed, or jerked away, as he had half expected after his lesson with the ferocious plants of Venus. Blake pulled a leaf off, then a few more. The plant acted quite plant-like, which pleasantly surprised him' (Campbell 1975: 765). The omniscient narrator here presents Blake's thoughts by report (rather than in inverted commas). Again, the narrator seems to take a back-seat and lets the events and characters apparently carry the narrative.

From the opening passage quoted above, it is apparent that the content of the speech presented is highly non-naturalistic. There is some effort to imitate the proximal deictics of genuine face-to-face conversation ('back there', 'you must admit', and the echoing vernacular syntax of 'It's their own fault if they can't find us – outlawing research on atomic power.'), but this is thoroughly undermined by the over-fluency and complexity of the rest of the syntax. Blake's last speech quoted contains far too many subordinate and coordinate clauses to be a realistic representation of everyday speech. Such utterances do sometimes occur in recordings of everyday speech of course, but the point here is that the literary convention for them is not being used.

Instead, the purpose of this sort of dense expository prose within speech presentation is to establish the framing episode, characters and their history quickly. As in the passage above, characters explain things to each other that they must know already, having shared the experience prior to the time-frame of the narrative text. The last speech is reported with the phrase 'Blake argued', but there is no need for him to adopt this tone with his partner Penton. The reason, of course, is to bring the reader up to date with the plot, but this clumsy presentation is very common in pulpstyle.

These potted updates on 'the story so far', are more or less the only sort of departure from the ongoing narrative time-frame of the story. Such flashbacks within direct speech are the only forms that appear in pulpstyle, and because they are contained by direct speech they seem to emanate from the characters' experience rather than the manipulating narrator. They refer beyond the time-frame of the narrative, representing prior history. Any other departure from the ongoing plot will tend to be within the time-frame of the narrative. Such departures are either extended generic expositions (detailed in 4.2.6 below) or flash-forwards, in which the narrative action jumps forward to a later point. As we saw in the discussion of Asimov's (1968) *I, Robot* in 2.2.1, such flash-forwards are often marked by a disjunction in the lines of the text, and by a shift in the temporal and spatial deixis to indicate that the action has moved on. In 'The Brain Stealers of Mars', each such disjunction is followed by an explicit focalisation through either Penton or Blake, rather than the narrator omnisciently and objectively re-setting the scene. This too is typical of pulpstyle.

4.2.6 The Register of Pulpstyle

The term **register**, within stylistics, relates to a general code of language patterning. Where dialectal variation is identifiable according to the speaker's geography, age, gender, race, social network, and so on, register is defined according to its situation of use. Identifying a particular register involves analysis at various levels of linguistic organisation, from syntactic ordering and patterning to individual lexical choices: the entire lexicogrammar, in other words. Clearly, all of the categories in this chapter that I am using to characterise pulpstyle contribute towards the generic register of pulp science fiction. So far I have mentioned lexical choices in naming patterns, neologisms and titles, and grammatical patterning in title-structure and narrative point of view. These all serve to identify the register of pulpstyle.

Literature itself does not have a register of its own, a 'literary register'. Instead, it is a mode of writing which borrows registers from other domains, and by placing them into a new context it effectively re-registers them (see Carter and Nash 1990). For example, as with the importation of scientific and technical source terms for neologisms, pulpstyle very often imports scientific and military registers. In general, register is usually defined along three dimensions: *field* (the setting and purpose of the interaction), *tenor* (the relationship between the participants) and *mode* (the medium of communication) (Halliday 1978:

31–5), and the organisation of the lexicogrammar will be appropriate to these dimensions. However, the re-registration into the literary context creates complex layers of patterning. Within the universe of the pulp story, the *field* is often an adventure scenario involving decision-making and action. The *tenor* tends to comprise scientists, adventurers, soldiers, and intelligent action-men. The *mode* (within the story at least) is direct speech, often taking the form of commands, orders, and the syntax of logical reasoning.

Of course, framing all this within a literary narration introduces other dimensions. The *mode* shifts to writing, which carries different norms of formality of syntax and lexical choice, even when attempting to imitate and represent spoken discourse. Literary texts rarely try to present conversation as it really is, with its normal disfluency, long pauses, and close deictic connection to the here-and-now; instead, speech in literature is tidied up, with a few markers retained to indicate that speech is being presented. The *tenor* also becomes more complex in the literary situation, with the basic participants framed as characters within a discourse between an apparent narrator (usually third person) and an addressee, which in turn is framed by an author and reader. The *field* is framed as a literary experience. (See Carter and Nash (1983), Short and Candlin (1986) and Downes (1994) for detailed discussion of re-registration in a literary context.)

All of this complexity makes pulpstyle very uneven, and pulp writers often seem unable to slip gracefully and seamlessly between different registers. It is commonplace, for example, to find the narrative temporarily suspended while an extended piece of exposition is inserted, explaining a particular point for the benefit of the reader. This can either be put into the mouth of one of the characters, as in Blake's speech in 'The Brain Stealers of Mars' extract above, or it can simply be narrated authoritatively. Such shifts of register into technical-sounding pseudo-science can often be quite abrupt. In Murray Leinster's 'First Contact' (as Taylor (1990) points out), the ongoing narrative of a survey ship encountering an alien craft in the Crab Nebula is quickly suspended for an extended exposition on the science of the nebula:

> [The ship] had come out from Earth to make close-range observations of the smaller component of the double star at the nebula's centre. The nebula itself was the result of the most titanic explosion of which men have any knowledge. The explosion took place some time in the year 2946 BC, before the first of the seven cities of long-dead Ilium was

even thought of. The light of that explosion reached Earth in the year 1054 AD, and was duly recorded in ecclesiastical annals and somewhat more reliably by Chinese court astronomers. It was bright enough to be seen in daylight for twenty-three successive days. Its light was brighter than that of Venus.

From these facts, astronomers could calculate nine hundred years later the violence of the detonation. Matter blown away from the centre of the explosion would have travelled outward at the rate of two million three hundred thousand miles an hour, more than thirty-eight thousand miles a minute, something over six hundred and thirty-eight miles per second. When twentieth-century telescopes were turned upon the scene of this vast explosion, only a double star remained – and the nebula. The brightest star of the doublet was almost unique in having so high a surface temperature that it showed no spectrum lines at all. It had a continuous spectrum. Sol's surface temperature is about 7,000° Absolute. That of the hot white star is 500,000 degrees. It has nearly the mass of the sun, but only one fifth its diameter, so that its density is one hundred and seventy-three times that of water, sixteen times that of lead, and eight times that of iridium – the heaviest substance known on Earth.

(Leinster 1979: 17–18)

This passage is an extract from almost 1700 words of uninterrupted narrative exposition. As noted generally in 2.4.5, such passages are marked not only by consistent third person narration but also by a shift in tense and aspect from the simple past of the rest of the story. The register here is mainly that of an encyclopedia entry, with lexical elements from scientific register prominent, such as dates and numerical measurements, and technical terms such as 'spectrum lines', 'mass', 'density', and so on. However, there is a good deal of register-mixing going on here too. There are evaluative terms ('the most titanic explosion', 'somewhat more reliably') that serve to shift the field of register towards popular science rather than the bald encylopedic statement of fact. And the 'gosh-wow' element remains in the translation of equivalent velocities and densities ('. . . an hour, . . . a minute, . . . per second', '. . . of water, . . . of lead, . . . of iridium'), which would be redundant in a genuine scientific register, but serves in pulpstyle to claim an incrementally greater sense of wonder with each comparison. This is part of the awareness in the text of the state of likely readerly knowledge, explaining velocities and densities in familiar terms, not assuming an education in classical antiquity in the helpful phrase 'long-dead Ilium', and pointing out the status of iridium.

Pulpstyle register, then, tends to be a mixture of military action-adventure, scientific description, and rational discussion and argument, all filtered through an awareness of the state of knowledge of the reader, and occasionally with lexis and syntax that express an emotional dimension, usually just hyperbolic fear and wonderment.

4.2.7 Lexical Variation in Pulpstyle

Circulating (probably apocryphally) around the pulp writers and publishing offices was a 'Said-Book', which supposedly contained synonyms or alternatives for the word 'said' when writing large sections of direct speech. It seems likely that, if it existed, the 'Said-Book' was simply a few torn pages from a decent thesaurus, but the lexical variation amongst reporting clause verbs in pulpstyle is clear to see. In 'The Brain Stealers of Mars', Penton and Blake rarely just 'said' anything; they 'argued', 'groaned', 'panted' 'yelled', 'decided', 'asked', 'sighed', 'gasped', 'explained', 'snapped', 'stated', 'agreed', and so on. Clearly, in a genre with a lot of direct speech, such lexical variations are needed to avoid clumsy-sounding repetition. But most pulp science fiction stories employ the same range of stock lexical verbs for reporting direct speech. Sometimes, direct speech is reported freely, without any reporting clause, but there is then usually an indication within the character's speech as to who is speaking (mainly deictic elements that help to orientate the reader).

More noticeable than these stock lexical variations are adverbial qualifications to reporting-clause verbs. This addition of adverbials helped the pulp writer to earn an extra few half-cents. Characters rarely just say or sigh or mutter something; they do it 'meditatively', 'savagely', 'bitterly', 'softly', 'curtly', 'briskly', 'carefully', 'doubtfully', 'uncomfortably', 'profoundly', 'heavily', 'dispassionately', 'beatifically', 'urgently', 'tiredly', 'unhappily', 'drily', 'unsympathetically', and so on. Even more profitably, pulp writers often expanded adverbial qualification into an entire extended phrase, so characters do things 'hurriedly and efficiently', 'slowly and thoughtfully', 'extending his arms in a similar gesture', 'in Rod Blake's voice', 'between a cough and a sneeze', 'sighting the iongun at the nine flapping, rapidly vanishing things scuttling across the red dusty planet', and so on.

Unfortunately, this money-spinning tactic occasionally produces some oddities, as in these extracts from 'First Contact':

> The skipper said *through tight-locked teeth*:
> 'They're doing something now. There's movement on the outside of their hull. Watch what comes out. Put the auxiliary blasters on it.'
> [. . .]
> 'Hmm', said the skipper *profoundly*.
>
> (Leinster 1979: 15, 38, emphasis added)

To illustrate to yourself that earning a few cents was more important than verisimilitude for Leinster on this occasion, try saying anything clearly 'through tight-locked teeth' or try to make 'hmm' sound profound. Sometimes, as in the opening extract from 'The Brain Stealers of Mars' quoted above, the choice of adverb is simply varied without much consideration for its aptness ('Ted Penton smiled beatifically'). Indeed Campbell's story is framed with adverbial ineptitude, from the first sentence to the last:

> Rod Blake looked up with a deep chuckle.
> [. . .]
> Rod Blake blinked slowly.
>
> (Campbell 1975: 764, 781)

I am not sure how easy it is to look up with a deep chuckle nor whether blinking is something that is done, by definition, quickly?

4.2.8 Lexical Co-Reference and Repetition in Pulpstyle

It is commonplace in most forms of writing, in the interest of keeping the text brief and fluent, to shorten phrases and ellipt certain words where the sense can still be understood in context. Pulp writers, of course, did not want to keep the story brief at all, so there are relatively few pronouns or ellipses in pulpstyle. Where continuity and cohesion between sentences is necessary, co-reference between lexical items is most typically handled by repetition:

> Blake stared. He stared with steady blank gaze at that perfectly impossible Japanese maple. He gawked dumbly.

[. . .]
Rod Blake sat down and laughed. He laughed, and laughed
again.
[. . .]
'Let's move'.
They moved. They moved hastily back across the sand dunes
to the ship.

(Campbell 1975: 766, 767, 769)

In most of these examples, the same word re-occurs. This typically
happens at pivotal moments in the plot and the short, curt sentences
seem to have the effect of heightening the dramatic tension. Where the
writer has some sensitivity to the potential clumsiness of over-repetition,
the word can be substituted by a synonym ('stared . . . gawked'), but
it is noticeable even here that Campbell is able to say the same thing
through the repetition of identical words ('stared', 'stared'), synonym-
ously ('gawked') and also with an extended synonymous circumlocution
('steady blank gaze'), to maximise his earnings.

4.2.9 Thematic Repetition in Pulpstyle

Connected with lexical repetition is the convention in pulp science
fiction of repeating the central theme of the story (noticed by Taylor
1990). In 'The Brain Stealers of Mars' a plant-like species called the
'thushol' have formed themselves into dozens of simulacra of Penton
and Blake. The central conundrum is how the real Penton and Blake
differentiate their respective partner from the thushol copies, and escape
back to Earth without taking any thushol with them to contaminate the
home planet. This problem is compounded by the fact that the Martian
thushol are mind-readers, and can second-guess any strategy Penton and
Blake devise. This theme is explicitly repeated several times throughout
the story, both by the third person narrator and in many discussions
between Penton and Blake (as well as in the title).

Besides allowing increased wordage again, this technique satisfies the
editorial emphasis on a single 'thought variant' that carries the narrative.
It is the origin of what Suvin (1979: 63–84) has termed the *novum*: the
central concept, whether a technical innovation, a social variation, or
some other element of alternativity, that more than any other marks
out science fictional poetics. It is especially apparent in the 'single shot'
short story, the foundation of pulpstyle.

4.3 The Pulp Reader in History

So far, I have been focusing on the relationship between the organisation of the text and its historical conditions of production. However, in 4.2.1, I briefly mentioned the importance of readers' response in shaping pulpstyle, through the instant feedback of readers' letters and the beginnings of science fiction 'fandom'. In the highly competitive market of the pulp magazines, responsiveness to the tastes of the readers was of ultimate importance. It seems reasonable, then, in this discussion of the effectiveness of pulpstyle, to consider some reader-responses to a pulp science fiction story.

4.3.1 An Empirical Approach to Pulp Value

The question of value in literature has long been a point of discussion, with various attempts to set out criteria of style that specify the grounds for 'good' canonical literature. This exercise is obviously doomed to failure since literary canons are drawn out of what is fashionable at the time, dictated by whoever happens to hold the institutional power at any single point. At the moment, post-Romantic ideals hold sway in the valuation of prose literature, so that fully psychologised and naturalistic characterisation, close thematic analysis of events rather than action itself, open-ended ambiguity and freeplay of meaning rather than plot resolutions and didacticism all form the basis for institutionally valued literature. Under these conditions, of course, science fiction and especially pulp science fiction tend to come off rather badly. Largely through identifying the sort of clumsy style I have outlined above, students of literature and literary academics tend to look on pulp science fiction as bad writing, having been trained to value these other criteria.

However, the stylistic basis of such judgements seems to be assumed rather than tested, and so 'taste' and canonisation often become universals by default. Pulpstyle is condemned for being 'crap' as an obvious truth. In order to discover some of the thinking behind this, I devised a small experiment which involved reader-responses to Campbell's (1975) 'The Brain Stealers of Mars'. This experiment was reasonably informal, and had the primary use of allowing me to establish how much knowledge of science fiction the students possessed at the beginning of a course they were about to take.

I gave the story to fifty final year English literature students in a British university: in effect, a representational group of semi-professional literary readers. In order to make their comments easier to tabulate,

I asked them what they thought of the story under the headings of general features of the text, characterisation, and the style of writing. I also left them space for their more open-ended comments on what they thought of the 'literariness' of the story's opening. For their specific responses, I devised a list of descriptive adjectives and phrases with which they were invited to agree or not on a scale of 1 (strongly disagree) to 5 (strongly agree). Their strength of viewpoint was thus numerically weighted. From these data, it was easy to calculate the disagreement scores (total ticks in response box 1 (doubled to indicate strong feelings) added to box 2) and agreement scores (total ticks in response box 5 (doubled) and box 4). Subtracting the disagreements from the agreements over all fifty responses gave a rank index score for each adjective, on a scale of +100 (strongly associated with the text) down to −100 (strongly not associated with the text). In summary, the rank index for all respondents was calculated on the basis of:

$$((\text{Box } 5 \times 2) + \text{Box } 4) - ((\text{Box } 1 \times 2) + \text{Box } 2) = \text{Rank Index}$$

Such a formula produced polarised results which enabled me to make a list of adjectives associated with the text (at the top of the list) to strongly disassociated from the text (at the bottom). The full set of results follow.

Reader-response results for 'The Brain Stealers of Mars'.

(Agreements are positive values; disagreements are negative values)

'Is it a piece of good writing?'	−29
'Is it a piece of classic literature?'	−78
'Is it a piece of classic science fiction?'	−2
'Does it have any literary merit?'	−14

General Description:

78	male-oriented
75	fantastic
73	clumsy
68	far-fetched
62	implausible
50	incredible
43	corny
22	entertaining

18	scientific
6	terrible
6	surprising
5	technical
2	exciting
0	original
0	funny
−3	complex
−6	easy to follow
−6	obvious
−10	literary
−16	metaphorical
−16	abstract
−18	artistic
−18	political
−19	hard to read
−20	imaginable
−22	witty
−26	simple
−28	clear
−30	allegorical
−30	wonderful
−34	ugly
−34	well-written
−36	dull
−43	informative
−44	relevant
−48	pleasant
−50	profound
−61	emotional
−66	subtle
−68	serious
−72	industrial
−74	classic
−76	believable
−80	gothic
−80	persuasive
−80	beautiful
−97	feminist

Characterisation:

41	macho
37	intelligent
34	corny
26	mechanical
25	clever
24	wooden
22	obvious
20	flat
0	psychological
−3	articulate
−10	believable
−12	imaginable
−25	well-written
−27	emotional
−36	sympathetic
−44	rounded
−47	subtle
−75	literary

Style of Writing:

97	inept
38	melodramatic
32	dramatic
27	plenty of character talk
22	full of clichés
20	scientific
19	descriptive
18	wooden
14	plenty of description
6	engaging narrator's voice
−1	carefully explained
−4	uninformative
−6	clumsy
−15	fluent
−20	full of metaphors
−22	too repetitive
−24	too much narrator intrusion
−27	too many adjectives
−28	evocative
−36	too much dialogue
−36	good style
−40	too dense
−41	contradictory
−42	stylish
−55	inappropriate
−58	elegant
−63	lyrical
−70	poetic

As an example of the method, and to test that my set of fifty students were normally socialised in current literary taste as I expected, I gave them a list of twenty-six authors including William Shakespeare, Geoffrey Chaucer, T.S. Eliot, John Keats, Emily Brontë, Alexander Pope, David Lodge, Doris Lessing, Arthur Conan Doyle, Colin Dexter, Stephen King and Enid Blyton, and asked them to record their 'literariness' (box 5) or not (box 1). The ranking came out as I have ordered them in the sentence above, which I suspect would more or less be most people's judgement.

Firstly, and in general, I asked the students whether 'The Brain Stealers of Mars' was enjoyable to read. Here are their 'raw' responses:

Box 1	Box 2	Box 3	Box 4	Box 5
'No' ——————————————————————— 'Yes'				
8	10	6	19	7

As you might expect, these are fairly evenly split between agreeing and disagreeing, with the edge towards agreeing. There is an index of plus 7, derived from the formula:

$$((7 \times 2) + 19) - ((8 \times 2) + 10), \text{ which is } 33 - 26 = 7.$$

However, there was more consensus in answer to the question of whether the story was an example of good writing (a final score of −29, that is, strongly 'no'; see results above). This feeling was even more emphatic when the students were asked if the text was a piece of classic literature (definitely not, with −78). There was less consensus on the issue of whether the story was a piece of classic science fiction, with each side of the formula balanced on −32 and 30, giving an almost even −2. However, when asked if 'The Brain Stealers of Mars' had literary merit, there was a leaning towards thinking that it did not (−14).

These general impressions are fairly easy to explain. As literature students, the informants seemed confident in their ability to spot classic literature, and so they answered confidently, and they were also reasonably sure of their ability to identify what counts as bad writing in this case. They were less confident in their judgements of whether the text was classic science fiction, largely because, as typical British mostly female young students of literature, they had not read much science fiction at that point. The poor score for literary merit seems to accompany the poor status of science fiction in these readers' minds. The first answer, on the enjoyability of the story, shows ambivalence partly also for this reason: admitting to enjoy 'crappy' fiction is almost an admission of poor taste.

The results for 50 general descriptions showed an interesting range (see the results above). There was a huge consensus that the story was 'male-oriented' and 'fantastic', but also 'clumsy', 'far-fetched' and 'escapist', 'implausible' and 'incredible', 'corny' but 'entertaining'. These, in fact, are all the stereotypical impressions usually connected with pulpstyle. At the other end of the scale, readers felt that the story was definitely not 'feminist' or 'gothic', not 'beautiful', 'persuasive' or 'believable', and not 'serious', 'subtle', 'emotional', 'profound' or 'relevant' either. However, the readers tended to disagree with the supplied descriptions more than they agreed with them (about two-thirds of the results are negative-value disagreements). This might be because the descriptions I supplied included mainly evaluative adjectives that are approving in mainstream literature, and only those words with generally negative connotations were applied to this pulp science fiction story. It became clear from these first results that pulpstyle, as represented by 'The Brain Stealers of Mars', seemed to be not valued.

There was a similarly predictable pattern in the judgements about characterisation. I supplied eighteen adjectives often used impressionistically to describe the presentation of character in literature, and the informants arranged them in relation to the pulp story. Penton, Blake, Loshthu and the thushol were all judged to be 'macho' though 'intelligent', 'corny', 'mechanical', 'wooden', 'flat' and 'obvious', though 'clever'. They were not 'literary', 'subtle', 'rounded', 'sympathetic' or 'emotional'. The polarisation between these two sets of epithets shows a strong consensus across the fifty students. It seems that pulpstyle tends to come off badly when measured against valued psychologising of character in this way.

It was in response to the style of the writing that there were the strongest reactions to extremes (with scores from 97 to −70 almost covering the whole available range). The greatest consensus is marked by the higher scores away from zero, as follows. There was 'plenty of character talk' (27) and not 'too much dialogue' (−36), which supports the impression that direct speech makes up a large part of pulpstyle and is an expected and approved feature. The students noticed that the writing was 'scientific' (20) and not really 'evocative' (−28). And the clumsiness of transition between registers, and other inappropriate or awkward phrasing, is perhaps apparent in the judgement that the text was 'wooden' (18) rather than 'fluent' (−15).

The strongest features (−70 to −42) that were not associated with the story at all were: 'poetic', 'lyrical', 'elegant' and 'stylish' – all prototypical features of high literary art, and this was thought appropriate for pulpstyle (that is, not 'inappropriate', on −55). The feature of style that received the greatest consensus was a judgement that the text was 'inept' (with 97, indicating almost total strong agreement across all the informants). This is a word which contains a perception that the writer was aiming at particular effects but failed to attain them, and is thus clumsy and inept, a poor writer. These projected effects must be assumed by the readers, of course, in order to make such a judgement, and I suggest that the assumed expectations are constructed by the students' experience of mainstream literature.

This suggestion is supported by the free comments that the readers were able to make on the literariness of the opening of 'The Brain Stealers of Mars'. Many evaluations concerned the writer's responsibility (passive forms such as 'contrived', 'clichéd', 'stilted', 'badly-written', and human traits transferred to the writing such as 'clumsy', 'slow', 'glib', 'sloppy' and 'poor'). Several comments concerned the effect on the reader ('undemanding', 'too obvious', 'ineffective'). And other comments were directly concerned with the textual style ('conventional', 'bland', 'antiquated', 'unrealistic', 'pulpy' and 'repetitive'). Of course, all of these judgements are made in relation to an assumed norm (not stilted, demanding, not of slow pace, not pulpy, not repetitive, and so on). Since these students had not read much science fiction previously, the norms for literary conventions that they held must have been developed by reading mainstream literature. In comparison, pulp science fiction was judged to have little value other than as escapist entertainment, and was described as 'trashy', bad writing.

4.3.2 The Historical Importance of a Parametric Principle

It seems, from such responses, that these inexperienced readers of science fiction have a fairly well-developed folk-theory of pulpstyle, sufficient to make evaluative comments with a fair degree of confidence and consensus. Their perception of pulpstyle is a general and cultural model, it seems, since they appeared to have actually read very little of it. For most of them, Campbell's (1975) story was their first contact. Nevertheless, they apparently have a ready-made stereotypical model as part of their repertoire of knowledge about literature and literary genres. Their experience of reading 'The Brain Stealers of Mars' is likely to have been assimilated into that worldview, and to have confirmed the relative prestige-value and status of pulpstyle science fiction and mainstream good quality literature.

It was noticeable that the most confident responses (the most extreme scores) in the questionnaire were shown when handling the value-terms most used within mainstream literature. Pulp science fiction, in short, is judged to be unpoetic, unstylish, clumsy and inept by comparison. Against this set of value-criteria, of course, pulpstyle *is* crap.

If this seems a bit harsh, then it is necessary to consider the framing criteria and state the obvious: pulp science fiction is not the same as mainstream literature. It did not develop from the same origins, and belongs to a tradition of literature that has a fundamentally different ancestry. It is commonplace for science fiction collections to assert their links with the metamorphoses of ancient mythology, folk-tales and fairy-tales, and old narratives set when the accepted technological and scientific framework of the time included the supernatural and magic. Joanna Russ (1975b) has pointed out the connection between the explanatory and pedagogic aspect of science fiction and didactic elements in the literature of the Middle Ages. Furthermore, the 'everyman' generic characterisations of medieval literature, symbolic naming patterns, stock lexical choices from religious or courtly chivalric registers, third person narration with hero-focalisation, and narrative repetition of images and themes echoing an oral, read-aloud narrative tradition all find their counterparts in pulp science fiction.

In addition to the perception of unvalued stylistic features in pulpstyle, modern readers (especially those professionally trained in literature) tend not to value it because it does not carry the antique patina and special historical circumstances of pre-Romantic literature. Post-Romanticism canonises the subject, encouraging realism and psychologised natural-istic characterisation over allegory, analogy and fantasy. It privileges a romanticised view of Nature over a social view of Technology. It is important to recognise that it is Romanticism, not science fiction, that is new-fangled. The origins and parameters of the fangling matter.

Enkvist (1989) invokes a *parametric principle* in the evaluation of genres: text-types should be judged as being well-formed (or not) if they fit the parameters of their general text-type (or not). Science fiction is explicitly mentioned by Enkvist (1989: 376) as a good test-case of the parametric principle in its evocation of a 'counterfactual' universe. The principle sounds so reasonable partly because of the circularity of its logic. Applied strictly, how does the analyst know where to break into the circle, since individual texts together comprise the generic text-type, which is supposed to determine the parameter for the individual texts? Of course, genre is not as rigid a concept as that, and the fact is that a reader's prototypical image of a genre is fluent and flexed by new encounters with specific texts.

The consequence is that all readers are able to form an opinion on the value of a specific text, and may do so with a sense of confidence. Experienced readers of science fiction are able to evaluate a pulp science fiction text within the parameters of the genre as a whole. These two sets of evaluations are equally valid for the readers, and are likely to be satisfactory for them, but within a framework of historical affective stylistics, there is an important general theoretical consequence. This suggests that the methodologies developed for the exploration of mainstream literature cannot give as satisfactory an account within the context of science fiction. Analysis, and the theoretical motivation for exploration, must be genre-specific.

This is not to say that fans and *fanzines* (fan magazines) have better things to say about science fiction than academic discussions, nor that a pecking order of 'I've-read-more-science-fiction-than-you-have' should obtain. But it does mean, at the very least, that a blanket approach will not do. A serious analytical treatment of science fiction should be aware of readership and the specific and special circumstances of every genre of literature.

To apply this version of the parametric principle, then, I have produced some reader responses to support the idea that pulpstyle is largely viewed as bad writing and is not highly valued. However, it was certainly valued, in the everyday sense, by its original audience: very broadly, adolescent boys, young men in office and retail jobs, and new immigrants to the United States for whom English was often a fairly poor second language. These were largely people without much social or economic power, who perhaps gained some vicarious control over their environment by stories of blaster-wielding heroes who won out by logical thought rather than economic status.

Furthermore, these were people for whom the writing of pulpstyle was easy to process. The texts were short stories or serialised novellas, which did not place a great demand on reading time and could be fitted into short periods of leisure. The limited domains of register typically deployed in pulpstyle meant that readers generally had the vocabulary to follow the story or developed it very quickly. If readers came across words they did not understand, it is likely that they would be neologisms or technical terms that would be defined in the text anyway. Readers inexperienced in literary reading would not be faced with tricksy patterns like embedded narratives, extended analepses or prolepses or lots of inferencing work; the scenario would be explicitly described or presented by one of the characters in direct speech. The characters were identifiable WASPy adventurers such as they – boys or immigrants after the American dream – aspired to be. Poor or slow readers would find that the repetition and lack of ellipsis at the level of sentence cohesion made reading straightforward and easy to follow. Brain-processing effort could be devoted to following the excitement of the plot rather than painstakingly decoding and processing the text. The repetition of the central issue of the story also contributed to this accessibility of processing. Finally, it made stories easy to compare, and foregrounded the good value of the magazines which carried dozens of stories that were obviously new and fresh.

Within these historical and affective stylistic parameters, pulpstyle is not clumsy or inept at all, but is entirely appropriate and perfectly matched to its reception.

4.4 The Pulpstyle Legacy

I have spent so long detailing the poetics of pulpstyle in this chapter because it is centrally important in the general traditional style of most of the science fiction of the twentieth century. A detailed analysis of subsequent material would require more space than I have here, and would in any case be largely a repetition of features already discussed in 4.2 above. In this section, then, I will briefly outline the basis for my claim that pulpstyle has left its mark very strongly on modern science fiction. Subsequent movements in the development of the genre have added to and refined the features of pulpstyle, rather than taking a completely new direction.

4.4.1 'Golden Age' Science Fiction

Though Asimov (1975) entitled his collection of early magazine science fiction *Before the Golden Age*, the movement into the short story science fiction of the 1940s and '50s from the pre-war pulps is almost seamless. Even the increasing number of novel-length works that appeared were more like long short-stories, with a single *novum* and resolution rather than a complex plot development. For example, Arthur C. Clarke's (1951) *The Sands of Mars*'s climax is the 'meson resonance' ignition of Phobos, one of the moons of Mars, into a second sun to re-climatise the planet. (Clarke (1982) re-uses this idea when the mysterious aliens in *2010* turn Jupiter into another sun.)

Though the pulps themselves had disappeared, magazine-based science fiction remained the bedrock of the genre. Where there was change, it was in the complexity of the conceptual content rather than in stylistic innovation. More stories seemed to be aimed at an adult readership, with the adolescent demand for 'gosh-wowery' being satisfied by the growing industry of science fiction 'B movies' in the 1950s. Like the transfer of the term 'pulp', the 'B movies' were sometimes not in fact the second presentation in a cinema, but the low-budget effects, merely workmanlike cinematography and stilted dialogue certainly gave many of them a 'B' quality.

However, films and literature shared the pulpstyle inheritance of the scientific and military register. Anthologies such as Nolan (1970), Moskowitz (1970), Asimov (1974) and Greenberg, Waugh and Waugh (1992) contain stories that span the late 1940s, '50s and early 1960s; and their titles, naming patterns, narrative viewpoint and focalisation, and source registers are all identical to the earlier pulpstyle stories. Only the different economic conditions of payment rates, cover price and available space altered the clumsy reliance on stock lexical variations and inappropriate adverbial phrases. This relatively greater prose fluency could also, of course, be a consequence of the new professionalisation of the writers: they tended not to write in several different genres any more, preferring to become specialist science fiction authors.

Exploration

■ Have a look again at the passages in 4.2.5 and 4.2.6 above, which feature encyclopedic 'drop-ins' characteristic of the pulpstyle manner of updating readers. Compare these with a later example. For illustration, here is a fairly recent piece from Greg Bear's *Legacy*:

> 'It wasn't the first time I've been sampled,' I said. 'I discovered a sub-zone and spent some time in it, looking for signs of a new flux.' Sub-zones, Redhill's encyclopedia said, were regions of peculiar specialisation within an ecos, where scions of unfamiliar characteristics sometimes emerged. Some scholars speculated that changes in sub-zones could be harbingers of fluxes. Others maintained sub-zones were actually small ecoi in themselves, serving specific needs for the larger zones in a symbiotic relationship.
>
> I hoped the encyclopedia was not hopelessly out of date.
>
> (Bear 1996: 56)

Here, the narrator, Olmy, is as unfamiliar with the planet Lamarckia as the reader, and has had to read the encyclopedia himself. This first-person point of view makes the insertion of the information appear much more natural.

4.4.2 Modern Traditional-Style Science Fiction

As more and more stories increased the intertextual universes of science fiction, the military-scientific register appeared so often that it became the default register of the genre. This heritage was then the conventional format for science fiction, against which modern stories through the 1960s, '70s and '80s were measured. Even science fiction writers who deliberately attempted to write against the grain of this convention (such as Vonnegut, Dick, Ellison, Aldiss and Ballard) did so by shifting focus within the pulpstyle pattern, for example by thematising the mental process of narrative focalisation in their texts (see this counter-style science fiction writing in chapter 3).

However, these departures from the conventional style are exceptions rather than the rule. The vast majority of science fiction published over the last forty years has retained the conventional pattern of fantastic content with prosaic stylistic delivery. Asimov, for example, continued writing in pulpstyle through the 1980s until his death. The stories in the collection *Azazel* (Asimov 1990) would not have looked out of place in a magazine of the '40s. Novels, too, tend to be written in a derivation of pulpstyle: Larry Niven's (1973) *Ringworld*, for example, reads as a three-hundred page short story. It has a single *novum* (the 'ringworld' itself, a solar system-encircling artificial ring-planet), third person narrative which is focalised through Louis Wu, exotic aliens with unarticulable names, lots of direct speech interspersed with the astronomical physics of the ringworld's technology, and an astonishing level of sexism in relation to the two female characters (a brainless, passive prostitute and a brainless, passive good-luck charm), all of which could have been written in the 1930s. The only addition is the inclusion of the sex which Louis Wu has with Harlrloprillalar and Teela Brown, though even here there is a coy euphemism in the technique of fading chapters out at the appropriate moment.

The modern traditional style of science fiction writing can be seen in the work of Poul Anderson, Greg Bear, Jerome Bixby, Arthur C. Clarke, Harry Harrison, Robert Heinlein, Ursula Le Guin, Walter M. Miller, Robert Sheckley, L. Sprague de Camp, Theodore Sturgeon, and many others. This is not to disparage these writers at all; their work represents some of the best writing in the genre. Even the pedestrian average surpasses the mundanity of much contemporary writing. Within the parameters of the conventional science fictional style, these authors still manage to construct narratives that are inconceivable in any other form of writing. Time travel in Heinlein's 'By His Bootstraps', for example, allows him to manipulate a single subjective narrative focalisation across different identities of the same character, something which is just not possible in any other genre except perhaps surrealism (see chapter 7 for more discussion of these sorts of possibilities). Jerome Bixby's (1974) 'It's a *Good* Life' is a brilliantly well-crafted short story, within the traditional science fictional style, which uses shifts in focalisation to convey a terror that cannot even be thought about or spoken (see 7.4). Most evolution out of pulpstyle seems to be within the dimension of narrative point of view.

4.4.3 The Narrative Kinesis of 'Cyberpulp'

In his preface to *Mirrorshades*, the seminal collection of 'cyberpunk' science fiction, Bruce Sterling writes:

> Cyberpunk is a product of the Eighties milieu – in some sense, as I hope to show later, a definitive product. But its roots are deeply sunk in the sixty-year tradition of modern popular SF.
>
> The cyberpunks as a group are steeped in the lore and tradition of the SF field. Their precursors are legion. Individual cyberpunk writers differ in their literary debts; but some older writers, ancestral cyberpunks perhaps, show a clear and striking influence.

(Sterling 1988: viii)

This sense of tradition is most readily seen in the blend of the literary self-consciousness of the '60s New Wave and a return to the hard science of the earlier Golden Age. At the conceptual and stylistic levels then, cyberpunk seems to have moved away from pulpstyle. However, many of the features of pulp are retained in the stories in the *Mirrorshades* collection: there is still the heavy reliance on the drama that direct speech provides (though it is more naturalistically vernacular), still diversions in register to explain technical innovations (though these are less abrupt), and still the enthusiasm for technical neologisms (though from computers rather than physics).

The developing stylistic self-awareness in stream-of-consciousness focalisation, conversational and colloquial syntax and the use of poetic metaphor are often seen as marking a shift away from traditional science fictional style. (See Warrick (1980) and the articles in Slusser and Shippey (1992) for examples and discussion of all these features.) It is this that contributes towards the identification of cyberpunk with postmodernist fiction, an argument outlined in 3.5.1, and to which I will now return.

In most mainstream fiction, authors can assume a readerly knowledge of present-day realities and the reader's environment that can be referred to rather than being explicitly stated and described. Science fiction, of course, cannot do this (see chapter 7 for its alternative strategies). It is the assumption of knowledge that enables McHale (1987) to call the mainstream predominantly *epistemological* fiction. He contrasts this with the foregrounding of explicit calling into existence of events and characters in postmodernist fiction and science fiction: this he groups as *ontological* fiction (concerned with existence). McHale cites the science fiction of Philip K. Dick as an example of ontological fiction.

However, I think this identification of science fiction with post-modernism (both its fiction and its usual bedfellow, post-structuralist deconstructive literary theory) is mistaken. The practical concern of science fiction, its heritage and history, and its explicitly contextualising effect, all serve to make science fiction itself a critique of postmodern-ism. For example, where postmodernism is satisfied with ontological uncertainty, or uses ambivalence to end texts without narrative closure, science fictional texts tend to resolve narratives (often spectacularly, cataclysmically or transcendentally). Even those that remain unresolved explicitly in the text hold out the possibility of explanation and under-standing. Where postmodernist fiction likes to blur rational boundaries and categories, science fiction recaptures fantasy and irrealism within the explanatory mode of science. The usual resolving instrument (science) is simply extrapolated from its current state and made to encompass ontology. Where postmodernism is generally concerned with groups of people, and characters are foregrounded as ciphers for groups, science fiction tends to deal with the ethics of individualism (see Butler 1996), a union of practical action and moral responsibility. Even the apparently amoral landscapes of cyberpunk often wear their amorality as a fore-grounded feature, making an issue of the ethics of the future.

McHale (1987) is right to say that postmodernist fiction is primarily ontological, but wrong to say that science fiction is thus limited. Sci-ence fiction can certainly be concerned with ontology (Dick is a good example), but there is no question that it also raises questions of episte-mology. The genre not only creates alternative universes, but it almost invariably sets up a dynamic narrative to explore what these are like and why (and the mechanisms – both textual and cognitive – that comprise this are the subjects of the second half of this book). The dynamism of the narrative – an inheritance from its populist pulpstyle roots – addi-tionally adds a third dimension to the genre: this might be termed *kinesis*. Narrative drive and the emphasis on action and a sequence of material events means that science fiction (especially including cyberpunk) is holistically epistemological, ontological, and kinetic.

4.5 Review

Pulpstyle provides the basis of the majority of science fictional style. Even those texts of science fiction which deviate most from this norm, such as those discussed in chapter 3, do so on the basis of a reaction to the central elements of what has gone before. They also retain the generic principles of a narratological progression of events that give what would otherwise be a reflective and static genre its excitement and narrative drive.

In this chapter, I have discussed the stylistic features of pulpstyle and related it to the current canon of value. In doing this, I am not trying to claim that pulpstyle has been unjustly marginalised. It had its historical place and has not travelled well, even though it has been influential. But the discussion demonstrates that valuation is a matter of cultural fashion and institutional standardisation, which is then attached to or detached from particular texts over time. By association, the stylistic features of those texts then seem to take on value, but we should remember that this is an effect not a cause. Value is not a matter that can be determined stylistically.

Explorations

■ Compare a pulpstyle story side-by-side with a cyberpunk story: for example, one from the Asimov (1975) collection and one from the *Mirrorshades* anthology (Sterling 1988). In your opinion, are the similarities due to traditions from the common science fiction inheritance or simply a result of the common short story format? (You might like to test this against a non-science fiction story.) If similar features are evident, how does cyberpunk re-contextualise them and use them differently?

■ Consider how science fiction has constructed children and childhood (especially in TV and film). Also consider the stylistic implications of viewing science fiction as 'juvenile' literature (both descriptively and judgementally). Much of the literature for children is often required to be primarily educational; escapism is not an option within this view of innocent childhood, but is reserved for adults. In spite of some of the escapist content, Campbell's policy emphasised the didactic element in science fiction, and many authors also write popular science. Why is play and entertainment, literature as a learning experience, not seen in the same way for adults? Do you think the didactic element in some adult science fiction makes it 'juvenile', or does it lead readers to see the function of science fiction as being different from other literature? Do readers do different things with science fiction?

Speculations

■ Though a parametric principle seems equitable, it has the extreme consequence that all literature is viewed as being equally valuable. The circularity of judging a text by the text-type of which it forms a part is then a problem. What about texts that set out to disrupt generic patterns? Is the question of literary value purely a socio-cultural matter, or can stylistic description inform it? Science fiction is even now still not treated as classic literature, except for those authors who are removed from the science fiction section (Orwell, Huxley, Pynchon, Vonnegut, Lessing, for example). Is it desirable that science fiction is canonised?

■ Most of the literary critical and analytical terminology used by most writers when discussing science fiction has been developed in relation to mainstream literary study and within the authorised view of literary history. Given, instead, a revised version of literary history that focused on 'alternativity' (as explored at the end of chapter 3), is it then appropriate to use such borrowed terms? Would it not be better to develop a historical poetics and critical theory from within the science fiction tradition? What would such a project look like, and how would it define itself in relation to the mainstream?

Further reading

The fascinating history of the science fiction magazines is described in Rogers (1964), Ashley (1974, 1975, 1976), Cawelti (1976), Carter (1977), and Cioffi (1982). Early precursors containing science fiction are detailed in Moskowitz (1974). Examples and approaches to the sort of reader-reponse criticism included in this chapter are to be found in Tompkins (1980), Freund (1987), Iser (1978), Fish (1980), Holub (1984) and Eco (1979). Discussion on cyberpunk and postmodernism, in addition to the further reading mentioned in chapter 3, appears in Broderick (1995), Shippey (1991), Slusser and Shippey (1992), and Warrick (1980).

CHAPTER 5

CENTREPOINT: RETROSPECTIVE/ PROSPECTIVE

5.1 Retrospect: History So Far

This brief central chapter offers an opportunity to reflect on where we have been and where we are going. The first half of the book has been concerned with the historical development of science fiction in a tradition. It has dealt largely with the textual and contextual side of poetics. I have discussed the internal history and evolution of science fiction within the twentieth century, and also suggested ways of thinking about the place of a literature of fictional alternativity in the more global scheme of things. The focus has been on language in science fiction and how science fiction has exploited aspects of linguistic organisation to achieve its special effects. I have tried to avoid claiming that science fiction is a fundamentally different order of literature from any other form. However, I have also tried to demonstrate that science fiction lays its emphasis on different aspects of narrative poetics. These include the characteristic patterns of framing and deixis as used in science fiction, especially the way in which past and future are handled; the way science fiction has used language and linguistic special effects; and the features it has taken from its own early history. All of these patterns are what makes it identifiable as science fiction. They also make discussions such as mine more generally applicable: science fictional poetics shows up features present in all narrative poetics but generally obscured, dormant or differently patterned in mainstream literature.

5.2 Mapping Science Fiction

In chapter 1, I introduced the cognitive linguistic understanding of prototype effects as a useful way of considering the category of science fiction. Having discussed some examples of science fictional poetics in the three chapters since, in which the notion of prototypes has emerged several times, the exploration can be usefully taken up again here.

So far I have been using the term 'prototype' loosely, as if there were an ideal image of a science fiction text, against which other texts are evaluated. In cognitive linguistics, however (see Lakoff 1987; Ungerer and Schmid 1996: 1–59), there is a careful emphasis on talking about 'prototype effects', rather than prototypes as such. This is because there can be no certainty about what constitutes a prototype, and human cognition seems to be sensitive to contextualising factors which produce prototypical effects from a range of categories within a domain.

It seems that individuals use *focal objects* as points of orientation for their cognitive worldview. Examples include children picking out a particular bright red colour as the 'best' example of redness in a range, or thinking about a certain sort of house that is 'normal' for their culture. These focal objects are more like the way I have been using 'prototypes' so far. It should be immediately apparent that there is a matter of perceptual salience here: individuals select certain items in the world as focal objects because the domain to which they are attached is important for them. The reasons why some people become interested in science fiction is a matter of childhood psychology and social theory that is beyond the scope of this book. However, once selected as being salient, the cognitive domain of 'science fiction' begins to be established with a focal object, generating a range of prototype effects from newly-encountered texts which are judged against it.

It should also be apparent from these brief examples that there is a cultural and contextual dependency in prototype effects. For example, an 'apple' might not be the best example of a fruit in Hawaii. If you read that the park Ranger got into his car, you are likely to picture a Land-Rover as the most likely example rather than a Ford saloon, say. Similarly, if you read in a science fiction text that the captain stood on the bridge of the ship, it is likely that you will imagine stars rather than waves out of the window.

The prototype effect of focal objects within radial categories is thus a social business. A generic characterisation of science fiction must recognise this. Bex (1996) has suggested that the social negotiation of genre works similarly to the spread of linguistic innovations as understood within sociolinguistics. For example, Milroy (1987) developed the notion of *social networks* from a study of speech variants among various communities in Belfast. Examining the social network of an individual involved tracking not only who knew whom, but also how closely-knit they were, whether they all had mutual friends, and whether they knew each other in a range of social roles and contexts. Milroy found that a dense and close-knit social network operated as a linguistic reinforcement mechanism: particular linguistic innovations were more likely to spread and become general usage from within such a network. Conversely, no matter how innovative the individuals, if they are isolated or not fully socially integrated, their innovations are less likely to be adopted generally.

Bex (1996) applied this notion to literature in proposing that institutional networks operate as generic reinforcement mechanisms. Institutions could include academic societies, journal editorial policy, publishing guidelines, fanzine discussions, and how science fiction is read and debated and taught. Individuals at the centre of academic study, for example, are more likely to have their views on a poetics of science fiction generally accepted than someone who only has coffee-bar conversations about science fiction, unless, of course, that person then goes on to a science fiction convention or club.

The category of science fiction – and its sub-genres – is set up as an idealised cognitive model that is socially negotiated and culturally shared. What counts as the 'best' science fiction varies according to its context: what is it being *used* for? Clearly the academic debate about the relationship of recent science fiction and mainstream literature is part of the current negotiation of cultural history. Science fiction is being claimed as a centrally important genre for turn-of-the-century society (by, for example, McHale 1987 and Jameson 1991), and the strategy involved in this argument is a linkage of, for example, cyberpunk, with wider cultural movements such as postmodernism.

What the nature of prototype effects within cognitive linguistics tells us, however, is that such arguments are a matter of social negotiation, institutional interest, and individual salience. In a very real and natural sense, the equation of postmodernism and recent science fiction is an act of corporate will. The debate should not be along the lines of whether the equation is accurate (this is a redundant question), but whether the equation is desirable. I think that it is not. Postmodernist fiction is a minority taste, and the popular genre of science fiction should not be shoehorned into an alien set of critical parameters. Postmodernist poetics only correlates with a tiny proportion of recent science fiction, and this serves to sever the connection with the genre's roots. Postmodernist fiction is ideologically allied to a set of critical practices (poststructuralist deconstruction, largely) which is founded on an outdated understanding and basic ignorance of modern linguistics, and is at heart anti-scientific (see, for example, the arguments in Tallis 1988).

It seems to me that a linguistically and cognitively informed poetics, which is developed from the study of natural language, and is adapted for the specific artistic context in hand, is a better critical tool for advancing the exploration of science fiction.

5.3 The Teaching of Science Fiction

Ideological preferences have consequences for a pedagogy of science fiction. This notion is primarily odd, in that science fiction is there firstly to be read rather than taught. The question arises, then, as to what is being taught. Science fiction itself is not taught, except in creative writing classes where, in my experience, nothing occurs that I would recognise as 'teaching'. I think that science fiction can be taught descriptively, within a framework of systematic stylistics; this is what I have been doing with my own students for the last few years. More generally what is taught are readings and reading strategies of science fiction. That is, seminar discussion takes place first at the level of interpretation and only secondarily (if at all) at the level of textual description. This means that science fiction is always placed into a context to justify its study.

For example, it is entirely possible to teach science fiction as a branch of speculative philosophy. There is certainly enough across the genre to address both fundamental and complex issues of ontology and epistemology. The use of logic and rationalism against faith and religion, the status of humanity in a technologised future, the nature of knowledge, progress and science are all dealt with in science fiction narratives. A course in science fiction then becomes a course in dramatised ideas, an applied practical philosophy. Though this is a perfectly legitimate use of science fiction, it necessarily involves disregarding certain aspects of the literary genre, such as the fact that it is a literary experience. The aesthetic dimension of science fictional reading, in this perspective, simply comes down to the attractive vehicle in which the philosophical ideas are carried and made more readable.

Science fiction has also been taught as cultural history. It is very important in this respect, especially in the twentieth century and in response to industrialisation and urbanisation in the nineteenth. Science fiction is now so much a part of both popular and authorised culture that it can be seen as a mode which is borrowed for all sorts of purposes (Broderick 1995). Its images, stylistic choices, terminology and narrative aspects such as action and resolution are apparent in every art form from film to billboard advertising. Even more significantly, science fiction has had an impact on the way our cities are planned, our transport systems are run, our politics operate, and the way we view the world today. The end of the Cold War coincided with Reagan's 'Star Wars' proposals for a nuclear 'shield' which placed medieval courtly language alongside the new mythology of science fiction. The images from the Gulf War were indistinguishable (indeed, hardly as good in quality) from computer arcade 'shoot-em-ups'. If you want to know about social history, especially in Britain, over the last 200 years, look to science fiction. The texts used in chapter 2 all encode their own period's view of the future, and this inevitably tells us about the time of these texts' production (see also the social historical approach to the development of the genre adopted by Aldiss and Wingrove 1986 and James 1994).

Within the expansive bounds of literary studies, where courses in science fiction mostly reside, old-fashioned snobbery has almost entirely given way to peaceful co-existence. Nevertheless it is depressing how much of the discussion still focuses on the canon, and which selected texts of science fiction merit inclusion in the curriculum. Even after all these years of rigorous theoretical awareness, the analysis of literary value still more or less comes down to authorised taste, rather than an examination of the concept of value in reception, and historical and cultural accidence. Different communities value different literatures for different reasons, and that is that. Science fiction studies have been around a long time in English Literature, but still a tremble of naughtiness accompanies their semesterly appearance in the syllabus.

Perhaps this is too idealistic, but the continuing sense of newness of science fiction in the rarefied air of English departments certainly offers a challenge to the entrenched customs and unnatural practices of literary study. The genre itself invites an intellectual synthesis of rigorous scientific knowledge and practice with the analysis of art. It offers to cloistered minds a reconnection with the wider community amongst whom they live and on whose taxes they depend. It can provide an example that popular art is not simple nor brainless. It supplies another context against which to evaluate and understand the rest of the literature that was being written around science fiction. It makes new connections and offers new perspectives on every period of literature.

Science fiction study, of course, can be more radical than this too. In demanding a history of its own, it can help to reframe not only the grand narrative of literary history but also the way that histories are perceived. In claiming its validation and value from its parametric readership it can suggest a means of investigating the value of all literature and art. In appropriating sympathetic and self-generated theoretical frameworks, rather than having ill-fitting approaches bolted on, it can demonstrate the importance of treating the literary experience as a natural process. Reading comes out of natural language use, and demands to be understood in that context, with the analyst armed with the most modern theoretical equipment.

All of this would be too idealistic and abstract if there were not evidence of it happening already. Increasingly the allusiveness, intertextuality, sampling and jargon popular across all art forms are resolving into a cultural aesthetic of integration. This is especially noticeable within the most popular forms of art: even mainstream studio films refer to older movies, with many sequels and re-makes; clothes fashion revisits its recent history as kitsch or irony; dance music samples phrases and styles from throughout the history of popular music, and even mainstream chart music mixes styles and samples; the spread of personal computers brings recording, publishing, re-mixing and image-manipulation technology to an individual level. The ironic freeplay associated with post-modernism across many art-forms seems in general to be becoming less nihilistic. My own students have shifted over the last few years from a general listlessness and apathy to a more political and outward-looking activism. In art and science, politics and social study, the importance of contextualised systems and holistic understanding has become increasingly explicitly stated and, more essentially, practised. Science fiction is a part of this, a central part both because it helped bring it to cultural consciousness and because it offers models of understanding it.

However, this is becoming a speculation, and the rest of this book must return specifically to science fiction. From here on, the book rolls its sleeves up and gets down to the intricate workings of the genre. If you want a user's guide to science fiction, that is what follows. You should remember, of course, that manuals don't tell you how to drive, only how the engine works; whether you become a better driver from this knowledge is another question altogether. The *Explorations* and *Speculations*, remember, are a means of test-driving your own mind. If you would like to discuss your ideas further, or have any comments arising from your reading of this book, I am on the web at the University of Nottingham (www.nottingham.ac.uk). Come and find me there.

5.4 Prospect: Mapping Reading Science Fiction

The chapters that follow are concerned with mapping, reading, science fiction, and mapping the reading of science fiction. The method of achieving all this is to integrate linguistics, cognition, and textuality into a rounded poetics of the genre. The nature of science fiction means that the discussion towards this has many points of relevance for a wider understanding of how literature works. In many ways, science fiction is a microcosm of fictional literature. It takes fictionality to the edge of impossibility but it is mainly realist. It defamiliarises the everyday absolutely; it presents new concepts in a familiar form. It can be poetic and lyrical; it uses the register of descriptive science and hard technology. It is visceral; it is cerebral.

This infinite variety in science fiction makes its study more generally applicable. In chapter 2, we have already seen how using science fiction to think about fictionality and fictional space allows us to develop our understanding of the comprehension process and how science fiction negotiates this deictically. This understanding can then be taken back to more general concerns in language where it was not so obvious. The process described here is one of metaphoric mapping which is common in understanding the world. An issue is mapped onto a metaphorical domain, worked out there, and the resolution mapped back.

For example, in science fiction, an issue that concerns the present day is figured metaphorically in a future scenario, and a resolution is reached that has implications for the present. For an example from politics, Hook (1983) and Chilton (1986) have documented the way that the Japanese government have tried to persuade their people to accept visits by nuclear-armed ships. Nuclear weapons are mapped as 'allergens', a small dose of which will desensitise people. In this way, mapping back again, protest against the arms race is seen as an illness which can be cured. The same metaphorical process operates in science fiction, which rehearses in glorious conceptual colour many of the monochromed poetics of mainstream literature. Understanding the workings of science fictional reading can assist in an understanding of literary reading in general.

This principle extends to the language system itself, since science fiction is also a form of linguistic usage. Many of the dimensions of science fiction involve the foregrounding or manipulation of narrative organisation. The presentation of new worlds involves new words, new syntactic structures, new semantic connections and new methods of understanding. The science fiction discussed in the remaining part of this book not only practises all of these, but also provides an education in learning how to read them and make sense of them.

Though this book uses linguistics to study science fiction, the study of science fiction can also be undertaken as a means of studying language. Many of the most illuminating examples of how language works can be found in science fiction texts. They explore the limits of what it is possible to do in language, and they even invent new forms of language on discoverable principles. Some aspects of this have been discussed in the first half of the book. The remaining chapters examine the workings of science fiction from the introduction of new words to the negotiation of new worlds, their poetic statement and their destruction. At each stage, science fiction is used to develop or refine models of language, reading, cognition and mind that will hold beyond the realm of science fiction.

CHAPTER 6

MICROLOGICAL: NEW WORDS

6.1 Preview

Science fiction presents an extreme of fictionality in as stark a realist presentation as it can manage. It blends the impossible, fantastic and barely plausible (fiction) with the baldest, plainest, most apparently objective style in which to set out a system of facts and knowledge (science). It creates new worlds by conjuring and coining new words. In this and the next chapter, I describe how this is done, and I explore some of the effects of new wor(l)ds.

6.2 New Words in Science Fiction

A feature of science fictional language, which is regularly mentioned by my students as being a characteristic, is **neologism**. One of the things that seems to deter new readers is the perception that science fiction texts are full of new words, and that these are 'hard words'. For those unused to the genre, it seems to encourage the exclusivity of the 'in-group', and alienate those who are not used to reading scientific terms. It is true that most groups in society (such as surgeons, computer technicians, teachers) are at least partly defined by the special terminology that they share. And it is also true that science fiction often alienates the reader in several senses (in Chapter 8, I explore ways in which this 'alienising' of the reader is a valuable and exciting peculiarity of science fiction). Indeed, neologism is the feature that most often appears in parodies of the genre, reflecting and ridiculing the perception of the miraculous technology that has powers in proportion to the complexity and obscurity of its name. The following, for example, is Douglas Adams's explanation of the invention of the 'Infinite Improbability Drive' in *The Hitch-Hiker's Guide to the Galaxy*. Adams's characteristic technique of blending pseudo-science with informal chat is exemplified here:

The Infinite Improbability Drive is a wonderful new method of crossing vast interstellar distances without all that tedious messing about in hyperspace.

It was discovered by a lucky chance, and then developed into a governable form of propulsion by the Galactic Government's research team on Damogran.

This, briefly, is the story of its discovery.

The principle of generating small amounts of *finite* improbability by simply hooking the logic circuits of a Bambleweeny 57 Sub-Meson Brain to an atomic vector plotter suspended in a strong Brownian Motion producer (say a nice hot cup of tea) were of course well understood – and such generators were often used to break the ice at parties by making all the molecules in the hostess's undergarments leap simultaneously one foot to the left, in accordance with the Theory of Indeterminacy.

Many respectable physicists said they weren't going to stand for this – partly because it was a debasement of science, but mostly because they didn't get invited to those sort of parties.

Another thing they couldn't stand was the perpetual failure they encountered in trying to construct a machine which could generate the *infinite* improbability field needed to flip a spaceship across the mind-paralysing distances between the furthest stars, and in the end they grumpily announced that such a machine was virtually impossible.

Then, one day, a student who had been left to sweep up the lab after a particularly unsuccessful party found himself reasoning this way:

If, he thought to himself, such a machine is a *virtual* impossibility, then it must logically be a *finite* improbability. So all I have to do in order to make one is to work out exactly how improbable it is, feed that figure into the finite improbability generator, give it a fresh cup of really hot tea . . . and turn it on!

(Adams 1979: 69)

Phrases such as 'Bambleweeny 57 Sub-Meson Brain' combine the sort of numerical nomenclature and Latin-based specialist scientific words, with a name blended from 'bamboozled' (deliberately fooled) and 'weeny' (small and childish), to undercut the seriousness of the usual computer-naming domain. This bathos is further developed by switching from multiple-word names ('atomic vector plotter') in a scientifically descriptive and formal register ('principle', 'generating', 'suspended') using real scientific terms ('Brownian motion'), to the colloquial ('say a nice hot cup of tea'). The connection of serious scientific research to sleazy parties mirrors this debasement, and the typical form of logical reasoning found in science fiction is used at the end to 'explain' the principle of infinite improbability. Here, the syntactic form ('if...then') places 'virtual impossibility' and 'finite improbability' as opposites, when they are nothing of the sort.

Of course, as with most successful parodies, this serves to satirise the procedures and features of science fiction partly because it is so close to actual science fiction style. Only the intrusion of the colloquial phrasing signals the humorous intent. Many of the naming features identified here by Adams occur in science fiction, and this chapter provides an organising system for discussing them.

The use of the referential power of language to help create a visual reality in the mind's eye is, in science fiction, the totem use of new words to signal to the reader that something very clever, advanced, and technological is happening. It is all part of the establishment of plausibility and verisimilitude.

6.2.1 The Scope of Neologisms in Science Fiction

In spite of the foregoing outline, there are not as many new things in the science fiction universe as might be intuitively thought. There are maybe half a dozen new inventions (and hence new words to refer to them) in the 'hardest' of 'hard' science fiction novels. Even episodes of that most neologising series, *Star Trek* (in all four TV incarnations), rate at most a couple of neologisms per programme. I am discounting, here, neologisms such as 'warp-drive', 'warp-core', 'transporter', 'photon torpedo', 'Klingon', and the like as being so familiar to even the most casual *Star Trek* viewer that they cannot really count as 'new' neologisms, having become a generally recognised part of the wider culture. Clearly, the perception that science fiction is full of new coinages must be because it is a feature that marks it out from other genres.

So it is not that science fiction is packed full of neologisms, but it is the case that it has more than are encountered in mainstream literature. There is a difference here as well in the type of neologism generally used. If you take the opening page of a few science fiction novels or especially short stories, you are likely to find new characters, new places, new machines, new social groups, new processes, and a host of new objects, all with new names invented by the science fiction author. Science fiction short stories tend to have an even greater concentration of such neologisms because the science fictional world has to be evoked in a relatively short space of text. But if you take the opening page of a few mainstream texts, the only new words you are likely to encounter will be new characters' names or invented new places. The paraphernalia of everyday life in mainstream fiction is simply there with its familiar terms attached.

In the scheme offered below in this chapter, the new words of mainstream fiction are almost always the result of *creation*, and they usually take the form of proper names ('Emma Woodhouse', 'Jane Eyre', 'Leopold Bloom', 'Yossarian', 'Mansfield Park', 'the Pequod', 'Wessex', 'Pooh Corner', 'Brideshead'). Otherwise, they merely *borrow* words already in existence to claim a correspondence with reality ('London' in Dickens, 'Dublin' in Joyce, 'Nottingham' in D.H. Lawrence). Whether creating people and places, or borrowing them from our own historical reality, mainstream fiction is limited in the things with which it can fill its world. Science fiction, essentially, is distinguished by new *concepts* and *things*, though it additionally has the capacity to use the same created and borrowed words as well. For example, H.G. Wells has his Martian machines with their death rays landing in the familiar areas surrounding London: 'I completely wreck and sack Woking – killing my neighbours in painful and eccentric ways – then proceed via Kingston and Richmond to London, selecting South Kensington for feats of peculiar atrocity' (Wells 1975: vii). Relative to mainstream literature, science fiction exercises its capacity for a greater number and a greater variety of types of neologisms.

In the next chapter, I will draw out a procedural model of the cognitive effect of such neologisms, in order to show how words and worlds are interdependent and constructive across the range of science fiction scenarios (for want of a better word than 'genres'): literature, film, video/TV, role-play game, computer game, comic panels, and so on. In this chapter, though, I will outline a simple structural description, based on a hierarchical taxonomy, of neologism-types. I have based this on a small lexical corpus of around 130 neological items (including variations on the root word such as 'UFO'/'ufologist', for example). This list was collected by taking the neologisms under the entry for 'Terminology' in *The Encyclopedia of Science Fiction* (Clute and Nicholls 1993: 1213), and adding more that students suggested in a science fiction seminar when they were asked to think of science fictional neologisms. This is not exactly a random sampling method (though, unfortunately, there is no semantically-tagged large computerised corpus of science fiction texts available to have a big sample), so comments on the distribution of real examples of neologisms across the types are to be taken as illustrative only.

6.3 Neologisms and Neosemes

It is important, firstly, to distinguish between new word-shapes and new meanings attached to existing words; only the former new words are usually called **neologisms**, from a literal etymological reading of the Greek *neo-logos*. However, both constitute new *uses* of a word and both are important in the linguistic practice of the genre. Since a distinction is to be made, I will refer to the second type as **neosemes** and will discuss **neosemy** (to coin a word) first.

Words undergo shifts in meaning from the moment they are coined until the moment they 'die', when no one uses them any more and they become archaic. **Neosemy** thus refers to meaning-shift. If a word shifts its meaning it can be said to be operating as a new word. **Neosemy** operates on all words in the language, and can be seen as a sort of linguistic entropy by which all words mutate or eventually disappear from current usage. Figure 6a (in 6.3.1) shows the distinction between **neoseme** and **neologism** proper, and outlines the various sub-types.

6.3.1 Broadening

The first sub-type of neosemy is **broadening**, which is a shift in meaning because of generalisation. For example, the word 'bird' originally referred only to a nestling, and a 'dog' was a specific breed. Finding similar neosemic shifts within science fiction is not easy, since the genre proper has been around for only the last century or so, and science fictional words have simply not existed for long enough to be affected by neosemy. Older science fictional words include 'utopia' (from the Greek *ou-topos* – 'no place'), in Sir Thomas More's (1910) narrative of 1516, for example. This proper name has since broadened its meaning to include any idealised imaginary society or state, and it is a word commonly found now in non-science fictional contexts such as political rhetoric and newspaper reporting. It has even developed a less widely used antonym, 'dystopia' (see chapter 9 for discussion of utopias and dystopias). The loss of the original etymological composition is apparent in

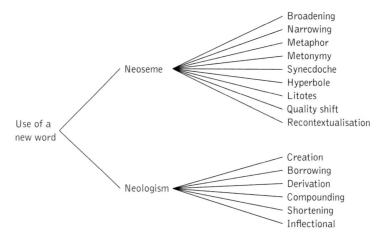

Figure 6a   Basic Typology of New Word Usage

this development, since, as Anthony Burgess has pointed out, 'cacatopia' ('bad place') would strictly be more apt. This shows how the original sense of the word as a neologism has faded to allow neosemic shift to occur according to anglicised rules, rather than Greek-based grammar. English has a history of adding its own morphemes to words borrowed from other languages.

6.3.2 Narrowing

The converse of broadening is **narrowing**, or the specialisation of meaning. 'Meat' in early Middle English meant all food, and 'deer' were all livestock. 'Alien' originally referred to strangers or foreigners, now frozen as in 'illegal alien', used mainly by immigration officials, or in formal idioms such as 'it's alien to me', and with derived forms such as 'alienate', 'inalienable', and 'alienation'. However, I believe that, largely because of the mass appeal of science fiction, the primary meaning of 'alien' has now narrowed to refer to extra-terrestrial life, and this is its prototypical denotation.

6.3.3 Metaphor and Metonymy

Metaphor, with reference to language change, describes the shift in meaning when creative metaphorical neologisms lose their original sense, as have 'bitter' (biting) and 'harrowing' (ploughed). These have become 'dead metaphors'; in fact, since they are no longer perceived as such, they are popularly not regarded as metaphors at all, but as having a literal coincidence of denotation and reference. 'Field', from the Anglo-Saxon 'feld', meaning open country, has become the metaphor for a conceptual space, as in 'academic field'. It is further used in science fiction as a contraction of 'force field' or 'energy field', and developed (for example by Iain M. Banks (1988, 1989)) into 'cutting field' and 'effector field'.

In contrast to metaphor, **metonymy** indicates conceptual proximity in meaning shift. 'Jaw' originally meant what we now call the cheek. It can explain why 'Frankenstein' (thanks to Boris Karloff) is popularly understood to refer to the monster rather than its creator, Victor Frankenstein, in the original 1816 novel by Mary Shelley (1998).

6.3.4 Synecdoche, Hyperbole, Litotes and Quality Shifts

The next four neosemic processes account for many words which have shifted meaning over the last millennium, but science fictional words are too new to show evidence of their effect yet. **Synecdoche** (part for whole meanings) describes the use of 'stove' (originally a heated room) and 'town' (a fence around a settlement). **Hyperbole** (exaggeration) explains the use of 'astound' (to strike with thunder and lightning); **litotes** (understatement) explains 'kill' (to torment). **Quality shifts** refer to changes in the connotation of words, which can be degenerating or elevating: both 'knave' and 'knight' originally meant a boy. I have not found any evidence in science fiction texts of these long-term linguistic changes.

6.3.5 Recontextualisation

Finally, **recontextualisation** is a global textual effect of changing the meanings of words, and this is the source of most neosemy in science fiction. Recontextualisation is where the peculiarities of the text world affect the semantic field of a word. Since science fiction deals centrally with alternative realities, there are many examples. The most famous concerns the use of the word 'pregnant', which (in its normal semantic composition) denotes 'carrying a child prior to birth'. There are limits on the words with which 'pregnant' can collocate: they must agree for the component 'femaleness' (and thus, by implication, not 'maleness'). Clashes of these components are normally judged ungrammatical. For example, 'The king was pregnant' is semantically odd, since 'king' (male) does not match the normal restrictions on the use of 'pregnant' (not male). In our reality, this is a semantic clash. However, semantic rules work within possible worlds, and the text world of Ursula Le Guin's (1981) *The Left Hand of Darkness* is the planet Gethen. There, biological gender is neutral most of the time. Within the Gethenian semantic system, in other words, 'king' is neither male nor female, and so 'The king is pregnant' is semantically well-formed (see 7.2 for further discussion of this). The science fictional text world has recontextualised the lexical meaning of an existing word (neosemy, again).

The case of the recontextualisation of London suburban place-names in H.G. Wells's (1975) *The War of the Worlds* is a similar case mentioned above. These do not refer to the real places, as they would on a map in our world, any more than Thomas Hardy's Wessex or Irvine Welsh's Edinburgh ever really existed in exactly that form. A simple, though not definitive, test of such cases of fictionality is to ask whether the novel containing the textual world exists in that world. No one in *Trainspotting* has read *Trainspotting*. Even in the most apparently realistic narratives such as 'gritty' TV soap operas, their world is not our world because no one in the soap watches the soap every night. Science fiction rarely experiences this reflexive problem, since it is founded on the notion of alternativity. In the science fiction novel, even familiar words are recontextualised into a different possible world. There they act as 'counterparts' of the real places in our world. I return to this idea in the next chapter.

Neosemic processes operate gradually throughout history on all words that are in living usage, but of these it is the process of recontextualisation that is most important for science fictional words. Neologism proper is much more central to science fiction, and Figure 6a indicates that there are six main sub-types. Figure 6b below gives a detailed breakdown of the variations within this scheme, and it is this detail which comprises substantially the rest of this chapter.

Exploration

■ A neologistic game is played out by Douglas Adams (1983) in his mock dictionary *The Meaning of Liff*. Here, everyday words such as the names of cities, towns and villages are given definitions and treated as neologisms. Try this recontextualisation yourself by providing alternative definitions for ordinary words, and consider how the component parts of your neologism bear any relation to the new sense you have attached.

6.4 Types of Neologism

Of course all words were once new, and thus any use of the term **neologism** involves a notion of 'relative recentness'. I also take a practical (pragmatic, in the everyday sense) view of the perception that words are 'English' words, rather than currently having a foreign flavour. Thus, the original English connotation of 'alien' is compared with modern usage above, though of course originally the word was **borrowed** (see 6.4.2) from the Latin *alienus* (other), and the Latin root was then forgotten. Furthermore, the sources of neologisms discussed below are various. Some are purely derived from science fiction, some have found their way into science fiction from real science, and some (e.g. 'cyberpunk') appeared in order to describe a sub-genre of science fiction. In all this, there is a problem in the overlap between science and science fiction, since hypothesis-formation and terminology in advance of discovery are types of fiction, and I return to this idea at the end. For the purposes of the typology below, I treat all these various neologisms and sources equally.

6.4.1 Creation

The prototypical form of neologism is **creation** (see Figure 6b for the typology of neologism which follows here). These are words which appear from scratch, and very often take the form of proper names: examples include the cultural groups 'Geshels' and 'Naderites' (Bear 1985, 1989a), the races 'Eloi' and 'Morlocks' (Wells 1953), and the philosophy of 'Odonism'. This last example is a reminder that sometimes various neologising processes come into effect. 'Odonism' in *The Dispossessed* (Le Guin 1975a) and 'The Day Before The Revolution' (Le Guin 1975b) is an anarchist movement founded on the planet 'Urras' (another created neologism) by Odo, and so 'Odonism' is a *derivation* by adding a suffix (see 6.4.3) to the proper name of the founder 'Odo'. The other examples too have taken plural inflections (see also 6.4.6) to create plural neologisms from singular proper name creations. Non-proper name examples of creations include Dick's (1972) 'kipple' (everyday accumulating litter) and Le Guin's (1981) 'kemmer' (the period of gender polarisation on Gethen).

Creation, though, is a particularly problematic category of neologism. Can there really be any genuinely new creations of new words, or are all words fundamentally implicated in other similar-looking words. As long as created neologisms look pronounceable (for example, not

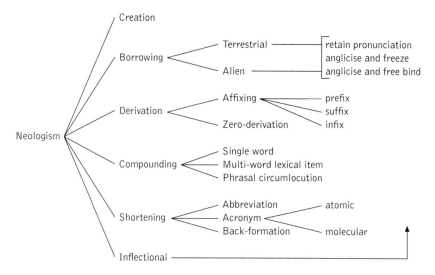

Figure 6b   Detailed Typology of Neologism in Science Fiction

'thrsklpttlegggbkggggrhntd' in English writing), readers often try to interpret them in terms of words they already know. I did this by trying to break down a lexical blend I perceived in Adams's word 'Bambleweeny' at the beginning of the chapter, and it is the sort of thing people do intuitively with nonsense poems such as Lewis Carroll's 'Jabberwocky'. If readers do this, then created neologisms are, in the practice of reading, subsumed as derivations or compounds of other meaningful chunks. There are, then, very few true examples of genuine creation.

Even proper names are often treated as being meaningful in literary reading. Incidentally, the pulp science fiction practice of listing consonant graphemes such as 'thrsklpttlegggbkggggrhntd' as alien words betrays a curious view of what words in the English writing system represent. It is obviously not a spelling from the history of English, so it looks like a new word intended to imitate pronunciation. However, even as an approximation of pronunciation, this word is impossible in English, because of the move from voiced to unvoiced 'bkg' and 'td' without an intervening vowel, for example. It may be possible to articulate in a mouth of alien anatomy, but it is doubtful whether human ears could then distinguish the phonemes, nor whether such a sequence of phonemes is physically possible as a sound wave at all. Clearly, such words are an index of alienness in science fiction, rather than contributing towards plausibility.

6.4.2 Borrowing

Throughout the history of English, **borrowing** has occurred from many other languages. These have either retained (usually through a non-English pronunciation) a sense of their origins ('chic', 'schadenfreude', 'et cetera', 'post-mortem'), or have been anglicised ('pistol', 'galleon', 'curry', 'banana') to the extent that most people do not even think of them as foreign words at all. In the field of science fiction, borrowing can be from ostensibly alien language systems, or from existing combinations of terrestrial languages. Whatever the origin of the word, the borrowing can then be affected by three possible processes of naturalisation: the pronunciation can be unchanged; the word can be anglicised in its form and pronunciation, and then frozen in this form; or, most adaptively, the word can be anglicised and free binding with other morphemes can take place. These processes are exemplified below.

The Latin word 'Terra' has become the standard term for the planet Earth in many English-language science fiction texts, which also use a similar source for 'Sol' (our own local star, the sun) and 'Luna', *the* moon, which is only one of many moons in the universe. 'Solar' is currently a highly adaptable word (solar wind, solar power); 'lunar' has long been used as an adjective (from T.S. Eliot's (1974) 'whispering lunar incantations' to NASA's 'lunar module'); but 'Terra' is almost entirely restricted to science fictional contexts in English, retaining this flavour even in derived current usages like 'terrestrial broadcasting'.

Examples of words that have been anglicised but only ever appear in one form include Bear's (1988) 'noocyte' (Latin, new cell), 'android' (Greek, man-like), 'clone' (Greek, shoot), 'cryogenics' (Greek, cold-producing) sometimes abbreviated to 'cryonics', 'dimensions' (Latin), 'cybernetics' (invented by Norbert Weiner in 1947 from the Greek *kybernetes*, helmsman), 'dianetics' (Greek, *dianoetikos*, to think through), 'tachyon' (Greek, swiftness) a faster than light particle theorised in the 1960s, and 'telekinesis' (Greek for distant movement). All of these are words that are widely used in science fiction. All are neologisms from real terrestrial languages, and they rarely vary in pronunciation or grammatical form. For example, 'android' might take a plural '-s', but does not appear in forms like 'androidal', 'androiding', 'androidness'. It has, however, been shortened by back-forming (see 6.4.5), unetymologically splitting the 'andro-' root to create 'droid', which is typically a non-human looking service robot.

These are all examples of terrestrial languages. 'Dalek', from the 1964 BBC series *Dr. Who*, seems to be extra-terrestrial. Le Guin's (1975a) instant inter-galactic communication device, the 'ansible' is either a borrowing from an ostensible alien language, or a creation, though it has suggestions of the German root *anschauung* (perception) and *anschluss* (union). The problem with apparent borrowing from an alien language is the fact that, since in reality we don't know any alien languages, the borrowing is always ostensible and therefore analytically speculative. This pretence is, of course, part of the whole process of verisimilitude in science fiction.

Words that are anglicised and allowed to be bound with other morphemes include the alien word 'grok' (Heinlein (1965), meaning a variety of interaction-types from talking to sex and close mutual understanding) which is used as a verb both transitively and intransitively, and participially as 'grokking'. Edward Bulwer-Lytton's 19th century coinage 'vril', an energy-giving substance, was combined with 'bovine' to give the real-world 'bovril'. The Greek 'telepathy' produces 'telepath' and 'telepathic'. The Latin *mutare* (change) gives us 'mutant' and 'mutation'. Latin and Greek are mixed in 'teleportation', 'teleport', and 'teleporter'. 'Pantropy' (from Greek, all-turning), gives 'pantropic', James Blish's idea of genetic alteration to make off-world living possible. 'Utopia' and its varieties have already been mentioned. Finally, 'robot' comes from Capek's 1920s play *RUR – Rossum's Universal Robots* probably from the Czech word for worker/slave, though the word has also meant an enforced labour law in eighteenth- and nineteenth-century Europe, and a traffic light in Afrikaans. In general usage, a 'robot' now includes any mechanical worker analogous to a person (such as the single arm in car factories), with human-like machines exclusively referred to as 'androids'. But 'roboticised' and 'robotic' are also in general usage outside science fiction.

Borrowing, of course, is a term that depends on a sharp distinction between different language systems. But sociolinguistic investigations have shown that the demarcation between many languages is actually very blurred, and that the condition of a dialect continuum is shown to exist in many cases. Understanding languages – especially closely related ones such as English, German, French, Italian and Latin – as being in a dialectal relationship with one another undermines the stability of the notion of borrowing. It also depends on a historical sense of the word's origins that might not be apparent in the process of reading. Science fiction seems to be eclectic rather than principled with respect to this: if it sounds apt, then it works.

6.4.3 Derivation

Derivation is the process of creating neologisms by adding morphemic elements. Properly, this is *affixing* morphemes to the front, end or middle of a word. Examples of *prefixing* include *Star Trek*'s 'dilithium crystal', which is produced by adding a prefix to the lightest metal 'lithium' (itself from Greek *lithius*, stone), and also compounded with 'crystal'. As mentioned, 'dystopia' is a prefixed form. Ballard's (1983) 'archaeopsychic', physicist Paul Dirac's 1932 coinage 'anti-matter', 'nano-technology' (first used in 1976), Asimov's (1960) 'psychohistory', and 'superman', 'hyperspace', and 'cyberpunk' are all prefix neologisms. Such prefixes tend to be Latin or Greek, as here, and mirror the common process of word-formation in the natural sciences. As will have become apparent, many neologisms are created by a combination of the processes listed in Figure 6b. For example, 'astrogation' (Latin *astrum*, Greek *aster*, meaning a star, to produce a word for navigating among the stars rather than simply by them) is back-formed (see below) from 'navigation' and then prefixed. The *Star Trek* 'tricorder' is back-formed from 'recorder' and also prefixed. This is a lovely example of the use of a prefix to make the object seem vaguely and mysteriously more complex. And 'psi' powers (telepathy, and other putative *psy*chological processes) are used as the prefix for their study, 'psionics'.

Suffixing creates Bear's 'Naderite', Le Guin's 'Odonism', pulp science fiction 'blaster' and 'disintegrator' weapons, and the 'communicator', when it means a device rather than a person. The abbreviation 'ESP' (Extra-Sensory Perception) from the 1930s gives 'esper', a person with such powers. Frequent radio-wave emitting astronomical objects that pulse, were in 1968 named 'pulsars', and the word has since figured in much space science fiction. Larry Niven, in 1971, coined 'corpsicle' for a cryonically preserved body, by analogy with 'popsicle' from 'icicle'. And all the names of races from the imagined and named planets are products of suffixing: 'Vulcans', 'Klingons', 'Cardassians', 'Romulans' and 'Martians'.

The final type of affixing, the *infix*, is very rare in English outside modern poetry (though it is common in some other languages, such as Turkish). Banks's (1989) robot drone uses infixing for exclamation at one point, declaring 'unbefuckinglievable!'. In everyday English, similar forms always seem to involve infixing a swearword.

A different form of derivation from affixing is to change the class of the word, not by adding a morpheme but by leaving the form of the word the same and changing its grammatical function in the context.

(In fact this is close to some forms of neosemy.) The noun phrase 'flat line' becomes the verb 'to flatline' in a narrative about students who deliberately undergo near-death experiences in which the cardiographic screen displays a flat line (i.e. no pulse). Another example is found in the generic term across much science fiction for the medium of monetary exchange of the future, the 'credit'. 'Credits' are paid and transferred, either deriving from the verb 'to credit', or shifting from a non-count noun ('give him credit') to a count noun ('200 credits'). And, as a last example, from the proper name, a 'waldo' is a remote control link.

6.4.4 Compounding

One of the main devices for the formation of new words in the Germanic languages, such as English, is **compounding**. This is the process of creating a new lexical item by joining two familiar words together. When the words are joined to create a *single word*, these are often lexical blends such as 'holodeck', 'orgasmatron' and 'cyberspace'. Words can be formed with noun and verb (N+V): 'warp-drive', 'terraforming'. Or even adjective and verb (Adj+V or V+Adj): 'Newspeak', 'doublethink', 'spindizzy' (anti-gravity). But the most common forms are the collocation of nouns (N+N): 'vidphone', 'ion-gun', 'wormhole', 'hive-mind', 'rim-world', 'spaceship', 'starship' and 'steampunk' (a back-formation (see 6.4.5) from 'cyberpunk' to describe science fiction novels set in an alternative Victorian era).

However, lexical items are not necessarily made up of only one word (consider 'red herring'). *Multi-word lexical items* are very common in science fiction because of their descriptive power and the flavour of a scientific register: 'dilithium crystal', 'shuttle-craft', 'tractor beam' (all from *Star Trek*), 'flying saucer', 'artificial intelligence', 'black holes', 'Dyson sphere' (an artificial globe around a solar system named after physicist Freeman Dyson), 'extra-terrestrial', 'ion-drive', 'Lagrange point' (of gravitational equivalence between objects in space), 'neutron star', 'suspended animation', 'virtual reality', 'white holes' (a back-formation (see 6.4.5) from 'black holes'), 'death rays', 'Dirac communicator' (after physicist Paul Dirac), 'force field', 'Frankenstein monster', 'gas giant' (invented by James Blish and then into science), 'generation starship' (in which the descendants of the original crew arrive at the distant destination), 'inner space', 'parallel world', 'pressor beam', 'space warp', 'time machine', 'time travel', and 'game world'. Many of these are actual scientific terms borrowed into science fiction. Several of them are in the form of a qualification or modification of a familiar entity (e.g. 'neutron star'), which illustrates the way scientific discovery, like science fiction, progresses most readily by understanding the new in terms of the familiar.

The last type of compound is the formation of a lexical item by a *phrasal circumlocution*. Lessing's (1981a) 'sense-of-we-feeling' (or its acronym 'sowf') is a complex noun-phrase used to describe a new way of thinking. It is common to find such clumsy phrases in speculative philosophical writing, where a particular and new difficult concept requires a precise statement. Other examples of phrases which retain a sense of their origins and newness (and are thus not perceived as single items in their own right) include: 'cultural engineering', 'galactic lens', 'hollow Earth' (though a Renaissance coinage), 'solar wind', 'space habitats', 'UFOs' (an acronym, also suffixed as 'ufologist' and 'ufonaut'), 'alternate worlds', 'Big Dumb Objects', 'Bug Eyed Monster' (BEM), 'matter transmission', 'positronic brain', 'time paradox' and 'slash fiction' to describe the sub-genre of science fiction that deals with two characters (e.g. Kirk/Spock). In Bradbury's (1977a) *Martian Chronicles*, all of the attempts to gesture towards Martian words are in this form: 'crystal pillars', 'wine sea', 'electric spiders'. Again, these phrases have a familiar headword, but the modifiers in each case create a landscape that is alien and poetic (recalling the Homeric 'wine-dark sea').

6.4.5 Shortening

Where compounding can be seen as the compaction of pairs of words and phrases into single items, **shortening** is a further process that reduces words themselves to an atomistic form. *Abbreviation* is a common means of shortening in science fiction: 'litvid' (from literary video), 'fax' (from facsimile), 'bionics' (from biological electronics), 'cryonics' (by analogy with the last, from cryogenics), 'parsec' (from parallax second, a measurement of astronomical distance), 'cyborg' (from cybernetic organism), and 'multiverse' (a multidimensional universe). Abbreviations in science fiction serve to create a pseudo-technical language, borrowing the same process that is often used when new current technology is marketed.

An extension of this, that also suggests a form of communication about advanced technology with which everyone is familiar, is the *acronym*. Taking the initial letters of words can either be *atomic* (in which every individual letter is pronounced) or *molecular* (in which the acronym is pronounced continuously as if it was a word). Atomic acronyms include 'AI' (artificial intelligence), 'ESP' (extra-sensory perception), 'ET' (extra-terrestrial), 'UFO' (unidentified flying object, though note also the more molecular 'ufologist'), 'BEM' (bug-eyed monster), and 'FTL' (faster than light). Molecular examples include Lessing's 'sowf', and Clarke's (1968) computer 'HAL' (derived from the previous alphabetical letters of the atomic acronym 'IBM'). As with abbreviations, three-letter acronyms (or 'TLAs' as they are mockingly known in the electronics industry) are very common in high-tech companies, again borrowing the image of science fiction to market the product and sound futuristic.

A particularly fruitful form of shortening, mentioned several times above, is *back-formation*. This is where a common word is wrongly split into false morphemes, and often then recombined with analogous chunks to produce a new word. For example, 'hamburger', falsely thought to involve ham rather than simply deriving from Hamburg, is thus back-formed to 'burger' and then recombined to give 'beefburger', 'cheeseburger', 'fishburger', 'veggieburger' and so on. The *Star Trek* 'tricorder' is back-formed from the more mundane 'recorder', as is the race of the 'borg' from 'cyborg'. 'White holes' are analogies of 'black holes', 'astrogation' is intergalactic navigation, and 'corpsicle', 'psi powers' and 'steampunk' have been mentioned above.

6.4.6 Inflectional Extensions

All words can take the usual **inflectional** endings found in English grammar: such as word-final '-s' to denote plurality ('Martians'), or possession on nouns ('Childhood's End'), or the third person verb ending ('he groks'), for example. In themselves, of course, these endings create new words that are extensions of the 'root' word, with new meanings added by the grammatical inflection. (The grammatical nature of the inflectional morpheme is what differentiates this class of neologism from the affixing derivation type.) All of the neologisms mentioned so far, and coined by the various means of *creation, borrowing, derivation, compounding* and *shortening*, are available to be extended into further neologisms by the inflectional process. Thus the noun-phrase 'flying saucer' can be extended into 'flying saucers', the verb 'grok' can lead to 'grokking' and 'grokked', and so on. Some would perhaps not consider such extensions as neologisms proper, but this classification is included here to complete the discussion of the way science fictional universes can be further extended.

The inflections which are available to add to neological root-words are a fixed class; innovation in inflections is very rare in the historical development of languages. At the moment the apostrophe in final possessive 's' (as in 'Peter's', to denote the missing 'e' from the Anglo-Saxon genitive case ending, 'Peteres') is being lost from the writing system of everyday usage, though the 's' inflection is still pronounced. 400 years ago, the second and third person verb endings '-est' (thou makest) and '-eth' (he runneth) were replaced by word-final zero-inflection (you make) and '-s' (he runs), but such inflectional innovation is very unusual. It would be difficult to imagine even a highly experimental science fiction narrative trying to invent new grammatical morphemes, for the simple reason that modern readers would be unable to make sense of the inflection without an explicit explanation. There are examples of science fiction texts which explicitly play around with linguistic categories (discussed in chapter 3), but even they tend to leave the grammatical inflections of English alone.

Exploration

■ Here is the list of neologisms used in this chapter. Their point of entry into the language is recorded in an etymological dictionary such as the Oxford English Dictionary (most useful here on CD-ROM). Some of these will not appear there at all. You can use the OED to find out about the sources and historical development of these words and their components. A concordance program will also give you the local textual context in which these words have been used. Using these research tools, you can build up a historical picture of science fictional neologism, its component sources, and the ideological basis of dictionary-compilation.

AI/artificial intelligence	alien	alternate worlds
android	ansible	anti-gravity
anti-matter	archaeopsychic	astrogation
Big Dumb Objects	bionics	black holes
blaster	borg	Bug Eyed Monster/ BEM
Cardassians	clone	communicator
corpsicle	credits	cryogenics/cryonics
crystal pillars	cultural engineering	cutting field
cybernetics	cyberpunk	cyberspace

cyborg	dalek	death rays
dianetics	dilithium crystal	dimensions
Dirac communicator	disintegrator	doublethink
Dyson sphere	dystopia	effector field
electric spiders	Eloi	ESP/esper
ET/extra-terrestrial	fax	flat line
flying saucer	force field	Frankenstein
FTL	galactic lens	game world
gas giant	generation starship	Geshels
grok	HAL	hive-mind
hollow earth	holodeck	hyperspace
inner space	ion-drive	ion-gun
kemmer	kipple	Klingons
Lagrange point	litvid	luna
Martians	matter transmission	Morlocks
multiverse	mutant/mutation	Naderites
nanotechnology	neutron star	newspeak
noocyte	Odo/odonism	orgasmatron
pantropy	parallel world	parsec
positronic brain	pressor beam	psi powers
psionics	psychohistory	pulsars
rim-world	robot	Romulans
sense-of-we-feeling/sowf	shuttlecraft	slash fiction
sol/solar wind	space habitats	space warp
spaceship	spindizzy	starship
steampunk	superman	suspended animation
tachyon	telekinesis	telepathy/telepath/ telepathic
teleportation/teleport/ teleporter		terraforming
terra	time machine	time paradox
time travel	tractor beam	tricorder
UFOs/ufologist	unbefuckinglievable	utopia
vidphone	virtual reality	vril
Vulcans	waldo	warp-drive
white holes	wine sea	wormhole

Some of these neologisms are specific to the text in which they appear, whereas others have become conventional in other science fiction texts, and some have even passed into the language generally. See if you can identify these three sets.

6.5 Neologism and Plausibility

So far I have focused on the types of neologism used in science fiction. What I cannot do (although it would be very interesting given a large computerised database of science fiction texts and a program to spot invented words) is to examine the spread of each of these types in science fiction. My guess is that mainstream fiction, as I suggested at the beginning, relies almost entirely on *creation*-type neologisms for characters and places, and these are almost always simply proper names. Science fiction seems to have a greater spread of types of neologism, with lots of examples of *borrowing*, *derivation*, *compounding*, and *shortening*, as well as creations of both proper nouns and common nouns for new objects.

It might even be possible to go further than this, and look at the frequency of occurrence of particular neologism-types in each of the sub-genres within science fiction. I suspect that so-called 'hard' science fiction would feature a greater concentration of borrowings, derivations and compounds of the single word and multiple-word lexical item types. These are the sorts of neologisms you find in scientific discourse. By contrast, science fiction that deals more with inner space and psychology is likely to have fewer neologisms as a total, and those it has might be phrasal circumlocutionary compounds and creations. Cyberpunk writing looks like it has lots of creations, affixed derivations and various shortened forms. Neologism then becomes part of the description and definition of genre and sub-genre.

Of course, another factor in this is not simply the type of neologism used but the source of the parts within the new term. If the words which are borrowed, compounded, shortened or which act as the roots for affixing come from particular lexical fields, then the neologism takes on the flavour of that source, and in turn it will contribute to the texture of the science fiction narrative. For example, the lexical blends and abbreviations often found in cyberpunk writing tend to rely on technological product terms and marketing language. The use of such neologisms helps to give cyberpunk worlds their atmosphere of advanced techno-capitalism. By contrast, the borrowed and derived words of 'hard' science fiction are often taken from the Latin and Greek roots commonly used by the natural sciences and medicine, and lend a scientific credibility to such science fictional worlds.

All of this contributes to the plausibility of the science fictional narrative, a feature that is a readerly effect of judging the expected patterns in the text. For example, a text which uses an unexpected set of neologism-types, and from a strange source, runs the risk of appearing badly written, or having an incoherent world, or it may even be a signal that the text is parodic (as with the mix of types in *The Hitch-Hiker's Guide to the Galaxy* passage at the start of this chapter).

Readers bring different such sets of expectations with them, of course. Part of the 'hardness' of 'hard' science fiction is that most readers are unfamiliar with the specialist technical terms that are likely to be used as the source domain for neologisms in that sub-genre. Part of the enjoyment of pulpstyle is that most readers know that the technical-sounding 'ion-guns' and 'hyper-drives' are fairly meaningless derivations designed to sweep quickly over scientific complexities in order to get on with the ripping yarn. In either case, the comfort or difficulty that different readers feel when meeting science fiction can partly be seen as a product of their familiarity with the sources of neologisms used in the text.

Exploration

■ Provide neologisms for the following new inventions and concepts:

- a tiny machine laced into chewing gum which manufactures tooth enamel
- a car security device which immobilises thieves by controlled electrocution of every muscle in their bodies when they sit down
- a new academic discipline which investigates the relationship between coincidences and people's perception of patterns in their lives
- a sub-genre of science fiction that is written by women but is neither overtly feminist nor traditionally male-oriented
- a form of transport that takes its driving energy from ley lines
- a mobile phone built into the ear with connections to the larynx
- a dairy cow which produces 'skimmed' milk
- a personal computer that digitises nerve impulses so it operates by thought.

For each, consider the type and source of the word you have created. Try to think of an alternative type for each and consider, if one 'sounds' better than the other, why this is so.

6.6 Review

In this chapter I have focused on the variety of types of new words which have been used within science fiction. But occasionally the discussion has also involved mentioning neologisms from commerce and industry as well as science and technology. The fact is that the creative processes involved here are the same. Framing a new concept for a science fiction narrative, and then finding a plausible name for it, is the same process as devising a snappy marketable name for a newly conceived product. Similarly, the process of forming a hypothesis to be tested in science is a similar creative process, and we have seen several examples (such as 'fax', 'black hole', and so on) in which it is not clear whether the term was borrowed by science fiction from science, or invented by science fiction and then subsequently discovered or invented in reality.

This issue involves the whole question of whether science really discovers anything in the world, or whether the terms in which it is framed structure our understanding of the universe to the extent that we mistake our forms of expression for real phenomena. In other words, we understand our reality through figurative language, and the conventionalised models that result from this process act as the filter through which any new ideas must come (see 9.2 for a development of this idea). This means that such new ideas will tend to fit our current reality-view.

For example, at the end of the nineteenth century, the common view of an atom was as a tiny solar system, with a solid nucleus and negatively charged electrons orbiting like small moons. There are early pulp science fiction stories in which the adventurer shrinks to the sub-atomic scale and does battle standing on the surface of an atom! Science in this century has reframed atomic structure and forces and presented metaphors of 'attraction' and 'repulsion', which are altogether less concrete. More recently, the model of the atom has moved from being a solar system to being like a 'butterfly in a cathedral', and the whole conception has become subject to far more chaotic forces than were previously thought. Armed with this new understanding, scientists have gone looking for predicted particles, and, unsurprisingly, have found them (or at least, since they are so small, indirect traces of them). There seems to be some truth in the observation that you always find what you look for in atomic physics.

Elsewhere (in Littlewood and Stockwell 1996: 3–4), I have mentioned the case of the 'discovery' of the circulation of the blood by William Harvey in 1616. To prove his theory, he invited other physicians to feel their own heartbeats and the blood flowing through their arteries, but none of these sceptics could feel anything at all. They couldn't observe what they didn't believe, and didn't have the terms or frame of reference to understand until Harvey provided one. In our own time, we have models of the human body based on western medicine, the Chinese tradition, and 'alternative' procedures, all fundamentally at odds with each another, with different terms for different aspects of bodily health, yet each claiming to account for symptoms and treatment that is often successful. And we paper over the conceptual contradictions inherent in this simply by terming the various systems 'complementary'. This all comes very close to the notion that reality is radically affected by being observed, and that naming is more than being creative simply verbally.

At this point, neologism assumes a fundamental importance as an act of creation that is not just conceptual but real.

Explorations

■ The neologisms for the modern technology that surrounds us encode a trace of its history. 'Computers' evolved from mechanical adding-machines to compute larger and more complex sets of numbers electronically. The electric light 'bulb' is so-called because someone thought its original shape was bulbous or bulb-like, though many 'bulbs' are now tubular. Similarly, we still 'dial' a telephone number, though in fact most phones now have push-buttons. Identify the neologism types and sources for some of the other machines and objects of the twentieth century. Try to imagine a different name for them, and consider the alternative imaginary history that this name would encode. For example, the Norman-French brought their word 'penne' (meaning a feather or quill) which replaced the Anglo-Saxon 'fether' so we now write with 'pens' not 'feathers'. And we eat pork sausages not pig sausage, have beef in our cow stew, and have a parliament not a talkhall. What if the (computer) 'mouse' was called an 'umbilical', a 'disc' was a 'square', an electric 'plug' was an 'outer', a 'credit card' was a 'paystrip', an 'autobank' was a 'transcash/tranny', a 'paper clip' became a 'twist', a 'filofax' was a 'lifepack', a 'traffic light' was a 'robot', or a 'hoover' was a 'mucksuck'? Imagine others and their counterfactual historical worlds.

■ Take two science fiction texts from different sub-genres (say an Asimov and a Gibson), and examine the neologisms systematically, using the framework given in this chapter, to see if there really is a difference in type and source. With this data, consider how the neologism usage fits in to the general characteristic style and themes of each text.

Speculations

■ We are used to the idea that using words is an act of reference either to an object in the world or to the idea of an object in our heads (more on this in chapter 7). Objects we call 'aliens' in science fiction are named and pictured as embodied (slobbery, tentacled monsters or humanlike variants) or as more abstract manifestations of pure energy (diaphanous shimmering fields with telepathic capacities). In both cases, they are named, usually with created neologisms. As with all naming, this separates the referring word from the referent to which it refers. Such aliens sometimes invade Earth society, and are resisted either immediately or once their cunning disguise is revealed. However, consider an alien race that has evolved beyond bodily form, beyond even a manifestation as an energy field, and has attained the status of pure conceptualisation. They exist not just as pure thought; they are thought itself. Thus, there is no distinction between the word for these aliens and their identity as aliens: they are the word that refers to them (though 'refers' has no meaning in such a context). An invasion of Earth by these aliens is effected simply by people thinking or saying the word for them, and the word passes like a computer virus through the minds of every human who is exposed to the word. We all have experience of invading waves of such aliens in the faddish words that sweep through popular culture. But which ones are simply our own neologisms and which are alien fleets? Consider 'cool', 'postmodernism', 'Microsoft', and 'module'.

■ Neologism has been treated in this chapter as a reasonably objective formal notion with features which define it. However, at the beginning I noted that all words are initially new, and so there is an aspect of 'relative recentness' involved in the idea having any substance. Of course, this aspect can only be judged by a person at a particular point in history, which means ultimately that the term 'neologism' only has any meaning in relation to an individual subjectivity in their social context, situation and experience. Taking this line seriously, we must view neologism as a thoroughly readerly notion. Unfortunately this means that *every* uttered word is a neologism since its meaning varies with every occasion of its use, and since the word will never have previously been used in exactly that situation in exactly that way, it is a new usage. This would apply equally to mainstream fiction as well as science fiction. It makes the differentiation between *types* of neologism even more important a factor in distinguishing science fictional from more general usage.

Further reading

Exploring the world of neologisms for yourself is only a science fiction book away. Almost any such text will contain a variety of neologisms, and investigating them can give you an insight into this central feature of science fictional writing.

The Oxford English Dictionary, or a good etymological dictionary, is an essential tool for investigating the history of words. Surveys of historical change in English range from the introductory (Baugh and Cable (1978), Jackson and Stockwell (1996), Leith (1983), and McCrum et al (1992)) to the more detailed and technical (Pyles (1971), Wakelin (1988), and Blake (1992)). The field of lexicology deals with investigating words, from Katamba's (1994) introductory book to the explorations by Hofmann (1993), Jackson (1988), and Hudson (1995). Meyers (1980) deals specifically with science fiction, Krueger (1966) and Niven (1976) deal with new words, and Nicholls (1978, 1982) discusses the relationship of science and science fiction.

CHAPTER 7

MACROLOGICAL: NEW WORLDS

7.1 Preview

All of the neologisms mentioned in the previous chapter serve to create new referential tokens in the ongoing text-world being processed by the reader. In other words, neologisms bring into fictional, hypothetical or virtual existence new objects or processes, and thus they effect a shift in the perception of the world to which they are attached. This chapter will develop the discussion of how this is done when reading science fiction.

I will first discuss the possible worlds which science fiction reading creates, and then go on to follow through the cognitive processes involved in 'filling out' such worlds into rich detailed universes of veri-similitude. The focus of this chapter will be on science fiction short stories. These are convenient in terms of length and concentration to allow a discussion of world-creation, but the short story can also be regarded as the prototypical format for science fiction, and much of the best of the genre can be found in this form.

7.2 New Worlds and Possible Worlds

The notion of **possible world** was developed in philosophical logic to resolve a number of problems to do with determining the truth or falsity of propositions. The basic premise of all possible worlds theories is that our world – the actual world – is only one of a multitude of possible worlds. To say that, 'Former president of the United States Ronald Reagan was an alien', is false in our everyday reality. The opposite ('Reagan was not an alien') is true. Our actual world is non-contradictory in this respect: only one of these statements (and not both at the same time) can be true. Correspondingly, in the actual world at least one or the other of these statements *must* be true: there can be no middle ground where both are false. In order to be possible, a world (like our actual world) must thus be made up of propositions that are non-contradictory and do not break the rule of the *excluded middle* (Ronen 1994: 54). In the science fiction film *Men in Black* (Sonnenfeld 1997), it is asserted on a video screen that Reagan was an alien. This film world is a possible but non-actual world since it does not break the rules of non-contradiction and the excluded middle, but in reversing the truth-value of the original statement above it is demonstrably not our world.

Possible world theory is also a useful way of accounting for *reference* to things which do not exist. Take the famous science fictional sentence (mentioned in 6.3.5), 'The king was pregnant' (Le Guin 1981: 89), in which 'the king' refers to the ruler of Karhide on the planet Gethen. In the traditional 'correspondence' theory of truth, statements about fictional characters are either simply false (Russell 1957) or neither true nor false (Strawson 1963), since the state of affairs does not have any correspondence with the actual world. In more recent 'pragmatic' theories of truth, epistemology (knowledge about objects) does not depend on the ability to refer (Kripke 1972, Rorty 1982, Putnam 1990), so statements about non-existent entitities can have a contextual truth-value in their own possible worlds. In the world of Le Guin's novel, the king of Karhide exists, and as a Gethenian is able to be male or female and thus to be pregnant.

From these brief examples, it should be clear that the notion of possible worlds is highly relevant to science fictional reference. Indeed, a thorough consideration of the matter could fill a book on its own, and this section is merely an introduction to some of the central issues. Several authors have used possible worlds to discuss literary narratives, usually focusing on prose and fiction (as Semino (1997: 86) points out and re-focuses by discussing poetry). The central concern in most of this work seems to be to account for the difference between the logical notion of possible worlds and the looser and more rich notion of fictional worlds.

Various schematic patterns have been produced (by, for example, Doležel 1988, 1989; Maitre 1983; Ronen 1994; and Ryan 1991a, 1991b), mainly concerned with specifying the relationship between actual, possible and impossible worlds. Thus, degrees of possibility and impossibility are produced, to distinguish, for example, between fantasy (which could never be actual) and science fiction worlds (which are unlikely but relatively possible). One way of specifying this further is to schematise the degree of 'accessibility' between our actual world and the fictional world (Ryan 1991a). Factors include correspondences of known physical objects, of chronology, of natural laws, of categories, of language, and so on. Degrees of possibility are judged on these dimensions of accessibility. Since they involve readerly judgements based on readerly knowledge and expectations, this could be seen as a specification of the notion of plausibility discussed in chapter 2. A 'principle of minimal departure' (Ryan 1991a: 48) is introduced to limit the divergence of the possible world to the differences that the text actually specifies: other than the stated *novums* of science fiction, the rest of the universe is treated as obeying the same natural laws as our own.

The problem with using such typologies to discuss science fiction, however, is that the authors tend to have a very narrow idea of what science fiction includes, and in general use their approach, circularly, to define what counts as science fiction. The boundaries of the possible and the impossible are also easy to revise for anyone with a wide reading in science fiction. For example, Eco (1990: 76) claims that statements pertaining in logically impossible worlds (such as contradictions or excluded middles) can be 'mentioned' but not 'constructed'. That is, we can read contradictory sentences literally, but we cannot process them conceptually. The problem with this is that, seen through a science fictional filter, it is difficult to imagine any syntactically well-formed sentence (and even many ungrammatical ones) for which it is impossible to frame a possible universe, however weird. And weirdness, of course, is the stock-in-trade of science fiction.

As an introduction to a practical consideration of a science fiction story, consider the following exchange:

> 'Today is Tuesday'.
> Harry scratched his head. 'Met a feller on the steps this mornin' – one of these here stage hands of yours. He said this was Wednesday'.
> 'It *is* Wednesday. Today is Tuesday. Tuesday is today [. . .] This is Wednesday. Yesterday was Monday; today is Tuesday. See?'
> Harry said, 'No'.
>
> (Sturgeon 1963: 50)

There seems to be a straight contradiction here. Saying it is Wednesday, in our actual world, entails that it is not Tuesday. Given the two possibilities that today can be either Tuesday or Wednesday, the passage seems to contain propositions that state that it is *both* Tuesday *and* Wednesday today. This logical impossibility would seem to indicate, at this point in the reading, that we are in an impossible world. However, there are a variety of ways in which these statements could be authenticated (Doležel 1989: 237): one of the speaking characters could be mad, or mistaken; a chronology different from our own could be in force, whereby different time-measurements proceed in parallel with each other (this is Ryan's (1991a) chronological correspondence); a linguistic system might be in use that treats words from similar lexical fields as synonyms and thus interchangeable (Ryan's linguistic correspondence); or the references to 'today', 'it' and 'this' are not co-references to the same thing but differentiating references. In the context of the rest of the science fictional world of Sturgeon's (1963) 'Yesterday Was Monday', the last reason is in fact the case. Today is Tuesday. The stage-set on which the characters are standing is a parallel world where '6:22am on Wednesday' is being prepared for the actors in 'reality' to perform. Harry Wright has accidentally slipped dimensions and is caught 'in the wings' of reality where it is Tuesday and the final set-up for Wednesday is being made by God the 'producer' and his stage-hands in Limbo. So, today is Tuesday, and 'this' is a stage-set for 'Wednesday'. (The story has a similar premise to the film *The Truman Show* (Weir 1998), in which a character realises his life is in fact being televised as a popular soap-opera.)

In this example, the surrounding short story provides a context which makes the apparently impossible world of the contradiction possible. The possible world of the rest of the story is not straightforward either. Harry lives in a possible world that is not our actual world. It seems to be set in a late-1930s American city. It has some corresponding characters and objects such as a picture of the boxer Joe Louis, 1930s cars, a telephone book, but the existence of the fictional mechanic Harry Wright amongst them makes them all part of a possible alternative world (albeit one easily accessible to our own history). Within this world is a further possible world into which Harry crosses. This is where real people are actors without realising it, and time is a series of stage-sets prepared in Limbo, in which God is the producer of a play, and the audience are, vaguely, 'Certain – Ones who may be amused' (Sturgeon 1963: 52). This embedded possible world seems at first glance to be less accessible and more improbable than the first. However, as Semino (1997: 81–2) points out, this impression assumes a reality for ideological assumptions that discount God, guardian angels, Limbo, parallel dimensions, and so on. Some people believe in these things. Given ideological disagreements about the universe, it is not so easy to be certain even about the conceptual content of the actual world, and without this solid foundation, notions of accessibility and degrees of fictionality and plausibility become increasingly relative.

'Doubled and Redoubled', a short story by Malcolm Jameson (1963), offers a series of embedded possible worlds. The unacknowledged prototype for the films *Groundhog Day* (Ramis 1993) and *12:01 PM* (Ripps 1990, and remake by Sholder 1993), the story concerns a character, Jimmy Childers, who is trapped into repeating a perfect day over and over again, many hundreds of times. On the original day, he wins an outside horse-racing bet, receives a cheque for a short story he has written, is promoted at work, foils an armed bank robbery, and proposes marriage to his girlfriend, who accepts. The day begins: 'The very first thing that startled Jimmy Childers that extraordinary, repetitive June day was the alarm clock going off' (Jameson 1963: 119).

The major events occur again every day from then on, with this phrase repeated. However, each day is not simply the same reiterated world, for Jimmy is allowed minor differences. For example, in an attempt to escape the time-loop, he boards a ship for South America at 11pm:

> If it were a dream, he ought to knock it now – different room, different bed, different environment, different everything. Jimmy closed his eyes. That night, the first for many a June 14th, he went to sleep with a ray of hope.
> *The very first thing that startled-*
> 'Oh, Heaven!' sighed a haggard Jimmy Childers, as he shut off the clock, 'another day of it'.

(Jameson 1963: 132)

Even though he insults his boss, Jimmy is always promoted. He deliberately avoids placing the winning bet, only to find that his bookmaker has placed it for him. He breaks his date with his girlfriend, so she telephones him to thank him for the ring sent to her by the jeweller and to accept his implicit offer of marriage.

The first day which Jimmy lives is a reasonably plausible possible world, accessible and close to our own actual world. The unlikeliness of Jimmy's run of good luck is sufficiently and normally unusual to be commented on with surprise and marked as a 'perfect day'. What makes each subsequent possible world progressively further from our own is not the events of each day but Jimmy's awareness that they have been run through before. He goes to see a psychiatrist on subsequent days, only

143

to have to explain the whole story from scratch each time. The status of each possible world, then, is a matter of character-consciousness, and the other characters, being unaware of the repetition, can be said to occupy different possible worlds of their own belief. In Doležel's (1976) terms, 'Doubled and Redoubled' constitutes a set of epistemic worlds held by the different characters, within an *alethic* world (with alternative laws of possibility). However, after an account of Jimmy's visit to a 'charlatan', who explains that the events were caused by a misfired blessing from a witch, the reader (and Jimmy) are able to rationalise the anomalous events of the embedded worlds within an explanatory framework. Jimmy is returned at the end to a possible world that is like our own (and his original day), except that in his world, possible departures from linear time exist as a plausible possibility.

The reader is skilfully guided through these embedded worlds, partly by a close focalisation through Jimmy's consciousness, partly by describing first the repeated day with the original as an embedded flashback, and partly stylistically by repeating phrases from the first account (as above). Of course, an approach simply through possible worlds theory is only able to identify the different worlds; it cannot specify how an interpretation is made in each world and how the reader negotiates the worlds. So far, I have briefly indicated that possible world theory tends to be limited in scope to sentence-level propositions, and it does not create rich worlds but only those sufficient to resolve the meaning of individual utterances. It is always possible to imagine a science fictional world to make any sentence mean something, or to be 'misled' by a well-crafted text into an apparent impossibility which is later 'authenticated' into the possible (as outlined above). Because of its focus on sentence semantics, traditional possible worlds theory has tended to be relatively static as a model. It rests on a stable and unideological notion of the actual world which much science fiction sets out to disrupt. It becomes very complicated when conceptually complex sentences are considered, such as presuppositions, speculative conditionals and metaphors. Later possible worlds theory (for example in the work of Ryan (1991a, 1991b)) has considered the more readerly and narrative-based aspects of fiction. I will return to this at the end of the chapter.

In traditional possible worlds theory, there is a reflexive problem in applying a logical model to science fiction. Imagine a science fictional universe in which a different local physics and mathematics operate: one in which the square root of nine is an even number, or in which beings live in only two dimensions, or where the inhabitants are able to perceive time as we perceive space. Such worlds might be beyond our understanding, mentionable but not constructable (in Eco's (1990) terms), but science fiction writers and readers have been able to conceive of them. The last two of the universes above exist as 'Flatland' and 'Tralfamadore' (Abbott 1962 and Vonnegut 1970) in science fiction, and someone could write a story about the first. The problem is that the basis of traditional possible worlds theory – logic – is as amenable to alternativity as any other system. Imagine a logic in which a particle could be matter and not-matter at the same time: a universe in which such logic, if allowed, would make both quantum physics and our own problem of the dark matter of the universe very much easier. If a different form of logic and logical rules is allowed in a different universe, then *any* world is possible and is within the potential scope of science fiction. What is important for a poetics of science fiction, then, is not so much the logical status of the imagined universe, but the mechanics of its readerly construction and negotiation. This is the subject of the rest of this chapter.

Explorations

■ Invent science fictional worlds for the following contradictories and excluded middles. Imagine the next sentence and the story to follow.

- Penton realised suddenly that faster-than-light travel was impossible but possible
- Mars was at once red and not-red
- We found ourselves in a universe of neither logic nor non-logic.

These involve a similar process to the recontextualised neologisms of chapter 6. Imagine and describe the science fictional world, as coherently as possible, in which the following are not semantically odd. In each case, it is likely that you will have to use the new context to adjust the special meaning of one of the words:

- That bald man is very hairy
- The dead writer's decomposing head is alive
- After tomorrow, yesterday will be a relief
- I am older than my grandfather
- Whispering lunar incantations dissolve the floors of memory.

Can you imagine non-science fictional worlds in which these make sense?

■ In Orwell's (1948) *1984*, 'doublethink' is the practice of holding contradictories together, occupying the excluded middle, and believing in both at the same time. Can you conceptualise the following?

- The man you remember from yesterday has never existed
- 2 + 2 simultaneously equal 4 *and* 5
- This statement is false

7.3 Re-cognising New Worlds

As Semino (1997) notes, possible worlds theory needs to be augmented with a cognitive dimension, if it is to have any usefulness in discussing how readers manage to construct worlds from texts. In this section, I offer an approach to understanding how readers construct a science fictional world from the first-mention of an entity in the narrative. This dynamic framework of reader-comprehension should be read in parallel with my discussion of deixis in 2.4. Also, in chapter 2, I introduced Emmott's (1997) model of narrative comprehension, and I will use this further in the next section (7.4) to extend the exploration of science fictional reading. In 2.5 I suggested that adding a readerly and cognitive dimension to deictic theory served to remove any need for a distinction between deixis and reference. If there must be any distinction, it is that the first-mention of an object is an act of creative reference, and all subsequent mentions, gestures or 'referrals' to the object are acts of indicative deixis. The next section discusses the former.

7.3.1 A Cognitive Model of Reference

Figure 7a below shows a basic model of memory structure that will serve for analytical convenience (adapted in general from Brown and Yule (1983), Seuren (1985) and Chafe (1987)). This simplifies a number of issues, such as the continuity rather than 'block' structure of memory, but it will do for the purpose at hand (it has some neurological support in Smith and Jonides 1997; Baddeley 1986, 1992). Here, memory (or consciousness, or awareness) has been divided into three bands: **active memory** (the here-and-now); **semi-active memory** (in peripheral awareness); and **dormant memory** (everything else in the known background). In relation to reading a text, **active memory** is composed of the most recently encountered items, probably up to about

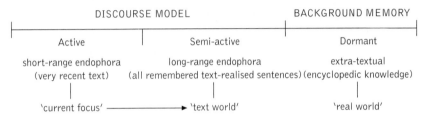

Figure 7a Basic Memory Structure

seven clauses, or meaning-units (see Miller 1956, Eysenck and Keane 1990). These items come from within the just-read text (they are 'endophoric'), and this *short-range* memory constitutes the **current focus** of the reader. The **semi-active memory** is constituted by *longer-range* endophorically referred items: that is, these are still sentences (carrying propositions) from within the text, but they are ones that the reader has encountered and remembered up to this point in the reading. They constitute the ongoing text-world which is the fictional but cognitively coherent world constructed by the reader out of the language of the text.

Together, the active and semi-active memory of the reader make up the **discourse model** of who is who in the text, what is going on, and what the fictional world is like. This still leaves the massively larger part of the reader's memory inactive as **dormant** background below the level of consciousness. As far as the current text being read is concerned, this is *extra-textual encylopedic* knowledge. Elements from this background knowledge are often brought to bear on the current reading. It might usually be said to constitute the **real** (default) **world** in which the reader lives when not reading fictional texts, though of course it accumulates memories of the real experience of having read fictional texts previously. The real world thus includes existent fiction.

In Stockwell (1994a), I argued the 'pragmatic' theory that reference in literary reading is not to the base-reality (the 'real world') of the reader, but is to a discourse model. (This is the premise of Van Dijk and Kintsch 1983; Brown and Yule 1983; Emmott 1997.) Newly-encountered noun-phrases in texts instantiate a new referent-entity in the reader's ongoing cognitive discourse model, which is then altered or engages in actions as a result of further reading of predicates in the text. Here I would like to clarify the consequences and possibilities of the model, and provide a practical analysis using it.

There are several possible procedural options for referent entities in Figure 7a, depending on a variety of factors such as: the newness of the reference, whether the entity is familiar or not, whether it has been repeatedly or recently mentioned, and so on. Unless something acts on them, the natural direction of referents in memory is to fade away to the right of the diagram: that is, to become less and less active. In other words, once a referent has been mentioned, it is central in active memory; but if it is never mentioned again, it fades into background knowledge and is replaced by other conscious items. (See Chafe (1994) for a more complex statement of this based in an account of psychology.)

A referent can be directly and newly created in active memory or moved there from dormant memory. We can call both of these situations **evocation**, and the referent is said to be 'evoked' for the reader. A referent can be already in the discourse model, and can be put into active memory from semi-active memory, or it can be kept in active memory if it is already there. These two situations 'invoke' a familiar referent, and can be called **invocation**. Finally, a referent can be allowed to fade gradually into dormant memory or it can be closed by the negation of its existence. The referent in both cases is 'revoked', and the process is **revocation**.

To summarise this cognitive typology of reference:

New evocation: directly into active
Old evocation: dormant to active
Recalling invocation: semi-active to active
Renewing invocation: keeping active
Gradual revocation: active towards dormant
Defeased Revocation: active to dormant almost instantly

The first of these cases, the evocation of a newly created entity into the active memory of the reader, includes neologism (see chapter 6). These words instantiate a new referent, which gathers attributes, traits and defining qualities from the context in which it first occurs, and then from the subsequent predications to which it is subject in the succeeding text. In other words, neither it nor any referenced entity remains stable in the mind, but they are continually redefined and modified in the experience of encountering new texts in which they occur (see also Cook 1994; Semino 1997: 119–224).

The second procedural dimension is the evocation of a referent which is familiar from the dormant memory into active consciousness. A first mention in a text of 'Nottingham', or 'the sun', for example, illustrates this operation. Decisions of which referents are part of a reader's background knowledge will vary with different readers, of course. It is possible to imagine dormant referents which are globally shared ('the sun', 'wind', 'children'), as well as those which are culturally shared or not ('Saltburn Pier', 'Dick Turpin', 'Alf Ramsay'), and referents which are peculiar to a specific 'interpretative community' ('the Mekon', 'Jean-Luc Picard', 'Joe Chip'). Where a text seems to mis-assume that dormant references are available to be evoked, then the reader is likely to regard the text as obscure and its referentiality as a failure. Such is the case when I read an advanced computer manual and am not familiar with any of the terminology used.

The act of recalling a recently-mentioned referent, by referring to it again, involves moving the referent from semi-active memory (into which it has faded by the intervening non-mention) to the active memory. This invocation by recall is what happens when previously-read episodes further back in the text are brought back into the focus of the plot and developed.

In contrast, renewing invocation can be seen as a shorter-range form of this. An active referent is kept active by constant co-referral. This can be done stylistically by lexical repetition, synonymy, use of a pronoun, ellipsis or substituting expression, use of an antonym, or by the use of a superordinate or subordinate term (Halliday and Hasan 1976) that renews the memory of the original referent within about seven or so clauses. If I write here the words 'Saltburn Pier', I am likely to effect a recalling invocation in your mind from the text of three paragraphs ago, which has probably faded into semi-active memory. If I now co-refer again to 'Saltburn Pier', or 'the pier', or 'the entity that we both know I am thinking of right now' or 'not Brighton Pier' or 'the structure', and I keep on mentioning 'it', then I keep 'it' active for you by repeatedly recalling the invocation, before 'it' has a chance to fade into semi-active or dormant memory. It should be noted that such repeated invocation strengthens the trace of items in the activated fictional world. In such a plastic or 'engram' model of memory, those items are recalled that are most, and most recently, used. Fictional worlds that are strongly coherent are often those with lots of invoking references. Saltburn Pier (just caught it!).

As already mentioned (and illustrated), referents fade into semi-active and eventually dormant memory if they are not referred to again. This is the revocation of referents, and the text must actively keep entities alive if the reader is to follow a coherent thread. Conventionally, central characters are not gradually revoked through the course of novels, but are constantly referred to regularly to keep them in the centre of the discourse world. It is probable that most of the individual neologisms in chapter 6 have by now been gradually revoked into the borders of your semi-active/dormant memory (remembering that the tripartite distinction is in reality a continuum rather than a convenient division). I could invoke some of them easily: 'utopia', 'kipple', 'dilithium crystal', or 'Saltburn Pier', 'Jean-Luc Picard', for illustration.

Of course, characters (and other entities) in fiction die, disappear, are unimportant, and are forgotten about, and there remains the possibility that they can be revoked out of active memory by a direct predicate relation. In other words, the referent is not simply allowed to fade away 'naturally', but is closed, most obviously, by negation. Other means of actively revoking characters are to have them die and take no further part in fact or remembrance in the plot, and of course the end of the text itself which closes all fictional co-reference and returns the reader to default reality where the fictional world becomes a domain in background memory.

A sentence can evoke/invoke with a noun-phrase and then immediately move towards revoking the referent with the following predicate in a verb-phrase: 'the ship (invocation of a previously mentioned ship) disappeared (revocation)'; 'aliens (invocation) do not exist (revocation)'. Such predicate revocation, as it were, 'flashes' the referent in the active memory. An even faster method of 'flashpoint reference' is when the noun-phrase itself contains the negation: 'no ships were near'. Here the entity is barely instantiated. The effect can be ghostly, or suggestive of a parallel alternate world which is not realised. Of course, such apparent moves towards revocation can easily be undone as well. If the next sentence continues to refer to the 'ship' or the 'aliens', then they are retrieved and continue to be invoked in the reader's active memory.

All referents eventually enter dormant background memory. Whether they are (days, years) later available for recall depends on whether they have been used (invoked) several times in the intervening period. At each occurrence, it is not the original memory that appears, but the memory of the last time the referent was invoked. This is the plastic model of memory, with referents overlaying older, unused items in the layers of background knowledge. It is a model of memory based on *decomposition*, the notion of an object that carries a trace of its own history and evolution. Active invocations are merely the most recently evolved version of the referent, available for further modification, as a character develops through the reading of a text. It is important to realise that this is a simple model of consciousness, rather than a direct model of linguistic reference.

Neologisms are disproportionately important in this model because they are the point of entry from which background knowledge is expanded. Science fiction, with its capacity for neologism, is well-placed to expand the potential of background knowledge in the same manner as science itself.

7.3.2 A Short Story Opening

In Stockwell (1994a), I applied the prototype of this model to the opening of Ray Bradbury's (1977a) *The Martian Chronicles*, in order to show how innovative evocation can also be poetically evocative in science fiction. The ideas around reference there were developed using empirical reader-response information, and I believe that an acknow-ledgement of the readerliness of meaning-construction is essential for any literary criticism. A cognitive model, such as that set out above, allows a general theory to be used to understand the various specific readings that different readers can produce within broad parameters. A text can thus be analysed and its artistry appreciated on the basis of likely readings measured by the likely background knowledge of certain cultural types of readers, without denying the possibilities for other culturally-informed readings. In order to track the mechanics of this, the following is an analysis of part of a short story by Roger Zelazny, 'The Keys to December', which is reproduced here.

2.
THE KEYS TO DECEMBER

BORN OF MAN and woman, in accordance with Catform Y7 requirements, Coldworld Class (modified per Alyonal), 3.2-E, G.M.I. option, Jarry Dark was not suited for existence anywhere in the universe which had guaranteed him a niche. This was either a blessing or a curse, depending on how you looked at it.

So look at it however you would, here is the story:

It is likely that his parents could have afforded the temper-ature control unit, but not much more than that. (Jarry required a temperature of at least −50°C. to be comfortable.)

It is unlikely that his parents could have provided for the air pressure control and gas mixture equipment required to maintain his life.

Nothing could be done in the way of 3.2-E grav-simulation, so daily medication and physiotherapy were required. It is unlikely that his parents could have provided for this.

The much-maligned option took care of him, however. It safe-guarded his health. It provided for his education. It assured his economic welfare and physical well-being.

It might be argued that Jarry Dark would not have been a home-less Coldworld Catform (modified per Alyonal) had it not been for General Mining, Incorporated, which had held the option. But then it must be borne in mind that no one could have foreseen the nova which destroyed Alyonal.

(Zelazny 1971: 33)

Clearly, it would be possible to comment mechanically and exhaustively on every referring expression in this passage, but this would be tedious, and so the analysis that follows selects only analytically interesting references.

The likely state of most readers' discourse models before reading this opening passage is that they will have read one story already, the title story of the collection, *The Doors of His Face, The Lamps of His Mouth*. This is a reworking of *Moby Dick* set on Venus, full of extended metaphors and literary allusions to nineteenth-century French novels and Renaissance poetry (unusual in science fiction texts, it must be said). Any reader used to short-story collections will know that the stories are usually self-contained and each therefore needs a separate text-world assignment.

The story begins on a new page; this, with a gap at the top and the numeral '2' signifies that this is a new text. '2' is understood to refer to the global sequence of the stories in the base-reality of the physical book. The story title uses definite reference to evoke two familiar referents ('keys' and 'December') from dormant to active memory, but it collocates them in a way which is semantically unacceptable in base-reality grammar. This in itself could conceivably cue a likely possible world (poetry, surrealism, fantasy?), but the existing discourse model from the preceding story can account for this as science fiction. In the reader's surrounding base-reality it is also assigned as the title of a story, which is being held in the reader's hands. (Later, 'December' turns out to be a company name, as well as having connotations of coldness, which is central to the narrative.)

The opening verb and prepositional phrase, comprising two familiar nouns ('Born of man and woman') evoke familiar attributes to attach to the later headword subject 'Jarry Dark'. This is a creative evocation, a proper noun neologism. Many of the previous neologisms are attributes which modify the Jarry Dark referent in the discourse model: 'Catform' is a single-word compound, and is itself part of a phrasal compound with 'Y7'. The register ('in accordance with [. . .] requirements') suggests legalese. 'Coldworld Class' evokes a single-word compound neologism, and puts it into a phrasal compound. Alyonal remains an unmodified referent. 'Alyonal' is clearly a neologistic evocation, but at this stage in the reading it links to a blank or empty referent in active memory, possessing only the possibility that it is a proper noun (suggested by the capitalised initial letter). In the last line of the quoted passage, the Alyonal referent is invoked by recall from semi-active memory (already primed, or made more active by the repetition of the word in the whole repeated phrase three lines above it), and the referent is filled in as being, probably, the name of a planet. The repetition of the phrase as a primer is skilful, in that the Alyonal referent is thus invoked ready to be assigned some meaning.

'3.2-E' seems to be some sort of measurement, but again it is evoked (a neologism combining a compound and a single-letter acronym) as an empty referent. 'G.M.I.' is equally obviously an acronym, but is unexpanded here. At the end of the excerpt, it is resolved as 'General Mining, Incorporated', but this is so textually distant that on my first reading I treated this full form as a new evoking neologistic proper name, without connecting it to 'G.M.I.', which by then had faded by non-mention (revocation) towards dormant memory. Only on my re-reading could I match it with the barely active G.M.I. referent, collapsing the acronymic neologism and the phrasal neologism together.

The rest of the passage invokes Jarry either by repetition or by pronominalising co-reference, keeping the referent active while modifying its referring expression with attributes. In other words, the referent entity, constantly invoked, evolves in on-line reading. '3.2-E' turns out to be a measurement of gravity; an experienced science fiction reader would have no trouble reading the 'grav-simulation' compound neologism as comprising an abbreviated initial element. The science fiction reader might then guess that 'E' is an acronym for 'Earth', and '3.2' is a multiplying value of Earth gravity. The invoked abbreviated referent would thus attract attributes while in active memory.

'The [. . .] option' evokes a familiar dormant word (legalistic again), but it is uncertain as yet how this fits in to this possible world. The repetition of the whole phrase 'Coldworld Catform (modified per Alyonal)' invokes the created referent back from its semi-active state where it had been gradually revoking by non-mention. 'The nova' (a definite reference) evokes an apparently specific entity of a known class. Knowing that a 'nova' (the Latin plural of *novum* is sufficiently borrowed and anglicised as to be used for a single entity of the class of 'novas') is an exploding star helps in the verbal revocation of the Alyonal referent: this is invoked and then quickly revoked (flash reference) out of the discourse model.

By the end of this passage, the reader is likely to be in possession of a text-world comprising genetic engineering, extra-terrestrial activity and life, a family and industrial structure. All this has been created, and a central character evoked and developed, in a few lines sufficiently for a reader to use it as a virtual world with which to read on and make sense of the story. The subsequent definite reference to this created world, active in the ongoing discourse model of the reader, is a relatively simple matter for the narrative which follows. It should be noted that the knowledge frame tracked in this section is not used in the same sense as Emmott's (1997: 238–41) 'contextual frame'. In her model, the Zelazny passage quoted above is unframed since it is a context summariser. My use of 'frame' additionally includes such 'establishing' knowledge and also other sorts of information about the science fictional world. In reading (science) fiction it is important to recognise these sorts of knowledge.

7.4 Negotiating New Worlds

In the previous section, I followed through in detail how an example of a science fictional world is created and brought into consciousness. Of course, reading a narrative involves a further ongoing process in which the evoked world is set into motion. Emmott's (1997) framework of narrative comprehension, first introduced in chapter 2, provides a means of understanding how readers manage and negotiate the contextual frame of the narrative, and I will use this model to end this chapter by looking at some of the peculiarities that science fiction uniquely allows.

7.4.1 Frames, Alternate Worlds and Points of Differentiation

The analysis of the opening of Zelazny's (1971) 'The Keys to December' in 7.3.2 above provided the detail of how entities are created and made available for subsequent referral. Extending Emmott's (1997) terms, the episode, and characters and objects, are bound in to the reader's current frame, and 'Jarry Dark' is primed and textually focused by the end of the passage. The reader is likely to have a frame for the story that is recognisably not our own actual world. However, corresponding with the principle of 'minimal departure' (Ryan 1991a: 48, see 7.2 above) in possible worlds theory, and as Emmott (1997: 129) points out, the alternate world is treated in general as being subject to 'real-world assumptions', with the same natural and conceptual rules as our own reality, 'unless there is some indication to the contrary'. It is in exploiting the possibilities of these contrary indications that science fiction manages the cognitive balancing act between newness and familiarity.

Though Emmott (1995: 92) suggests that her framework is primarily cognitive and not stylistic in nature, the model can be augmented by identifying the stylistic textual presentation of cognitive entities. The 'science-fictionality' of many short stories depends on the reader identifying the 'indications' that mark out the alternativity of the narrative universe. In science fiction the **points of differentiation** between the fictional universe and our own reality are often marked stylistically to assist the reader in negotiating unreality. This can be illustrated using Jerome Bixby's (1974) terrifying story, 'It's a *Good* Life'. Here is the opening, containing two points of differentiation:

> Aunt Amy was out on the front porch, rocking back and forth in the high-backed chair and fanning herself, when Bill Soames rode his bicycle up the road and stopped in front of the house.
>
> Perspiring under the afternoon 'sun', Bill lifted the box of groceries out of the big basket over the front wheel of the bike, and came up the front walk.
>
> Little Anthony was sitting on the lawn, playing with a rat. He had caught the rat down in the basement – he had made it think that it smelled cheese, the most rich-smelling and crumbly delicious cheese a rat had ever thought it smelled, and it had come out of its hole, and now Anthony had hold of it with his mind and was making it do tricks.
>
> When the rat saw Bill Soames coming, it tried to run, but Anthony thought at it, and it turned a flip-flop on the grass and lay trembling, its eyes gleaming in small black terror.
>
> (Bixby 1974: 356–7)

The first alternativity marker consists of the inverted commas around 'sun'. The second is the unusual syntactic positioning of Anthony's thoughts: 'playing with a rat' and 'he had caught the rat' are at first unremarkable; making it think it had smelled cheese could be just a physical trick; but when 'Anthony had hold of it *with his mind*', then something unreal is happening if the sentence is read literally. This point of differentiation is confirmed by the verbal construction 'Anthony thought at it', and this might cue the reader to re-evaluate catching and playing with the rat as extraordinary and unusual ways of catching and playing.

The story continues with such points of differentiation arranged in-frequently through a story that is otherwise very ordinary and everyday, featuring shopping, shelling peas, watching television, playing a piano for neighbours, exchanging simple presents: only 26 sentences mark points of differentiation in a story of roughly 7,000 words. However, these points alter the whole interpretation of the other events, and are central to the story *as* science fiction. Briefly, since he was born, Anthony Fremont has controlled the environment of Peaksville according to his childish whims: making it rain so that he can smell the woods, creating a pool for small animals, and also killing any of the town's inhabitants who think nasty thoughts. This means that no one is able to think freely, and must always stress the fact that Anthony's world is 'fine', 'swell,' and unremittingly 'good' (which gives the story its title).

This absolute imperative to say and think nothing that might upset Anthony is imitated in the style of the narrative, in which the points of differentiation that mark the true horror of the townspeople's situation are expressed indirectly, vaguely, by evasion and in terms that are very underspecific:

> The one time somebody had started to sing, Anthony had looked over from the top of the piano and done something that made everybody afraid of singing from then on.
> [. . .]
> The children of Peaksville were never, ever allowed near the Fremont house – not since little Fred Smith had tried to play with Anthony on a dare.
> [. . .]
> Tobacco was precious. It was only pure luck that Pat Reilly had decided to try to grow some in his backyard just before what had happened to Peaksville had happened.
> [. . .]

'Bad man', Anthony said, and thought Dan Hollis into something like nothing anyone would have believed possible,
and then he thought the thing into a grave deep, deep in
the cornfield.

(Bixby 1974: 368, 368, 369, 373)

The lexical and phrasal choices throughout these representative excerpts
are always underspecific ('somebody', 'done something', 'what had
happened', 'something . . . the thing').

Only almost at the end is the absolute isolation of the framing context of the town indicated:

It did no good to wonder where they were . . . no good at
all. Peaksville was just someplace. Someplace away from the
world. It was wherever it had been since that day three years
ago when Anthony had crept from her womb and old Doc
Bates – God rest him – had screamed and dropped him and
tried to kill him, and Anthony had whined and done the
thing. Had taken the village someplace. Or had destroyed
the world and left only the village, nobody knew which.

(Bixby 1974: 374)

The 'sun', at the beginning of the story, is thus not our sun at all, but a
vague bright glow that shines out of the 'nothingness' that surrounds
the town.

7.4.2 Enactors and Frame Projection

It should be clear from these examples that there are several 'belief
frames' (Emmott 1997: 164–6) in which the world is seen differently.
Anthony's view of the world is one over which he has absolute control.
The townspeople's view of Anthony is that he is evil, but it is dangerous
to articulate this even in their own minds, so they mumble and appear
mentally confused to Anthony, while outwardly mouthing optimism
and contentedness ('That's a real *good* thing', 'A good thing', 'Such
talk is *good*' – Bixby 1974: 366). It seems appropriate, then, to think
of **frame projection**, in which the reader constructs not only the contextual frame to make sense of the fictional world, but also imagines
the contextual frames that the characters might have within their own
world. In Werth's related text-world theory, such embedded frames

are termed 'sub-worlds' (Werth 1994, 1995a, 1995b, 1999). Some sub-worlds (such as those described in the narration, or with connections to the actual world) are accessible by the reader. Others, such as character-memories and anticipations are only 'character-accessible'. Though, of course, characters in fiction are not really real, the principle of minimal departure embodied in Emmott's framework means that readers expect characters to be like real people, and will often fill in the traits and characteristics that are not explicitly stated in the text.

At the stylistic level, there is some overlap between the belief worlds of the townspeople and the world presented by the omniscient narrator. In the overall frame, the reader sees into Anthony's thoughts when he is primed and focused, and so shares some of his power. However, the inarticulateness of the townspeople is also taken into the overarching frame, as in the last line of the story: 'Next day it snowed, and killed off half the crops – but it was a *good* day' (Bixby 1974: 374). Here, as in the underspecific and evasive quotations above, the reader's narrative frame shares some of the perspective of the characters' viewpoints: the final phrase is incorporated into the narrative voice without speech marks. Not only must the reader project the character-accessible frame, but the stylistic form of the narrative throughout the story effects an element of *frame-mixing* of belief frames that serves to draw the reader into the unreal fictional world.

Science fiction allows this overlapping of different belief frames fairly easily, since many science fiction short stories are centrally about a revaluation of the universe as a result of a new piece of technology, a new cultural turn, or a new scientific perspective. What distinguishes science fiction from explanatory popular science or pure philosophical writing is that it dramatises these issues with characters and action.

In possible worlds theory and in text-world theory, characters who initiate a sub-world (such as thinking of a flashback or a comparative situation) present an earlier, younger or unrealised hypothetical version of themselves. The reader has to keep track of two representations of the character, with slightly different attributes: Emmott (1989, 1992, 1997: 180–90) develops the notion of **enactors** to account for this feature of reading (see also chapter 2). Science fiction can do some very strange things with enactors.

The best example of science fictional manipulation of the enacted versions of a character is contained in the work of Ryder (1998), who uses Emmott's framework to explore two famous short stories by Robert Heinlein (1959a, 1959b): 'By His Bootstraps' and 'All You Zombies'. Both of these are time paradox stories, a science fictional feature which allows the same character to interact with earlier and later versions (enactors) of him/herself. (The inclusion of both male and female pronouns here is especially apt since, in 'All You Zombies', the main character has a sex-change and he impregnates herself: only in a science fictional universe is this grammatical!)

'By His Bootstraps' features five characters who all turn out to be enactors of the same 'Bob Wilson'. As Ryder (1998) shows, Heinlein cleverly exploits the ambiguities of co-reference in names and pronouns to enable a single narrative line to be taken round and round in time. The strong focalisation through Bob Wilson's linear experience means that the same scene is repeated several times from different points of view, without shifting out of the focalised character's consciousness. Enactors of the same character thus exist in the same place and time, and are treated by the other enactors as they would treat different characters. However, the reader's realisation that each 'Bob Wilson' is an enactor only applies retrospectively to each previous playing of the same scene. The reader is thus taken through the process of realisation along with the constant perceptually-sequenced 'Bob Wilson'. In base-reality, chronology is constant and perception (memory, anticipation) can be non-linear. In this story, perception is constant and chronology is circular and repetitive. This is only possible in science fiction.

7.4.3 Frame Overlay and Repair

There appear to be several frame-switches during the story, but it turns out that these are all versions of the same scene, played repeatedly, set in Bob Wilson's student room. Ryder (1998) terms this a *frame overlay*, and it is a feature that is used widely in science fiction. For example, Ryder also discusses the even more complex plot structure of Heinlein's (1959b) 'All You Zombies', which she summarises as follows:

> The story opens in a bar, Pop's Place, in New York City, November 7, 1970. Pop, the bartender, who is also a temporal agent, a time traveler who patrols the time stream, is working on recruiting a younger man known as the Unmarried Mother because he writes stories on that subject for confession magazines. The Unmarried Mother tells the temporal his life story, which is as follows.
>
> He started out life as a little girl named Jane who was left on the steps of an orphanage in Cleveland in 1945. He/she

grew up there, became a 'mother's helper' at eighteen, met a man who seduced her and then disappeared. She had the baby at which time the surgeon discovered that she had both sets of sexual organs, neither completely mature. He removed the now-damaged female ones and turned her into a young man. The baby survived, only to be kidnapped from the hospital, presumably by the baby's father. When 'Jane' recovers enough, she moves to New York City and becomes a confession writer.

When the Unmarried Mother finishes his story, the temporal agent offers to put him in contact with his seducer if he'll consider taking a job the agent has for him. He agrees and the agent takes him by time machine back to Cleveland to a night in April 1963. Giving him some expense money, the agent indicates that the seducer is through a door, says he will come back to retrieve him, and leaves.

The agent then goes to March 1964 and kidnaps 'Jane''s baby from the hospital and takes her, now revealed to be Jane herself as well, back to 1945 to leave at the orphanage. After that, he goes back to April 1963 to retrieve the Unmarried Mother, who has just finished seducing Jane. He takes the Unmarried Mother to 1985 to be inducted as a recruit in the temporal patrol. After wrapping up a few loose ends, he returns to the temporal patrol base in 1993, determined to move from recruiting to operations. It's revealed in the last few scenes of the story that all these characters are actually the same person.

(Ryder 1998)

As Ryder points out, the story works by a clever manipulation of focalisation and point of view. Though written in the first person, Heinlein embeds different belief frames, for example by having the 'Unmarried Mother' tell his own story (in the second paragraph of the summary above) within the overarching frame of the narrative. The reader's contextual monitoring necessary to make sense of all this involves a great deal of frame projection and frame overlay. Together with keeping track of each of the characters, the reader must project the fact that each character has a different belief frame in relation to their environment. The 'Unmarried Mother' knows less than the seducer, and the temporal agent knows more than either of them. After reading the twist at the end of the story, the reader has a lot of frame repair to do. The projected belief frame of the temporal agent must be repaired to include the fact that he knew all along who all the other characters were; this revised belief frame then serves to provide an explanation for all his motives during the story. The separate belief frames of what were assumed to be different characters have to be overlaid onto a single character's frame, with different belief frames being held by different enactors of that character. Finally, the frames used to contextualise different scenes throughout the story need to be recalled and overlaid on each other to realise that the same event has been described several times over.

In Emmott's (1997) model, frames are primarily based on the space which is occupied by characters. *Frame modification* occurs when characters are bound into or bound out of the frame by entering or leaving the space. As in reality, time is assumed to be a linear experience which can be recalled or anticipated, handled cognitively by frame switches and frame recalls, and stylistically by flashbacks or speculation, with tense and aspect shifts and other deictic markers, for example. In time-travel science fiction stories, however, this basic assumption is shown to be experiential and ideological. In 'All You Zombies', character and space are relatively constant and it is time that serves to differentiate contextual frames. The categories of frame recall and modification depend on time being linear and available for back-tracking by a constant character. Science fiction literalises such character-perception by making recall and anticipation tangible in the form of time-travel. The fact that Emmott's framework is stretched to the limits of its categories is an index of the mind-bending cognitive manipulation that is achieved by this sort of science fiction.

Frame repair and frame overlay are manipulated in much science fiction to deliver a 'twist in the tale'. These single shock revelations or final explanatory resolutions, presented with a stylistic flourish of some sort, match the conceptual pattern of science fiction short stories with their single *novum* and explanatory scientific framework. Where time-travel stories uniquely work by overlaying what appears to be a sequence of frames onto a single multi-temporal frame, most other types of science fiction stories work by overlaying or repairing belief frames. This involves the reader re-evaluating the memory of the previous text to conclude with a switch in perception and often a resolution of anomalies which the story had presented.

One of the best examples of this is Arthur C. Clarke's (1974) famous story, 'The Nine Billion Names of God'. In this, two computer technicians are commissioned by a Tibetan monastery to set up a program to print out all the possible permutations of letters making the name of God. The monks believe that the completion of this task is God's purpose for his creation, and that the universe will then end. Throughout the story, the focalisation is through the technicians, and it is their sceptical belief frame that provides the reader's contextual frame. The last few lines of the story effect a radical switch of belief frame:

> 'Look', whispered Chuck, and George lifted his eyes to heaven. (There is always a last time for everything.)
> Overhead, without any fuss, the stars were going out.

(Clarke 1974: 23)

This strategy is typical of Clarke, in that despite his grounding in science and technology, mysticism seems to replace science as the final belief frame. This is not, though, anti-scientific in the end, since the mysticism (as in this story) is not left ambivalent but is validated as being true. Clarke's stories end with a switch to a definite belief frame, rather than in ambiguity, and the mysticism serves then as an index of our current poor understanding in relation to far-advanced science which we can perceive only as magic or supernatural.

Twists in the tale in science fiction are often made more surprising by textual strategies which deliberately encourage the reader to monitor the narrative using the 'wrong' frame. Charolles (1983, 1989), arguing that coherence is a cognitive issue, refers to psycholinguistic research that shows that readers do not hold ambiguous meanings together, but rather adopt one interpretation and try to follow it as long as possible. This interpretative 'line' seems to be determined by being the one that has the most salience or relevance for the reader, involving the minimum processing effort. Charolles (1989: 6) calls this the 'garden-path strategy' of reading. The success of 'twist in the tale' narratives depends, as it were, on the wrong frame being followed successfully. Emmott (1997: 160–74) treats such readings as repairs or reappraisals. It is important in science fiction to differentiate interpretations that are simple mistakes (due to inattentive reading) from those that are obviously set up in the story as a pre-text to a twist.

An example would be Ray Bradbury's (1976a) short story, 'Skeleton'. The plot is basically as follows. Hypochondriac Mr. Harris is shown X-ray photographs of his skeleton. He becomes fascinated by the bones within, weighing up his legs and arms, cracking his knuckles. His wife,

Clarisse, laughs at Harris as he realises his ribs float, his kneecap moves, his nose-bone does not form the whole of his nose. He becomes obsessed with the idea of this skeletal image of death inside him. The obsession becomes worse and worse, until he talks to the skeleton as an enemy and believes it is trying to kill him. He has a Mr. Munigant come round to his house, where, in a few obscure paragraphs, he is treated very painfully. The story ends with Clarisse returning home and screaming:

> Many times as a little girl Clarisse had run on the beach sands, stepped on a jellyfish and screamed. It was not so bad, finding an intact, gelatin-skinned jellyfish in one's living room. One could step back from it.
>   It was when the jellyfish *called you by name* . . .
>
> (Bradbury 1976a: 46)

The story contextualises Munigant as a doctor, but it is only in this final paragraph that information is provided to make the reader realise that Harris has had his skeleton removed. Details of the contextual frame are then recalled and revaluated: the earlier painful bone-treatment is the point at which Munigant ripped out Harris's bones through his mouth; the description of Munigant leaving the house chewing and licking at a long white thing reframes him as a cannibal, not a doctor; and the breadsticks he was eating at Harris's first meeting were probably not breadsticks at all.

7.4.4 Frame Replacement

In science fiction stories (and in the related genre of detective fiction), the objective and end-point is often a conceptual resolution and explanation of a puzzle or anomaly. As mentioned above, Emmott (1997: 129) assumes a principle of minimal departure: 'unless there is some indication to the contrary', the fictional universe operates as our reality does. I would suggest that this principle also forms the motivation for readers' effort and enjoyment of science fiction. The genre has to introduce its innovations within an explanatory framework (if it is not to be surreal, absurd or purely fantastic), and readers' natural instincts aim towards resolving anomalous phenomena in narratives.

So far the examples discussed have involved frame overlay, switching or repair. Twists in the tale usually involve a shock anomaly at the end of a short story that causes the reader to revaluate the contextual frame as a type of repair. Some science fiction narratives involve such a radical and thoroughgoing revaluation, however, that 'repair' seems an inadequate term to apply, and the contextual frame is replaced entirely.

To illustrate **frame replacement**, we must consider the *informativity* of the fictional world. Working from the notion that readers bring certain real-world expectations to a reading, De Beaugrande (1980) suggests that texts have three orders of informativity (information-content matched against the known 'facts' of the world). Occurrences in a text which are fully expected when matched with the reader's world-knowledge are of *first-order informativity*. There is usually nothing remarkable about them. Unusual occurrences, with a middle-order of probability, are classed as *second-order informativity*. Occurrences outside the expected range of probable options convey *third-order informativity*; these are a serious challenge to world-knowledge which activates a motivation search to resolve ('downgrade') the discrepancy (De Beaugrande 1980: 105–10).

Discrepancies are a threat to coherence and plausibility. They can often be resolved by looking back into the contextual frame, reanalysing as described above. If this is successful, the deviant occurrence is downgraded to second- or first-order informativity. In a story, a tree with one trunk has first-order informativity. A tree with two trunks has second-order informativity. But a tree would have third-order informativity if it had no trunk at all and its branches were impossibly suspended in mid-air. Such an anomaly could be downgraded by deciding it was part of a science fictional text-world.

Science fiction often has third-order occurrences that are downgradable by discoverable principles. For example, in the novel *Ubik*, by Philip K. Dick (1973), the boss of a large corporation, Gene Runciter, is killed by an explosion on the moon. Miraculously, Joe Chip and the group of people with him escape serious injury. However, then the third-order occurrences come thick and fast. Things in the world begin to regress conceptually, so a modern car becomes an old car, which becomes a Model T Ford, which becomes a bicycle, and a horse and cart, and finally disappears altogether. Joe Chip's new coins regress to being old coins that are no longer legal tender. Even people suddenly become piles of shrivelled rags. No explanation is given for any of this, and no clues to provide a downgrading.

Joe is able to communicate with what is left of Runciter's brain in a Zurich 'moratorium' (a sanitorium for the dead), but his consciousness fades further and further with each communication. It is only near the end of the novel that the reader is told that in fact the lunar blast killed everybody including Joe Chip at the beginning, but Gene Runciter alone survived. And it is they and not he who are preserved in brain patterns in Zurich. As they become weaker, so the world around them seems to regress. At this point, the whole cognitive universe of the novel needs to be replaced, since the only way the downgrading can be effected is to realise that the contextual frame is a perception in the mind of a dead man.

This is a thorough *frame replacement*. It is not really a *frame modification*, since the same characters remain bound to the same frame, but their attributes (dead rather than alive) are suddenly reversed. It is not a repair, since the alteration is too radical, and the fact that the same world, time, objects and events have taken place mean that it is not really a frame switch either. *Ubik*, and many other of Dick's narratives, work by a large-scale belief switch applied to the whole narrative per-spective, which is thoroughgoing enough to be regarded as a frame replacement. It is a sort of paradigm-shift in comprehension. Of course, the experience of reading the novel also involves a memory of the previous 'false' contextual frame that was 'corrected' at the end, and the original can then be seen as a 'counterpart frame'. Attempting to fit this into Emmott's (1997) framework would involve re-binding enactors from the 'false' reading to the 'correct' contextual frame. The reader's perception becomes involved in the central issues of the text in this way: identity and the logical status of reality, hallucination, imagination and the truth-value of different perspectives. Frame replacement is a favourite strategy of much science fiction.

7.5 Review

This chapter has been concerned with how the science fictional world, already created, is negotiated and managed in the course of reading. The framework of *possible worlds* was only able to take us so far in under-standing this process, and was augmented by a cognitive dimension. This enabled the discussion to examine some peculiarities of worlds that science fiction exploits.

We are also now in a position to reconsider the concepts of possibility and impossibility raised in chapter 2. Within traditional possible worlds theory, if a proposition is contradictory or breaks the rule of the *excluded middle*, then the world it is attached to is an *impossible world*. Furthermore, any sentences which do not carry propositions (because they are incomplete or grammatically badly-formed, for example) cannot be judged either true or false, and so the possibility or impossibility of their world does not arise. This leaves a great deal of science fiction out in the impossible cold, and suggests that the traditional framework is too limited.

More recently, possible worlds theory has attempted to address notions such as readerly *accessibility* (Ryan 1991a, 1991b) and the representation of *impossible worlds* in literary fiction (Allen 1989). This work promises a new direction in narratology, and seems to be a useful way of developing the traditional concerns of possible worlds theory into reading and interpretation. Some of the points which arise by applying a cognitive framework such as Emmott's (1997), for example, could also be handled within this developing narrative possible worlds theory.

At least we can say that adding a cognitive dimension brings in the reader's judgement as an element of *plausibility*. In context, contradictories and ungrammatical sentences in science fiction (such as bits of alien language or computer code, imitations of speech or thought, and so on) can be placed into a conceivable universe and are thus possible. This means that anything that is expressible in language is possible. I want to reserve the realm of the impossible only for that which cannot be articulated and conceptualised: it is hardly worth speaking of since we cannot imagine it.

I offer, then, some redefinitions. If we are to employ the terms *possible* and *impossible* in any useful way, they must be made relative to the reading process and experience. As with the Sturgeon (1963) example used earlier, a world can be apparently impossible at one point in the reading, and then apparently possible later. The reader's judgement of how close and accessible the fictional world is to the actual world will determine whether the fiction is plausible or implausible. What does this mean in reality? Plausible science fictional universes probably exist; implausible ones probably do not, but might exist; universes which remain impossible neither exist nor can be imagined nor described.

Explorations

■ Take ten texts (such as: science fiction, romance, travelogue, diary, timetable, recipe, street sign, Macbeth, the gospel of St. John, chapter 3 of this book). Decide on the possible worlds that they involve, and put them in order of accessibility from our base-reality.

Do any of them have sub-worlds embedded within them (such as gas or electric cooker alternatives in the recipe, unrealised but imagined narrative possibilities in the science fiction, and so on)? Is the sub-world accessible from the actual world of base-reality, or is it within the consciousness of one of the participants within the world and so is only character-accessible (such as things they say or think about their previous lives)? How does the form in which these texts are realised (that is, their genre) relate to their world-accessibility? Try the same considerations on 10 literary texts from different periods.

■ Point of view manipulation is essential in managing twist-in-the-tale narratives. Ryder (1998) points out that an omniscient version of Heinlein's *By His Bootstraps* could barely work, since you would have to tell all of it simultaneously:

> The student noticed someone come in who is a slightly later version of himself after he's gone through the time gate and met an older man who cleans up the bruises he got from a fight he hasn't yet had with the student and then tells him about the set-up in the future (several pages left out) until he is convinced to come back and recruit himself, although he, that is the first 'he', doesn't know this at the time. They get into a discussion when a third man comes in who is also the same as the first two men except that he's also gone back into the future world (several pages elapse) and decided the whole thing is a bad idea . . .

> (Ryder 1998: 3)

You could try this revision with other twisted tales. Apart from the removal of the element of suspense, what other effects are lost or are different as a result of switching the point of view?

Speculations

■ Though the central concern of this book is science fiction, some of the issues which the study enagages with could be generalised to other genres, and to non-fictional uses of language. I have been concerned to point out the characteristic patterns of science fictional poetics, but the genre sits in relation to other linguistic phenomena, with connections and similarities, as well as differences. (Russ (1973: 56) points out how 'A reader judges the science-fictional-ness of what happens by what he himself knows of the actual world; that is, *the reader carries his frame with him*'.) This means that the refinement of the framework, which shows

167

up under science fictional application, is likely to apply to all other language events as well, but is simply not so evident in those circumstances. Emmott's (1997) framework and my modifications to account for science fictional peculiarities could apply to the way we negotiate base-reality as well.

■ The ultimate form of downgrading of anomalous events in a text is for the reader to condemn it as nonsense and incoherent. Downgrading at least to a satisfactory resolution is an important part of science fictional organisation. In De Beaugrande's (1980) scheme, *upgrading* is also suggested: the search for a less probable explanation for an obvious occurrence. This can provide one account for the interpretation of underspecific utterances, such as 'My husband is a human being', implying that he is so non-descript and boring this is the most that can be said about him. Conspiracy theories, paranoid delusions and nutty global ideologies that travel in the dark shadow of science fiction are all forms of upgrading: UFO sightings; flying saucer causes of crop circles; alien or supernatural explanations for cow mutilations, aircraft lights, weather balloons and the amnesiac or psychotic episodes of the feeble-minded; and so on. The popular acceptance of these forms of upgrading explains the success of science fiction such as *The X-Files* television programme, which plays on the anti-scientific tendency to reject the simplest explanation and accept the most complex.

Further reading

The main work on possible worlds theory is contained in Rescher (1975), Bradley and Swartz (1979), and Lewis (1973, 1986). It is applied to literature by Ronen (1994), Semino (1997) and in the collection by Allen (1989), and to science fiction by Suvin (1990). Theories of reference, especially within discourse analysis, are discussed in Wilson (1975), Hirst (1981), Brown and Yule (1983), Hoey (1983, 1991), Seuren (1985), Carter (1987), Givón (1989), McCarthy (1991), McCarthy and Carter (1994), and in narrative by Rimmon-Kenan (1983).

Discussions of Heinlein include Panshin (1968), Slusser (1977a), Olander and Greenberg (1978) and Franklin (1980). Sturgeon is discussed by Diskin (1980) and Menger (1981). Zelazny is discussed by Sanders (1980) and Lindskold (1993). Bradbury is discussed by Greenberg and Olander (1980), Slusser (1977b) and Touponce (1984), among many others.

General short story theory is addressed by Hanson (1989), May (1995), Hunter (1996) and Kaylor (1997), while Huntington (1989) discusses the science fiction short story specifically.

CHAPTER 8

MICROLOGICAL: POETIC PLANES

8.1 Preview

Beginning her book on metaphor, the science fiction and fantasy writer and theorist Christine Brooke-Rose (1958) observes a discrepancy in the treatment of the subject:

> Most studies of metaphor, from Aristotle to the present day, have been concerned with the idea content, rather than with the form: what is the mental process involved in calling one thing another? Now metaphor is expressed in words, and a metaphoric word reacts on other words to which it is syntactically and grammatically related. The effect of this interaction varies considerably according to the nature of this grammatical relationship. Remarkably little work has been done on these lines [. . .] Limited though a purely grammatical approach to metaphor may be, it seems to me necessary if only to restore the balance.
>
> (Brooke-Rose 1958: 1)

The whole field of metaphor is centrally important for science fiction poetics: science fiction is fundamentally about defamiliarisation, 'cognitive estrangement' (Suvin 1979: 4), the mapping of earthly knowledge onto alien environments, and understanding new things (Suvin's (1979: 63) 'novums') in terms of existing familiar knowledge. All of these concern the conceptual level of metaphor, and, as Brooke-Rose points out, this level has been the most studied theoretically. It will be discussed macrologically in chapter 9.

Metaphor at the surface level, where it can be manifest as poetic imagery, or an explanatory analogy, covers the dual function of science fiction's mission for entertainment and didacticism. At the micro-level, an examination of the range and types of metaphor in science fiction can illuminate the genre's specific workings. In this chapter, general points raised previously in relation to the register of science fiction are illustrated by specific examples. As an antidote to the perception that science fictional style is mainly explanatory or purely functional in the narrative action, the examples also serve to show how poetic, in the everyday sense, science fiction can be.

In this chapter, specific metaphorical forms are discussed along a set of dimensions set out in the next section. The examples are all taken from science fiction texts, and in order to be illustrative, the selection in this chapter mirrors the selection of texts in chapter 2. I selected eleven books from my collection completely at random, to form the basis of a small corpus of metaphoric forms. The texts are as follows (with original publication date distinguished from the date of the edition used):

Text and original publication date	Author and reference
The Drowned World (1962)	J.G. Ballard (1983)
Fahrenheit 451 (1954)	Ray Bradbury (1976b)
The Shockwave Rider (1975)	John Brunner (1988)
Do Androids Dream of Electric Sheep? (1968)	Philip K. Dick (1972)
To Your Scattered Bodies Go (1971)	Philip Jose Farmer (1974)
Shikasta (1979)	Doris Lessing (1981a)
The Marriages Between Zones Three, Four and Five (1980)	Doris Lessing (1981b)
On The Beach (1957)	Neville Shute (1966)
The Time Machine (1895)	H.G. Wells (1953)
The War of the Worlds (1898)	H.G. Wells (1975)
We (1924)	Yevgeny Zamiatin (1972)

8.2 The Visibility of Metaphor

Brooke-Rose's (1958) work was a pioneering study of the range of possible surface realisations of metaphor, and the more recent discussion by Goatly (1997) is largely based on her work. Goatly's framework, however, takes a more rigorous linguistic approach. He discusses both the surface expression of different types of metaphors, as well as the processes that are involved in the interpretation and conceptualisation of metaphoric expressions. The scheme for exploring metaphors in science fiction in this chapter is based on Goatly's (1997) treatment of surface metaphors (see also Stockwell 1994b), as follows:

Types of Metaphoric Realisation

Copula constructions
Apposition and other parallelisms
Genitives
Premodification
Compounds and blends
Topic specification across different parts of speech

(adapted from Goatly 1997: 198–228)

These will all be explained in the course of the illustrations throughout this chapter.

Goatly (1997: 169) suggests that the processing effort demanded of the reader to resolve these metaphors increases the further down the scale the metaphor is realised. For example, the copula construction 'The brain is a city' is easier to resolve than the specification across parts of speech involved in the famous science fictional sentence 'The door dilated'. This is partly because both of the terms (traditionally called *tenor* (the brain) and *vehicle* (a city)) involved in understanding the metaphor are present on the surface of the first sentence, but only one of the terms is present in the second sentence. For this, the reader has to conceive of the pupil of an eye (which ordinarily dilates) and see the door in those terms. Goatly (1997: 86) calls the process of resolving metaphors, especially of the second sort, *vehicle-construction*. The basic suggestion is that the degree of difficulty experienced by the reader can be placed on a cline.

Goatly (1997: 137–67) develops a cline in relation to the notion of processing effort, though the idea of arranging metaphoric manifestations along a cline of reader-accessibility has also been suggested by Nair, Carter and Toolan (1988) and Stockwell (1994b). In the latter article, I differentiated between metaphors which are *visible* and those which are *invisible*. The former are those in which the two domains involved are represented directly by linguistic tokens, and are thus *visible* in the text. 'The brain is a city' is an example of visible metaphor, and most of Goatly's types in the list above fall into this class. Examples such as 'The door dilated' require a degree of inferencing to access the metaphoric meaning, and can thus be termed *invisible* metaphors. (The latter will be considered in 8.3 below.)

At either end of Goatly's scale are manifestations of non-literal language that are only arguably metaphors. For example, it could be suggested that invisible metaphors such as sentence metaphors (like proverbs), text-length allegories, and fiction in general allow a conceptual mapping of the text onto a whole complex set of ideas. In one sense they thus point to a metaphorical process of thought, though they are not traditionally presented as being types of metaphor (also considered in 8.3). Most visibly, at the other end of the scale, extended metaphors, analogies and similes are likewise not usually considered as metaphors, though again there is a metaphorical aspect to their conceptualisation. They are highly visible since both terms are usually provided to make it easy for the reader to resolve a meaning. These forms are considered first.

8.2.1 Simile and Analogy

In chapter 4 we saw how early science fiction grew partly out of journal-istic popular science. It is not surprising, therefore, that science fiction makes use of the sort of **analogies** that are common in popularisations of scientific ideas. Goatly (1997: 225) adds **similes** to his list of meta-phoric realisations, arguing that they involve a mental operation which corresponds with metaphor proper. An analogy is a sort of extended explicit simile. Popular science (and science fiction) also features *extended metaphors*, which can be grouped in this category also.

For example, the popular science writer Carl Sagan (1981: 279) presented an *extended metaphor* over 368 words in which he explained the development of the brain in terms of the historical development of New York City. Here are some excerpts from the long passage:

> The evolution of a city is like the evolution of the brain: it develops from a small centre and slowly grows and changes [. . .] In New York City, the arrangement of many of the streets dates to the seventeenth century, the stock exchange to the eighteenth century, the waterworks to the nineteenth, the electrical power system to the twentieth [. . .] the slow accretion of new functions permits the city to work more or less continuously through the centuries [. . . The] use and restructuring of previous systems for new purposes is very much like the pattern of biological evolution.
>
> (Sagan 1981: 279)

The conceptual metaphor that underlies this is BRAIN IS CITY. This idea can also be minimally expressed as a *modifier-headword metaphor* in the form, 'urban brain'. These two realisations foreground different concerns. The extended form develops the idea of the city evolving over time with some areas becoming redundant; the minimal form figures the brain as constituted by institutional laws, or composed of individual elements with conflicting interests, perhaps. The meanings of the two utterances are thus divergent, though the underlying metaphorical proposition BRAIN IS CITY remains the same. *Modifier-headword metaphors* are harder to process because there are minimal cues for a resolution. Though they are *visible metaphors* (with both domains mentioned and available), the reader has more inferencing work to do than with *extended metaphors*, in general.

The most visible and easily accessible metaphor realisations are *extended metaphors* like Sagan's, *explicit analogies, straight explanatory comparisons,* and *similes.* The function of Sagan's book is clearly explanatory; it is 'devoted to the communication of science in an engaging and accessible way' (Sagan 1981: xiii). In such a context, long extended expository **analogies** have proven to be efficient textual strategies of teaching (from biblical parables to modern school-books). Long *extended metaphors* (to be distinguished from *allegory,* about which more in 8.3) tend to be rare in novel-length science fiction (and, I suspect, in most modern fiction), perhaps because they have for so long been associated with pedagogic registers, or with the 'epic similes' of Miltonic verse and the metaphysical 'conceits' of John Donne.

However, as discussed in chapter 4, early short-story science fiction from the pulps shared the pedagogic function of Sagan's later popular science. The clumsy insertion of scientific explanation through analogy (see 4.2.6) with no regard for consistency of register, is commonly manifest as extended metaphor in pulpstyle. Isaac Asimov comments that

> It was the mark of the early and rather unsophisticated science fiction stories of the 1930s [. . .] that they often opened with one scientist lecturing others on subjects those others could not fail to know in real life (but of which the readers had to be informed).

> (Asimov 1975: 46)

Though this explanatory concern persists, with more subtlety, into later science fiction, here extended metaphors also have evocational effects. Ray Bradbury, for example, describes a nuclear exchange as sowing and reaping (with obvious biblical connotations):

> Perhaps the bombs were there, and the jets, ten miles, five miles, one mile up, for the merest instant, like grain thrown

over the heavens by a great sowing hand, and the bombs drifting with dreadful swiftness [. . .] as quick as the whisper of a scythe the war was finished.

(Bradbury 1976b: 151)

The metaphorical idea presented here is WAR as FARMING, within which bombs and jets are grains of wheat to be harvested. However, the idea is developed through several similes which evoke other notions: the human controllers are made divine by the mention of the 'heavens' and the 'great sowing hand'; the whole process is speeded up, ending with a simile combining both reaping and death ('the whisper of a scythe'). Bradbury is thus able to create several different evocative effects by extending the basic metaphorical idea. Extended forms such as this are often composed of elements appearing within Goatly's classification proper. Following Goatly's (1997: 169) suggestion, extended forms which are a combination of other metaphoric realisations should offer many different possible resolutions to the reader. Part of the evocative effect in the context here is in the connotations attached to each different domain suggested by the different metaphorical forms.

Of course, extended forms can also be used explicitly to provide a clear explanation. Such a textual device is used, self-consciously, in the New Wave science fiction of John Brunner. In this passage, two characters are discussing the technological manipulation of people by the computer society:

'One might as well claim that the tide which runs pebbles smooth on a beach is doing the pebbles a service because being round is prettier than being jagged. It's of no concern to a pebble what shape it is. But it's very important to a person. And every surge of your tide is reducing the variety of shapes a human being can adopt.'

'Your extended metaphors do you credit', Freeman said.

(Brunner 1988: 109)

This extended metaphor assists in its resolution by providing the proper term or topic, 'a person', before taking up the metaphor again in the succeeding sentence.

Clearly, the Brunner passage is also an **analogy** in the explicitness of its comparison. This is signalled by the phrase 'one might as well claim that', which distances the speaker from the metaphor that follows. An analogy looks like an extended explanatory comparison, with the comparative dimension often made explicit. Analogies often have logical conjunctions ('as in', 'so') and a *syntactic parallelism* that invites the comparison of content; these can be seen in this example from Bradbury (the character is, illegally, reading from a book):

> 'As in filling a vessel drop by drop, there is at last a drop which makes it run over, so in a series of kindnesses there is at last one which makes the heart run over.'

> (Bradbury 1976b: 72)

This analogy explains, in a particular way, an emotional experience, but it still retains the flavour of being primarily explanatory. H.G. Wells uses an analogy to rationalise the working of a time machine:

> 'You know how on a flat surface, which has only two dimensions, we can represent a figure of a three-dimensional solid, and similarly they think that by models of three dimensions they could represent one of four.'

> (Wells 1953: 9)

Again, the analogical comparison is signalled explicitly by the numerical parallelism and by the adverbial 'similarly'. It is noticeable also that the last three examples are all in the form of direct speech, and thus represent, to a greater or lesser extent of subtlety, the direct explanation to the reader observed by Asimov (1975: 46) as characteristic of early science fiction.

Goatly (1997: 225) adds **similes** to his scale, and one way of distinguishing between **simile** (A IS LIKE B) and **metaphor** proper (A IS B) is by seeing the former as syntactic rather than semantic, with the same underlying proposition. In support of this, it is illuminating that, for example, in the passages from Ballard (1983) below, there is much slipping between **simile** forms and **copula constructions** (Goatly 1997: 202–8). In Brooke-Rose's (1958: 24) original work, verbs of appearance and transformation (such as 'to seem', 'to signify', 'to become', and so on) are included as 'more timid or cautious forms' of copula metaphor. Although she regards **simile** as different in kind from **metaphor**, on the grounds that it does 'not present any syntactic problems' (Brooke-Rose 1958: 14), within Goatly's model it can be seen as a form that is relatively easy to resolve, since it merely claims similarity rather than identity.

Explorations

■ The following are examples of simile-forms from science fiction texts:

The bar [. . .] was like the stern castle of a ceremonial galleon [. . .] while the divided central stairway was a bad film set of Versailles.

(Ballard 1983: 93)

The olive-green light [. . .] filled the lake [. . .], drifting over the surface like vapour off a vat. A few moments earlier the water had seemed cool and inviting, but now had become a closed world, the barrier of the surface like a plane between two dimensions [. . .] Even the men swimming below the surface [. . .] turned into gleaming chimeras, like exploding pulses of ideation in a neuronic jungle.

(Ballard 1983: 101)

The bright gold of yesterday['s dress] was like a bird's plumage in a wrong season.

(Lessing 1981b: 118)

He could see the helicopters falling, falling, like the first flakes of snow [. . .] the helicopters fluttering like torn bits of paper in the sky [. . .] out of the sky, fluttering, came the helicopter like a grotesque flower.

(Bradbury 1976b: 125 and 129)

Consider the different effects that these forms seem to have. Do some of them seem to be more explanatory or more evocative to you? In thinking about the two passages from Ballard (1983), what sort of familiar knowledge seems to be assumed in the text? Can you imagine the second of Ballard's examples in anything other than a science fiction context? What do you think Lessing's (1981b) example means? Explain your reading of it.

■ The last example, from Bradbury (1976b), seems to suggest that **similes** are more amenable to coherent mixing than **copula metaphors** (of the form A IS B, see below). Perhaps the relatively smaller effort involved in interpreting similes (according to Goatly 1997) is matched by a smaller degree of reader-commitment to the mapping. A simile seems less of a commitment to a metaphorical mapping than a copula-form. The difference between simile and copula metaphor thus seems to lie in their relative strength rather than in a qualitative distinction, and the difference is evocative rather than explanatory.

8.2.2 Copula-Construction

Goatly (1997: 202–8) discusses **copula–constructions** proper (A IS B) together with forms using the verb 'to become' and 'to make' (C MAKES A INTO B). Brooke-Rose (1958: 132–45) deals with 'to make' forms separately from copulas. I expected to find many examples of this form in science fiction, since

> it states the actual process of changing the proper term into metaphor, as well as the agent who performs or causes the change. It is like a visible fairy turning the pumpkin into a coach before our eyes, instead of the poet telling us that the pumpkin is a coach.
>
> (Brooke-Rose 1958: 132)

Such explicitness would accord well with the rational system which most science fiction texts rely on to explain their imaginary world. Brooke-Rose goes on to say that it is the rarest of forms in English poetry, partly because it is so explanatory in tone. Although I thought this would make it a good candidate for use in science fiction, I could find no examples of this form, even after a considerable search of my eleven books. Perhaps, as with the over-explanatory use of analogy mentioned above, science fiction has become too sophisticated for such obvious devices.

However, there were several examples of copula-like constructions using the verb 'to become' or other variations. Here the process of the identification is foregrounded:

> Had she then become earth? A clod?
>
> (Lessing 1981b: 233)

> [. . .] the surviving partner will often seem to close up.
>
> (Lessing 1981b: 295)

> It was as if some invisible jet impinged upon them and flashed into white flame. It was as if each man were suddenly and momentarily turned to fire.
>
> (Wells 1975: 29)

> [. . .] the jerking sun became a streak of fire, a brilliant arch,
> in space.
>
> (Wells 1953: 24)

Such a transformation of the entities referred to is often unavoidable in science fiction, which attempts to describe events governed by different or unfamiliar physical laws. For example, the last sentence quoted above seems **metaphorical** when decontextualised here. However, in context, it seems much more like a literal description of the view from a forward-speeding time machine of the sun passing across the sky. This is a good example of how apparently metaphorical language can be interpreted in the science fictional context as being a literal description.

From the corpus of fifteen poets examined in her book, Brooke-Rose (1958: 105) finds that the **copula form** is almost the least frequently used. She speculates that this is because it is the most obvious with both terms present (A IS B), it sounds didactic and authoritative, is gratuitous with banal metaphors, and it allows paradoxes. These disadvantages for the poetry Brooke-Rose discusses are the positive foundations of science fiction, and so it is not surprising that examples of copula forms were very easy to find because of their frequency in my eleven texts. 'Pure' copula forms, such as the following, seem to be very common in science fiction texts, contributing to the quality of 'cognitive estrangement' (Suvin 1979: 4) that is the science fictional aspect of literary defamiliarisation:

> It seemed to him that half his realm, the female half, was a dark dangerous marsh, from which monsters might suddenly appear.
>
> (Lessing 1981b: 220)

> It may be that I am no longer a phagocyte calmly and in a businesslike way devouring microbes (with blue-veined temples and freckle-strewn faces): it may be that I am a microbe and, again, it may be that there is in our midst a thousand such microbes by now, still pretending to be phagocytes, as I am pretending to be one.
>
> (Zamiatin 1972: 130)

> 'My God, I am a dead man!'
>
> (Farmer 1974: 5)

Examples like these illustrate again the importance of a *contextual* view of metaphor, since the sentence from Farmer (1974) could easily be read as a conventional (literally and figuratively 'dead') metaphor at first, but the succeeding text of the novel reveals that the character is indeed literally dead and existing in the imaginary Riverworld with every other human who has ever lived. Again, the science fictional context serves to literalise what appears at first to be a metaphor. 'I am a microbe' can only be resolved as a coherent metaphor by seeing it in context as characterisation of the speaker, named D-503 (discussed also in Stockwell 1994b).

8.2.3 Apposition and Parallelism

Next down the cline from *copula constructions* are what Brooke-Rose (1958: 24) calls **pointing formulae**. There are four main types of this textual device: **apposition**, **parallelism**, the **demonstrative** and the **vocative** (Brooke-Rose 1958: 68). Goatly (1997: 209–15) discusses apposition and subsumes the others with further types of parallelism. Such forms all rely on some sort of co-reference by the metaphoric term (B) pointing back to the topic (A). In all these cases, the **metaphor** is visible since both terms are mentioned in the text. Even with **vocatives**, the topic (A) is evident as the addressee (Brooke-Rose 1958: 101).

The following are examples of **appositional** metaphors. The first is the final sentence of the novel:

> So he [A] left the lagoon and entered the jungle again, within a few days was completely lost, following the lagoons southward through the increasing rain and heat, attacked by alligators and giant bats, a second Adam [B] searching for the forgotten paradises of the reborn sun.
>
> (Ballard 1983: 175)

> He [A] knew that when he returned to the firehouse, he might wink at himself, a minstrel man [B], burnt-corked, in the mirror.
>
> (Bradbury 1976b: 11)

The topic for these metaphors is, in both cases, 'he'. Though both domains (A and B) of the metaphoric mapping are thus visible on the surface of the text, there is a greater degree of effort required of the reader in perceiving the co-reference and identification between A and B, than is required with the direct copula.

The difference between **apposition** and **parallelism** is that, with the latter, the co-reference of A and B is indicated by a close repetition of syntactic structure, sometimes extending to more than one metaphorical term (C, D, E . . .). Clearly, the difference is one of degree rather than kind, as the first of the following examples shows. Because of the variation in the demonstrative expression, this could almost equally be classified as apposition:

> [. . .] those unpleasant creatures [A] from below, these whitened lemurs [B], this new vermin [C] that had replaced the old, might be more abundant.
>
> (Wells 1953: 59)

> [The heat-ray] [A] was sweeping round swiftly and steadily, this flaming death [B], this invisible, inevitable sword of heat [C] [. . .] it was as if an invisible yet intensely heated finger [D] was drawn through the heather.
>
> (Wells 1975: 29–30)

Obviously, there is a **demonstrative** component which indicates the co-reference in these examples as well. Such difficulty of classifying actual examples should be apparent from the following:

> [. . .] the proliferation of organic possibilities [A], the harvest of potentiality [B] which is [the planet] Shikasta.
>
> (Lessing 1981a: 16)

> [White people [A] have arrived.] [. . .] these sticks [B] of people.
>
> (Lessing 1981a: 200)

> As I watched, the little star [A] seemed to grow larger and smaller, and to advance and recede, but that was simply that my eye was tired. Forty millions of miles it was from us [. . .] Few people realize the immensity of vacancy in which the dust [B] of the material universe swims.
>
> (Wells 1975: 12–13)

And as I looked at this wide expanse of houses and factories and churches [A], silent and abandoned [. . .] I thought of [. . .] the innumerable hosts of lives that had gone to build this human reef [B].

(Wells 1975: 181)

All of these examples seem to me to gesture towards a sense of striving for a parallel explanation. It is as if there is no easy analogy to be made, so several possibilities are presented in parallel. The style is similar to the uncertainty which would feature in directly spoken discourse, and the science fiction borrows some of this verisimilitude as a result.

These examples vary in the textual distance between the *vehicle* (B) and its *topic* (A). In the second example, the *topic* 'white people' occurs 24 lines previously in the text, with detailed description in between (Lessing 1981a: 199–200). In the last two examples, the two terms are relatively close in the text. Such textual distance must have an effect on the processing effort required to resolve the mapping of the metaphor by identifying it with its topic.

Within Goatly's (1997: 209–15) classification then, I would argue that there is a sequence down the cline depending on the textual distance between the elements (Goatly 1997: 225 also regards this as an issue). The examples given above illustrate that the identification of the two mapped metaphoric domains is most evident with **direct parallelism**. **Apposition** is very similar, but requires the reader to infer the co-reference between *topic* and *vehicle* from syntactic juxtaposition rather than overt, lexically realised connectors. The **demonstrative** form can be seen as metaphor with a textually close realisation.

Increasing reader-effort would be a very abstract and idealised concept if taken simply in its own right, since in practice the co-text and context would always interfere with the measurement. However, the references to 'reader-effort' here signal a correspondence with the scope available to the reader for multiple interpretation. In brief, the more processing effort required of the reader, the more potential there is for the reader to find a range of possible resolutions for the metaphor. The ambiguities introduced by greater textual distance are one illustration of this.

Requiring more reader-effort, and thus with a large potential for multiple interpretation, would be a metaphor with topic realisation that is contextual rather than explicitly given in the text. This is what Brooke-Rose (1958: 99–104) calls the **vocative** form of metaphor. Goatly does not consider it, and strictly it is not a textual form of metaphor at all but rather a sort of 'discourse metaphor' between text and reader. Almost all of the examples of vocative metaphor given by Brooke-Rose are from Renaissance and Romantic poetry, and occur in the form: PROPER TERM + COMMA + METAPHOR. It seems to be much rarer in prose texts, and I could only think of one example of the direct vocative from science fiction. This is the opening of the short story 'The Night' (Bradbury 1976a: 154–62; also discussed in Stockwell 1991): 'You are a child in a small town. You are, to be exact, eight years old, and it is growing late at night' (Bradbury 1976a: 154). Obviously, this direct address to the reader is not in the prototypical form for vocative metaphor. However, it can be regarded as closely associated with the vocative form if the reader is seen as the contextually present topic (A), with 'You' and 'a child' as vehicles (B) given in the text. This example is debatable as a metaphoric form at all, though I would argue that there are metaphoric mappings involved. You might like to consider what such a text is 'doing' to you when it seems to know more about you as a constructed character than you know about yourself.

8.2.4 Genitive Forms

Forms which include the possessive 'of' as a means of specifying the topic of a metaphor are used particularly in popular scientific texts (Goatly 1997: 215), and so it is not surprising that they are also found commonly in science fiction. Brooke-Rose (1958: 146) suggests the prototypical form is A = THE B OF C, in which A (the topic) is sometimes not mentioned explicitly at all. Often, one of the reasons for this is that the language lacks a literal term for the topic, and a metaphor or neologism is therefore necessary to 'plug' the linguistic gap that has opened up because of the need to express a new concept (this effect of metaphor on language change is the concern of Dirven (1985) and Stephens and Waterhouse (1990)).

The need to express previously unlexicalised concepts is obviously central to the speculative nature of science fiction, and is apparent in the following: 'She had, in the past, not used words, not even in her mind. She had felt her closeness to them [her friends], as part of the fabric [B] of her life [C]' (Lessing 1981b: 115). While 'the fabric of her life' is metaphorical of something, it is difficult to find a term (A) to express it literally. It could be roughly glossed as 'her emotional life', or expanded into an extended surface metaphor such as: 'part of the emotional cloth that was her life, with her friends woven into it and their feelings inseparable from hers as the pattern is inseparable from the weave', and so on. This, of course, is merely to 'explain' a metaphor in terms of another explicit metaphor. Clearly, in order to establish the meaning of A (and the total meaning, with connotations and implications, of the entire metaphoric mapping), the reader has some inferencing work to do.

This is also apparent in the following example from H.G. Wells: '[. . .] that luxurious after-dinner atmosphere, when thought runs gracefully free of the trammels [B] of precision [C]' (Wells 1953: 7). It is important to notice that the final term (C) does not remain literal in this context. 'Trammels' (literally, an entangling net) maps the attributes of fishing onto the lexical domain of 'precision'. Again, the topic (A) is difficult to express literally. Phrases like 'logical constraints' are merely variations on the given metaphor. The topic is so abstract that it requires metaphorical expression.

8.2.5 Premodifications, Compounds and Blends

Metaphors expressed by a MODIFIER + HEADWORD (such as 'urban brain', in 8.2.1 above) represent a movement towards minimal realisations of metaphoric mappings. The last of the **demonstrative** examples quoted in 8.2.3 above – 'this human reef' (Wells 1975: 181) – contains such a **premodification**. The following (underlined) are other examples from science fiction:

> She hurried out through the dim, echoing caverns of the dead aircraft carrier.
>
> (Shute 1966: 265)

> The flapping pigeon-winged books died on the porch and lawn of the house.
>
> (Bradbury 1976b: 11)

These examples show variations on the prototypical form, with multiple modifiers collocated with the headword. They are near the borders of visibility because one of the terms is not given on the surface of the text fully. For example, the first metaphor has the underlying proposition AIRCRAFT CARRIER IS AN ANIMATE CREATURE. 'Aircraft carrier' is the topic, the literal element. The underlying element ANIMATE CREATURE is the vehicle, with 'dead' as the minimal surface realisation for this inference to be made. Resolving the meaning of this is what Goatly (1997: 86) terms *vehicle-construction*. The second example, presenting BOOKS ARE

PIGEONS, contains the vehicle as part of a compound within the phrase. The burning leaves of the books literally flap, but this attribute is also a feature of birds, and the horror of the scene depends on seeing the birds burning in the books.

Goatly (1997: 222–3) lists compounds as being in many ways 'semantically equivalent' to premodified structures, and lexical blends as being 'at a level still more intimate than compounding'. Taking 'urban brain' as the premodified form, this could be compounded as 'urban-brain', and made into a lexical blend as 'urbrain' or 'suburbrain', for example. The syntactic differences between these are increasingly minimalistic, and Goatly's cline suggests that it is this that allows greater scope for reader-interpretation.

As discussed in detail in chapter 6, science fiction texts create many compounds and lexical blends as neologisms. For example, Doris Lessing (1981b) differentiates 'Gene-Father' and 'Mind-Father' in a society with different patriarchal roles from our own. Philip K. Dick (1972) has a 'mood organ' on which emotions can be dialled, a 'regular' being someone who is legally allowed to reproduce because not damaged by radiation, and 'chickenhead' for a mentally retarded person. John Brunner (1988) has 'three-vee' for holographic television, and 'veephone' for a similar telephone. As Brooke-Rose (1958: 42n, 149) observes, such forms have a metaphoric foundation. Lexical blends bring together as one lexical item two words from everyday usage, thus mapping the familiar meaning onto the new meaning. Neologisms are given a new meaning in context, and this process can be understood as *vehicle-construction*.

8.2.6 Topic Specification Across Parts of Speech

The final category on Goatly's cline of metaphoric realisation involves the most processing effort and potentially the most interpretative possibilities. It is possible to create a metaphorical interpretation by collocating a noun and a verb which do not normally occur together. Brooke-Rose (1958: 147) calls these **verb-metaphors**, in that nouns are modified indirectly. She goes on to say that a verb used metaphorically does not replace another action, but implicitly changes the noun with which it is collocated. This allows metaphorical ambiguity (Brooke-Rose 1958: 212), or an imprecision that allows potential for poetic evocativeness:

The wind died.

(Bradbury 1976b: 155)

The silence, all at once, penetrated.

(Dick 1972: 154)

In him his mind, his hopes, drowned.

(Dick 1972: 159)

The collocations here implicitly change the meanings of the nouns in the following ways: wind becomes capable of animacy; silence is made substantial and piercing; mind and hopes are made animate and 'him' is made watery. If the underlying mapping of the first example were WIND IS A PERSON, then clearly the vehicle has to be constructed from the usual collocations of 'die'.

This 'deviation' in usage can also be seen as metaphorical in itself:

> As Isidore knocked on the apartment door the television died immediately into nonbeing. It had not merely become silent; it had stopped existing, scared into its grave by his knock.

(Dick 1972: 50)

In this case, the metaphor in the first sentence is reinforced by the reassertion of the mapping of animacy in the verb-metaphor 'scared' and in the associated noun-metaphor 'grave'. The television gains consciousness, and is killed metaphorically. This is even more pertinent in context, as Isidore is about to enter a room in which androids are hiding, themselves fearful pieces of technology given a sort of consciousness.

8.3 Invisible Forms of Metaphor

All of the metaphoric forms mentioned above depend on syntactic marking to be perceived as metaphors in the first place. However, many metaphoric forms simply involve the replacement of one linguistic element with another semantically different element but in the same syntactic position. For example, the sentence 'The saucer dropped to the ground' could be read literally and unremarkably, and does not contain any apparent syntactic deviation or markedness. However, if the context indicates that 'saucer' refers to an alien spaceship (as in the

185

now almost dead metaphor 'flying saucer'), then a metaphorical noun-replacement has occurred, and a metaphoric interpretation is required. Such metaphors in themselves are **invisible**:

> The proper term is replaced altogether by the metaphor, without being mentioned at all. The metaphor is assumed to be clear from the context or from the reader's intelligence.
>
> (Brooke-Rose 1958: 24)

This definition characterises simple noun-metaphors as being invisible and requiring reader-effort to perceive them. Whereas syntactically marked forms of metaphor (as outlined in 8.2) provide access to the mapping through the immediate context, simple replacement forms can be 'decoded' by recourse to the more general context. Brooke-Rose (1958: 32–4) points out that this is common in Symbolist poetry, and in puns. In these cases, there is a literal meaning of the term which makes the sentence literal, but also a punned literal meaning which makes the sentence metaphoric. (Of course, the assumption is that the reader has perceived the metaphorical level in the first place, otherwise the sentence is not read metaphorically at all.)

The problem with **invisible metaphors** is that they can be processed as being literal and unremarkable. They require additional effort of further motivation in perceiving a possible metaphor, identifying the mapping, and resolving it. Usually the preceding context provides some motivation. In the following examples, the necessary contextual information needed to identify the topic (A) (or even, in some cases, perceive it at all) is provided in square brackets, and the vehicle itself is labelled [B]:

> [The waters of a deeply flooded city have been pumped away, and the streets [A] drip with molluscs and crustacea.] At the first corner they turned away from the sounds of revelry coming from the other side of the square, and walked westwards down the dim dripping canyons [B].
>
> (Ballard 1983: 125)

> [Al·Ith, a princess of Zone Three, has been instructed to travel to Zone Two to marry there [A]. Her friend, Murti, is left behind.] It is enough to suggest that if she suffered in an indirect and difficult way from Al·Ith's sojourn in the watery Zone Four, she was bound to experience, too, at a

remove, something of what Al·Ith did – and would – feel in her slow osmosis [B] with Zone Two.

(Lessing 1981b: 295)

[Montag has hidden books [A], which are illegal, in his house, against the wishes of his wife.] Some were missing and he knew that she had started on her own slow process of dispersing the dynamite [B] in her house, stick by stick.

(Bradbury 1976b: 101)

[The Time Traveller has just finished telling [A] his story.] Consider I have been speculating upon the destinies of our race, until I have hatched [B] this fiction.

(Wells 1953: 97)

[On the mood machine, it is possible to dial an emotion, such as numbness [A].] I was in a 382 mood [B]; I had just dialled it. So although I heard the emptiness intellectually, I didn't feel it.

(Dick 1972: 8–9)

The information, in square brackets, necessary to decode the replacement metaphors here derives from the general context. This can be composed from the previous few lines (Bradbury 1976b), or one or two pages (Dick 1972), or a couple of chapters (Ballard 1983), or in the cases of Lessing (1981b) and Wells (1953) the perception of the metaphor depends on having read the whole previous text. In all but the first of the above examples, the topic (mentioned and labelled [A]) does not have a surface linguistic realisation in the previous text. These metaphors are therefore not only **invisible**, but require a great deal of effort of the reader to resolve a relevant mapping. However, the collocational clash, often characteristic of these forms ('hatched a fiction' instead of an egg, for example), can cue the reader towards the presence of a possible metaphor. The example from Bradbury (1976b: 101) above can be read literally in the sentence (dynamite can be dispersed around a house), but the previous context makes this reading unlikely in not mentioning dynamite at all. There is thus an inter-sentential semantic collocational clash that cues the reader towards a metaphoric interpretation.

It is possible that the reader might not even perceive such sentences as being open to a metaphorical interpretation. The metaphoric interpretation is often motivated by the reader's literary competence and by his/her desire to find the relevance (the 'point') of the narrative. So, for example, metaphoric sentences in the negative, proverbs, allegories and parables are all included as **invisible** forms of metaphor. Of all types of metaphor, it is these forms that require the most effort of the reader to be perceived and made meaningful, and which potentially have the most scope for variant interpretations The reader has first to notice that there is a possible metaphoric interpretation of the literal sentence, before identifying the mapping and resolving the relevance of which attributes are mapped (Goatly 1997: 283–318).

There are many other types of **invisible metaphor**. Most obviously, *negative* forms can allow a metaphorical interpretation without being syntactically deviant or even semantically odd. John Donne's famous 'No man is an island' is literally true, and yet most people would acknowledge that it is amenable to a metaphoric interpretation. Negatively formed metaphors can only be seen to have relevance ('a point') if the literal reading is mapped onto a metaphorical interpretation. Pointedly, I could find no examples of negative-metaphors in my science fiction texts. It is possible that such negation would work against the positive plausibility of the created science fictional universe, and are thus avoided.

More common in science fictional contexts are *sentence metaphors*, *allegory* and *fiction*, all of which can be considered as types of metaphorical representation. Where there is no suggestion of a surface linguistic representation of the topic, the metaphoric mapping is made on the basis of inferencing from textual and extra-textual knowledge. For example, the following sentence has a perfectly literal interpretation in isolation: 'He strode in a swarm of fireflies'. However, this reading would probably not be satisfactory to most readers in context:

> [With a kerosene hose in his hands, and] with his symbolic helmet numbered 451 on his stolid head, and his eyes all orange flame with the thought of what came next, he flicked the igniter and the house jumped up in a gorging fire that burned the evening sky red and yellow and black. He strode in a swarm of fireflies.

> (Bradbury 1976b: 11)

In context, the sentence refers metaphorically to the sparks of the fire. The metaphoric connection is made in order to preserve the coherence of the succeeding sentence. This is also the case with *proverbial sentences*: 'Coming events cast their shadows before' (Lessing 1981a: 288).

The inverted commas serve to cue the reader to identify the points of contact between the proverbial expression and the previous text, and make it relevant by mapping events of the story into the proverb. If the entire narrative consists of such forms, then it can be said to be an *allegory*: 'Without [. . .] [the link to the proper term] the passage becomes a brief allegory, applied whole to reality, like a code. Or it can be taken literally' (Brooke-Rose 1958: 66). Such texts can be read purely literally. They become allegories if the reader interprets each element in the narrative as referring to another coherent domain. Note that it is *readings* and not *texts* which are allegorical from this perspective; the reader-effort required is correspondingly high, and the scope for variant readings is great. So, for example, Bradbury's (1976b) *Fahrenheit 451* can be interpreted, not as a literal story about a future society in which all books are banned, but as an allegory on the repressive cruelty of Nazism. This is the interpretation made by Francois Truffaut (1966) in his original film version of the book (reviewed approvingly by Bradbury (1966) himself).

Allegorical reading is only exceeded in difficulty by texts of *fiction* which are not immediately amenable to a systematic metaphorical interpretation. For example, critical responses to Doris Lessing's (1981a) *Shikasta* and its sequel (1981b) discuss the state of our world and current gender relationships in a variety of ways (see Sage (1983), Rubenstein (1975, 1979), Fishburn (1985), and Lessing's (1975) own comments on the diversity of interpretation of her books). The growing volume of divergent critical studies illustrates how different readers can work hard to produce different interpretations from the same surface linguistic text. The wilful production of new interpretations is the most effortful mapping operation of all, since it involves denying the validity of established mappings in order to generate another resolution. Goatly (1997: 135, 164) suggests that *fiction* is a type of *large scale metaphor*, and I would also argue that these global processing strategies represent types of 'discourse' metaphor.

Exploration

■ Play the metaphor game with a small group of people. Write the following words onto slips of paper and put them face-down on a table: *book, bottle, chair, dog, electricity, hand, ice, love, music, night, oil, patience, rain, rose, shoe, stars, television, time, truth, wine*. In turn, each player selects 9 slips and must combine the words in sequence in place of the letters A, B, C in the sentences below:

- *Copula form:* (The/a) A IS (the/a) B
- *Simile form:* (The/a) A IS LIKE (the/a) B
- *Genitive form:* (The/a) A IS THE B OF (the/a) C
- *Modifier-headword form:* A–B

(Bracketed words are optional, and you might have to add a morpheme to the last example, such as '-ish' or '-ly', to make it work.)

Write the sentences out, replace the slips, and the next player selects 9 slips for insertion. Consider the following, which go to the heart of metaphor theory:

What does the metaphor mean?
Which elements of B (and C) are mapped onto A?
What is the effect of reversing A and B?
Does the metaphor create a new idea or is it just a poetic effect?
Are there any meaningful differences between the four forms?
Are all the sentences metaphors, or can some be read literally?

Imagine the sentences as literally-interpreted forms within a science fictional universe.

8.4 Dimensions of Metaphoric Reading

Goatly (1997: 38) suggests five clines or dimensions along which metaphors can be placed. These are as follows:

1. Approximative Similarity——Distant Similarity/Analogy
2. Conventionality————————Unconventionality
3. Marking——————————————No Marking
4. Non-contradictoriness——————Contradictoriness
5. Explicitness————————————Inexplicitness

(Goatly 1997: 38, 317)

In comparing texts of popular science with both modern novels and modern poetry, Goatly (1997: 317–18) discovers that the *scientific texts* were **explicit** where the *literary texts* were inexplicit, ambiguous and less well marked. In general, it would seem that explanatory scientific or pedagogic genres would employ metaphors towards the left of these five clines. That is, they would feature metaphoric expressions that involved **similarity**, were **conventional, marked** as metaphors, were **non–contradictory** and **explicit**. *Creative literary texts* would, by contrast, feature **dissimilar, unconventional, unmarked**, evocative **contradictory** and **inexplicit** metaphoric forms. Given that science fiction is, to a large extent, a blend of these two poles, some consideration of these five dimensions might be interesting.

The difficulty, which is immediately apparent even just across the eleven texts used in this chapter, is that different science fiction texts shift along the five different dimensions. On most counts, Bradbury's (1976b) novel would be further to the right on all the dimensions than Wells's (1953) *The Time Machine*. This accords well with the intuitive sense that Bradbury's science fictional prose is more evocative, poetic and 'literary' than Wells's rational explanations. The unexpectedness of much science fictional metaphoric expression is part of the pleasure of its reading.

The first dimension involves the **similarity** of the two domains involved in the metaphoric mapping. If, within our culturally defined conceptual system, both *base* and *target* domains are similarly structured, then a mapping between them would present fewer processing problems than a mapping between two conceptually dissimilar domains. For example, one of the difficulties in reading Zamiatin's (1972: 130) metaphor of the narrator and a phagocytic microbe lies in the complete conceptual **dissimilarity** (within our present understanding of microbiology) of these two entities. In contrast, Bradbury's (1976b: 11) mapping of sparks and fireflies allows of resolution by fairly easy access to **similar** points of contact (size, movement, and so on).

In general, when technological innovations or scientific ideas are presented in science fiction narratives, they are expressed using *analogies* and *metaphoric* forms in which there is an approximative **similarity** already existing between the two domains. Often, in the surrounding narrative, less similar metaphors are used for their 'literary' flavour. There is thus a blend between *explanatory* and *expressive* metaphors, a distinction which is taken up in the next chapter.

The second dimension, the conventionality of the metaphoric mapping, is a matter of the degree of the reader's familiarity with the *base domain* (as predicted by Gentner 1982). However, the degree of unfamiliarity of the *target domain* is also important. It is these two factors that determine whether a metaphor is *illuminating* or *defamiliarising*, and the science fictional negotiation of alien targets makes this a central issue.

The bar [...] was like the stern castle of a ceremonial galleon [...] while the divided central stairway was a bad film set of Versailles.

(Ballard 1983: 93)

Here are a *simile* and a *copula-construction* metaphor. For a reader brought up in the film-rich culture of the West in the twentieth century, the *base domains* would probably present few problems of familiarity here. The cultural knowledge evoked is of cinema images of antique ships and the recognition that 'Versailles' means the royal palace of that town. Equally, the *target domains* of an ornate bar and a majestic staircase would not be unfamiliar to the same reader. The metaphor can be said to be an illuminating and **explanatory** one, and while not a dead metaphor, it is at least not utterly **unconventional** or startling.

Compare this with the following *defamiliarising metaphor* which occurs only a few pages later. Though in similar form, it would be more difficult for the same reader to process because of the unfamiliarity with the base domain:

> Even the men swimming below the surface [. . .] turned into gleaming chimeras, like exploding pulses of ideation in a neuronic jungle.

> (Ballard 1983: 101)

Who, besides a brain-surgeon trained in radiography, would find this last *base domain* familiar? By contrast, the *target domain* (men swimming in water) is a familiar one, and so the effect of *defamiliarisation* is all the more striking. The processing of this metaphor might even be regarded as sufficiently **unconventional** as to reach the point where the language is *thematised* (the novel concerns the reverse evolution of humanity into the 'archaeopsychic' past, the reptilian depths of the brain, a theme to which the above metaphor stylistically contributes).

A further determinant of **conventionality** is the reader's awareness of a cultural consensus on readings. It is, for example with *allegory* and *fiction*, more effortful to overturn an established literary critical interpretation of a text than it is to simply take up that reading and acquiesce in it. Feminist readings of Lessing (1981a and 1981b) have become the culturally dominant and accepted meanings (see, for example, Kaplan and Rose (1988)). If, as already argued in 8.3, fictions are large scale metaphors, then such readings are also metaphorical representations of the literary text itself, which the reader of the criticism is invited to engage in and evaluate.

On the third dimension of **marking**, science fiction texts tend to show a degree of sensitivity to the knowledge needs of the reader. As illustrated in chapter 6, even completely innovative neologisms are explained either directly or by the context, and often the form of this explanation is metaphorical. In the examples of *invisible metaphors* above (8.3), I gave the *topic* that was replaced in square brackets. This information was derived from the previous text, but the textual distance covered in each case showed considerable variation. The example from Bradbury (1976b: 101) of 'dynamite' for 'books' occurs over only a few lines of the novel. The 'books' referent is even instantiated indirectly by the co-referential phrase 'some of them' in the same sentence as the metaphoric expression 'dynamite'. Because of the textual proximity, this example would be easier to resolve than two of the other examples quoted (Ballard 1983: 125 and Lessing 1981b: 295) in which the *topic* is inferred from whole previous chapters. Even more difficult is the meaning of 'a 382 mood' (Dick 1972: 8–9), which is never mentioned and must be generally inferred from the previous text.

Such a contextual view makes it apparent that 'slipping' occurs between syntactic realisations of metaphors. Sometimes a form which would in isolation be ambiguous (such as the lower elements in Goatly's (1997: 198–228) scale, in 8.2), is accompanied by elements that assist in a resolution. For example, in 8.2.6 above, an example was given from Dick: 'In him his mind, his hopes, drowned'. The context of this is as follows:

> [Isidore has just found out that his religion is a sham, invented in a film studio.] Pris, with the scissors, cut yet another leg from the spider. All at once John Isidore pushed her away and lifted up the mutilated creature. He carried it to the sink and there he drowned it. In him his mind, his hopes, drowned, too. As swiftly as the spider.

> (Dick 1972: 159)

The verb–noun metaphor slips, in the final sentence, into simile, which Goatly's scale indicates makes it easier and less potentially ambiguous.

The main point here is that metaphoric resolution is greatly facilitated by the degree to which metaphoric forms are **explicitly marked** as metaphors. As mentioned above, some forms, such as *sentence-metaphors* and *allegories*, can coherently be read literally, without recourse to metaphoric meaning at all. (In these cases, a metaphor cannot really be said to exist, since the reader in question is not aware of it. To reiterate, a metaphor is a way of reading and not a textual feature.) *Visible metaphors* generally present few problems of recognition, in that some sort of semantic collocational clash is involved, which immediately cues the reader into a search for resolution. Apparently invisible metaphors, however, can be supported by a subsequent expression that renders the metaphor visible and marked. This can be done simply by drawing attention to the metaphoric expression, as in Dick's (1972: 50) assertion that 'the television died', followed immediately by the additional metaphor 'it had stopped existing, scared into its grave'. This qualifying metaphor adds to the mapping of animacy onto the television. Alternatively, as in the example quoted from Brunner (1988: 109), the self-referentiality can be overt: ' "Your extended metaphors do you credit", Freeman said'. This greatly assists the reader in the primary task of recognition, and is also, of course, a knowingly self-conscious example of post-New Wave style.

The fourth dimension, **contradictoriness**, shows variation across science fiction texts for the same reasons as the similarity/analogy cline. Scientific explanations are likely to be **non-contradictory**, while poetic expression is often **contradictory**. The next chapter considers examples in which the explanatory power of **non-contradiction** is sacrificed in favour of a suggestive resonant poetic image.

With any of the examples of forms of metaphor, the degree of reader-effort required is lessened if the specification of the metaphor is made explicit. However, if the metaphor is spelled out too obviously, the resulting effect can sometimes seem over-explicit and heavy-handed for a literary context. For example, if an allegory or fiction ends with an explicit moral or authorial interpretation (as in some children's comics), then this itself constitutes the topic of the overall mapping. This severely limits the potential for multiple interpretation, since the assertion of authority presents itself as the sole legitimate mapping. This textual strategy serves a useful pedagogic function (typical of parables and their exegesis), but would perhaps seem too didactic for modern literary conventions. It is possibly for this reason that such formulae are often associated with children's fiction such as fables, fairy-tales, and superhero cartoons, and also find their place in pulpstyle texts.

The explicitness of the metaphor can provide cues for the reader, not only to point to the presence of a mapping (marking), but also to indicate which attributes need to be mapped in order to derive a coherent mapping and resolution. Shute's (1966: 265) 'dead aircraft carrier' and Bradbury's (1976b: 11) 'flapping pigeon-winged books' both signal the attribute that is most relevant to map, in, respectively, AIRCRAFT CARRIER IS ANIMATE and BOOKS ARE PIGEONS. Such specificity makes the scene described vivid for the reader.

Finally, the effort required of the reader is to some extent always dependent on the amount of energy s/he is prepared to expend in any given situation. In other words, the disposition of the reader is a factor in the identification and resolution of any metaphors. This is especially true of those more 'literary' or poetic metaphors which allow much ambiguity and openness in interpretation, and resist an easy resolution. However, such metaphorical expressions are often what makes the texture of reading enjoyable.

Exploration

■ Much literary criticism of science fiction – especially, for some reason, studies of individual authors – is impressionistic and intuitive. Points are made largely through metaphor and other imagery, and are rarely systematic or analytical at all. You could track the dominant metaphors in a piece of such criticism, to see how far the metaphor actually structures the argument. For example, consider the readings of the science fiction writers mentioned in this chapter that are listed in the 'Further Reading' at the end. Is the metaphor essential? Could the same argument be expressed with a different metaphor, or even without being so strongly metaphorical in the first place? What is the point of such criticism, presented in this way?

8.5 Review

This chapter has developed a framework of metaphorical reading in order to examine the detail of some science fictional poetry and poetics. The discussion of forms of metaphor has been applied to other text-types by Goatly (1997). The main point is not that there are features of metaphor that are exclusively peculiar to the science fiction text-type, but that science fictional texts typically illustrate a range of characteristics that differ, very generally, from the texts of other genres.

The type and distribution of forms of metaphor seem to differ quite markedly across the history of the genre, as discussed in chapter 2. The explanatory tone of early science fiction is reflected in the use of visible metaphors. In particular, there seems to be a large proportion of those forms that require the least effort of the reader: *extended metaphors*, *analogies* and *similes*. This accords with my argument that pulpstyle reflects the requirements and abilities of its original readership.

By contrast, as Taylor (1990) observes, later manifestations of science fiction, and specifically the New Wave of the 1960s and after, were more concerned with the sort of literary *defamiliarisation* and *self-referentiality* that was becoming popular in mainstream fiction. Forms of metaphor from texts of this period reflect this by including many *invisible metaphors*, which require greater reader involvement with the text. More *visible metaphors*, when they occur, are often marked by metalanguage, as in examples in this chapter from Brunner (1988: 109) and Dick (1972: 50). Of course, this is a great generalisation: I have pointed out how Asimov (1990) continued to write in pulpstyle into the 1990s, and Zamiatin (1972) was writing in the style of the New Wave as long ago as 1920.

In this chapter, the form of metaphor was discussed in the context of its reading, and the cultural factors carried by texts and readers. Linked to this is what might be called a conceptual consensus on the way we perceive our world, that is constituted by biology and experience as well as culture (see Lakoff 1987). The identification of semantic collocational clashes depends on a particular perceptual configuration of the world and which entities in it are categorised together or not. If this config-uration is seen (as in De Beaugrande 1980: 111) as having merely the status of our default version of reality, then clearly what are perceived as metaphors in the language system that represents and constructs that reality might be literally true in realities perceived differently. The con-struction of such alternative (views of) realities is the business of science fiction. From a moving time-machine, the sun *is* 'a streak of fire, a brilliant arch' (Wells 1953: 24); in a science fictional universe, emotions *can* be dialled (Dick 1972: 8–9); stars, planets, ships and computers can be animate and intelligent, and abstract concepts can be dramatised in narrative. Fundamentally, science fiction literalises metaphors.

Explorations

■ Metaphors – especially invisible forms – are more open to readerly interpretation, which works against the didactic function of some sci-ence fiction. This fact would predict that there are fewer metaphors in explicitly didactic or children's science fiction, and more in post-New Wave and adult-oriented science fiction. You could investigate whether this is the case.

■ Against this prediction must be laid the explanatory aspect of meta-phor, especially *simile, analogy* and *extended metaphor* often found in scientific exposition (see also 9.2.2). Do different science fiction texts use metaphors differently in predictable and principled ways, or is the story more complicated than that? You can test this for yourself across a range of texts.

Speculations

■ Metaphor is a readerly effect; it does not reside in sentences but in interpretation. Some deviant sentences can be read metaphorically, and then a balancing equation comes into play, as follows. A metaphorical reading of a deviant sentence is metaphorical in the world of base-reality (for example, 'Juliet is the sun'). Reading that metaphor literally involves relocating the meaning of the sentence in a non-actual or 'metaphorical' world (Juliet is literally the local gas-burning star). A literal reading of a possibly metaphorical deviant sentence cues up a science fictional (or surrealist, or magical, or other alternate) world (the sun has consciousness and can influence events in Verona). In this way, science fiction can be seen to treat metaphorical expressions and metaphorical worlds differently from other genres.

■ Science fictional poetry is a flourishing sub-genre within science fiction, though science fiction seems bound up as having a default as narrative (see Samuelson 1980). Though poetry can be narrative too, it is more prototypically lyrical, and founded on arresting imagery. However, if science fiction is seen as the process of literalising a context for metaphor, this robs science fictional poetry of its 'poeticness'. Certainly (as chapters 3 and 8 have illustrated) science fiction can be poetic, and also there is much modern mainstream poetry laid out in a prose typography. The poetry/prose distinction (like the identification of metaphor) would only seem to make sense if it is regarded as a readerly construct. Readers of poetry usually engage in a high awareness of form and a willingness to link it to content, function, connotation and association. Poetry is poetic if it is read as poetry.

Further reading

There is a mass of material on metaphor, though most of it is about the conceptual issues involved rather than the surface expression: see, for example, Black (1962, 1990), Ricoeur (1977), Lakoff and Johnson (1980), Paprotte and Dirven (1985), Cooper (1986) and Ortony (1993). Brooke-Rose has also written on science fiction and the fantastic (Brooke-Rose 1981).

Studies of individual authors mentioned in this chapter are common and of variable quality. Useful places to start are as follows. On J.G. Ballard, Pringle (1979), Juno (1984) and Jones (1996). On John Brunner, De Bolt (1976), Monk (1985) and Benson and Stephensen-Payne's (1992) critical bibliography. There is an industry of critical readings of Ray Bradbury, much of it fairly low voltage in analytical content: see the listing under the further reading for chapter 7. Philip K. Dick also receives much critical attention: Levack (1981) is a bibliography, Umland (1995) is more up-to-date, and there is a study by Warrick (1987). There is a bibliography of Philip José Farmer (Stephenson-Payne 1990), and a study by Chapman (1984). Doris Lessing has a mass of critical material, some of it on her science fiction, such as Clare (1984), Kaplan and Rose (1988), Rowe (1994), Greene (1994). Smith (1976) is a study of Neville Shute. Kern (1988) is a collection of essays on Yevgeny Zamiatin, and his work is included in the study by Edwards (1982). The mountain of material on H.G. Wells includes a sizeable proportion that manages to pretend he was not really a science fiction writer! More representative studies include Bergonzi (1961), McConnell (1981) and Parrinder (1995).

CHAPTER 9

ARRIVALS: THE ENDS OF THE EARTH

9.1 Preview

As the previous chapter illustrated, science fiction can be poetic in its figurative imagery as well as being explanatory in its general poetics. The notion of metaphor itself is central to the poetics of science fiction, and in this final chapter I explore how science fiction works conceptually and cognitively at a metaphoric level. Throughout this book, I have been concerned with describing and exploring science fiction texts and how the universes of science fiction work in the reading experience. I have tried to keep the notions of readership and interpretation in the forefront of the discussion, and this chapter encompasses this work within the theoretical frame of *cognitive poetics*. Briefly, this is the understanding of literary reading informed by cognitive linguistics – the study of language and mind.

After outlining some of the key ideas from cognitive poetics, the chapter goes on to use these ideas to discuss those aspects of science fiction which are most concerned with re-figuring new perceptions in a variety of ways: utopias, dystopias, apocalyptic visions and the use of new media. These are the ends to which the Earth is put in science fiction.

9.2 Cognitive Poetics

Fundamentally, a metaphor involves at least two areas of information: a new topic area and a familiar area, and the new information is presented in terms of the old. For example, in 'Juliet is the sun' both terms are visible in the sentence; the sun is familiar, Juliet is the topic and unfamiliar, and Juliet is presented in terms which invite similarities to be drawn with the sun. All metaphors, whether visible or invisible, involve this conceptual process. (I have tried to be as neutral as possible in my choice of words since there is a massive amount of theoretical debate around metaphor and certain terms belong to certain arguments. The connection between the two domains of information forms the basis of most of the disagreement: comparison, substitution or similarity; the replacement of one set of ideas with the other, or the integration or interaction of the concepts; metaphor as mere ornamentation or as essentially meaningful. There is not the space here to rehearse all these arguments again: see the further reading at the end of this chapter. In this chapter I will present one view of metaphor that has come to be central to 'cognitive poetics'.)

9.2.1 Metaphor as Structure-Mapping

The interaction of the two domains of knowledge involved in process-ing a metaphor can be seen as a **mapping** of the familiar *source* domain onto the unfamiliar *target* domain. Thus, to take an example from chapter 8, 'the flapping pigeon-winged books' maps the two domains PIGEONS and BOOKS, and the specific books in this case are figured as pigeons. Our knowledge of the attributes of pigeons (flapping-wings, living things) serves to structure this new mention of books, so that the wings are mapped onto the pages, which flap in the fire, and the books are presented as being alive. It seems to me also that the mapping is a two-way process in this case, so that the mapping of 'life' onto inanimate books makes it easier to see them *as* pigeons that are being burned in the fire. This makes the scene more terrible by giving real life to the books and invoking the horror of burning birds, so that the fireman's blaze is seen as the destruction of life in general. (This is an interactional view of metaphor, after Black (1962, 1990); see also Stockwell (1999), and Forceville (1995) for a contrary view.)

In this example, the conceptual structures of the domains of PIGEONS and BOOKS are mapped onto each other (a corresponding operation is known in mathematics as *isomorphism*: following Chilton (1986) I will use this term for a conceptual mapping to differentiate it from surface metaphor). The isomorphism underlying a metaphor can thus be seen as a **structure-mapping** (Gentner 1982) between domains of know-ledge. These domains altogether constitute an individual's knowledge and perception of the world, based on the totality of their experience, and these *idealised cognitive models* ('ICMs' – Lakoff 1987) are the psy-chological means by which we make sense of the universe. Science fiction is often concerned with the manipulation of ICMs and the isomorphisms involved in new concepts, as the rest of this chapter will illustrate.

In most accounts of cognitive linguistics, the isomorphism of meta-phor is treated, as described so far, in terms of the mapping from source to target of old familiar knowledge onto new unfamiliar areas. The familiar source tends to be concrete or tangible and the new target tends to be relatively abstract or intangible. The source is grounded in experience. Source domains tend to be *basic-level* categories such as 'dog' (rather than 'terrier'), 'car' (rather than either 'vehicle' or 'VW'), 'eat' (rather than 'scoff' or 'nibble'). The examples discussed widely by, among others, Ungerer and Schmid (1996), Lakoff (1987), Lakoff and Turner (1989), and Kövecses (1986, 1988), all tend to be of this prototypical type: 'Juliet is the sun', ARGUMENT IS WAR, LIFE IS A JOURNEY, ANGER IS A HOT LIQUID IN A CONTAINER, for example. However, when I looked back at all the metaphoric expressions in chapter 8, it is noticeable how many science fictional metaphors disrupt this prototypical pattern. In many of them, the domain presented as if it is familiar is in fact as alien as the target it is supposed to structure and clarify: I AM A PHAGOCYTE, THE HEAT RAY IS AN INVISIBLE INEVITABLE SWORD OF HEAT or AN INVIS-IBLE YET INTENSELY HEATED FINGER, WE WERE BLIND IN A HEAVY HOT WEIGHT OF SUSPICION, BOOKS ARE DYNAMITE, FIRE-SPARKS ARE A SWARM OF FIREFLIES, and men swimming are EXPLODING PULSES OF IDEATION IN A NEURONIC JUNGLE. In each of these, the second domain is less familiar to me than the first domain, though the latter is presented stylistically as the source.

This is most clear in the opening to Gibson's (1984) *Neuromancer* (discussed in chapter 2 and in Stockwell 1999): 'The sky above the port was the color of television, tuned to a dead channel' (Gibson: 1984: 9). Here, both domains, SKY and TELEVISION TUNED TO A DEAD CHANNEL (itself containing the metaphor 'dead channel'), would be familiar to most modern readers. However, SKY seems to me more of a basic-level category and more familiar relative to the TELEVISION, especially since this source domain is further sub-categorised by the addition of the specific sub-domain TUNED TO A DEAD CHANNEL. The SKY is treated as the target domain, being typically presented in topic position in the sentence. Ordinarily, this would indicate that SKY is more unfamiliar than TELEVISION TUNED TO A DEAD CHANNEL. What Gibson is doing here, of course, is neatly dramatising in a single visible metaphor the technique of immersing the reader in the cultural assumptions and view-point of the future. The most readily accessible reading that resolves this metaphor is simply that the sky is a grey colour. But the metaphor also suggests that televisions are more basic and natural than sky. The 'pathetic fallacy' of mainstream literature, whereby nature imitates human emotions, is reversed so that nature is alien and technology is familiar and comforting. This is further reinforced by mapping the attribute of a capacity for life onto the 'channel', which is 'dead'. The potential for life is claimed for technology.

9.2.2 Explanatory, Expressive and Constitutive Isomorphism

Gibson's sentence is an example of a metaphor which is apparently simply explanatory being used in an expressive, poetic way. Within cognitive linguistics, the distinction between **explanatory** and **express-ive** metaphors is usually held separate, with scientific analogies and explanations differentiated from literary imagery and figurative expression. Gentner (1982) suggests that a high degree of *clarity* is achieved by **explanatory** metaphors with a one-to-one mapping of attributes, and a high degree of *richness* is gained by **expressive** metaphors which map a large number of attributes and relations. She points out that there is often a trade-off, such that clear scientific metaphors tend to be less rich, and rich poetic metaphors are less clear. As the Gibson example shows, science fiction has the capacity for integrating the scientific and literary to produce **explanatory** poetic metaphors that are both rich and clear on different levels of reading.

As an example of the sort of straightforward explanatory isomorphism that is very clear but not very rich, here is Clarke's simile to explain the 'slingshot' effect obtained by an oblique entry into a planet's gravitational area of influence:

> Like a ball on a cosmic pool table, [the spaceship] *Discovery* had bounced off the moving gravitational field of Jupiter, and had gained momentum from the impact. Without using any fuel, she had increased her speed by several thousand miles an hour.

> (Clarke 1968: 128)

The obvious features to be mapped here are the trajectories of POOL BALLS and ASTRONOMICAL OBJECTS (the spaceship and Jupiter). This is very clear and not particularly poetic or rich. In fact, if the reader tries to go further than this level, the isomorphism tends to become invalid, since the ship and the planet are different sizes, one object has a massive gravitational field, the ship increases its speed, and is capable of using fuel, all very unlike pool balls.

Within the **explanatory** metaphors of science, a further distinction has been made (Ungerer and Schmid (1996: 146–52); Boyd (1993: 486)) between those metaphors that are plainly *exegetical* and those that are **constitutive**. Straightforwardly explanatory or exegetical metaphors become **constitutive** when the isomorphism is seen as the only way to represent the target concept. In other words, the metaphor itself structures understanding, and is used to develop further scientific theory. Since Clarke's example above does not have very high clarity or richness under close examination, it begins to border on being an invalid mapping, and must remain as a simple explanatory isomorphism. Ungerer and Schmid (1996: 148–9) suggest a much better worked-out isomorphism: the scientific model of the atom as a miniature solar system is an example of a constitutive mapping. **Constitutive isomorphisms** are most likely in cases where the target is very abstract or utterly unfamiliar, such as the alien and alternate universes of science fiction. Looking back at the metaphors in chapter 8, it is difficult to find examples that are not **constitutive** in some way, and it may be the case that there is a constitutive dimension to all science fictional metaphors, in the sense that within the projected universe of the text, every item of knowledge is unfamiliar until specified. This is particularly true in the introduction of the science fictional *novum* in the narrative, but it may also more generally be the case in the presentation of the entire alternative universe in which the narrative takes place.

Since every science fictional text (by definition) has an element of alternativity about it which differentiates it from our reality, any reading of a science fiction narrative involves an act of generic isomorphism between the real world and the text world. And if, as suggested above, every isomorphism has the capacity for re-framing our view of categories in the universe by being at some level constitutive, then science fiction possesses a fundamentally powerful capacity for altering readers' perceptions and habits of interpretation. If, as argued in 9.2.1 and Stockwell (1999), the 'flow' of information in isomorphism is two-way and interanimating, this means that the constitutive patterns in science fictional reading are brought back to habits of reading and interpreting in reality. In mainstream fiction, this generic power is reserved for allegory and those parts of fiction which have cues to indicate symbolism or another salient significance. (Delany (1971: 143) points out the linkage between science fiction and symbolist poetry, for example.)

Science fiction has this power as a defining aspect of its poetics. Less systematically isomorphic than allegory but more salient than general fiction, those science fiction texts which exploit this dimension in their narrative organisation can be termed **architexts**.

Though all science fiction has the capacity as an essential part of its generic make-up to alter readers' paradigms, only those which explicitly make use of this feature can be considered as architexts. An **architext** is any science fictional narrative which configures a fully worked-out, rich world, and also provides stylistic cues that encourage a mapping of the *whole* textual universe with the reader's reality. The rest of this chapter comprises a brief exploration of four of the main architextual templates in science fiction: **utopia**, **dystopia**, **apocalypse**, and the dramatisation of isomorphism itself that new media allow.

9.3 Utopian Architexts

Utopias are the essential form of science fictional architext, configuring an entire rich universe in which the details of the social, political and natural environment are the main concern.

> Central to utopian fiction, and to the entire mode of romance, is the alternative world imaged by the author. What in the realist novel would be considered 'mere' background setting becomes in traditional utopian writing the key element of the text.
>
> (Moylan 1986: 36)

Often the most interesting and thought-provoking part of reading utopian texts is not so much in the eventful narrative progression (if any) but in the lyrical description of the environment. This is stylistically expressed either in tiny incidental details or in encylopedic detours that account directly for the utopian society. For example, the unique calendrical system of Le Guin's planet Gethen is suggested in the sentence, 'It was always the Year One here' (1981: 9), and also set out fully and systematically in an appendix to the novel (1981: 254–6). Both strategies contribute to the whole conceptual architecture of the projected universe. In utopia, it is the environment itself that is symbolically and isomorphically significant in reading, and this is what makes utopia centrally architextual.

The fundamental issue at the heart of utopian writing is captured in Thomas More's (1910) original 1516 conflation of 'eutopia' (good place) and 'outopia' (no place): the perfect social architecture can never exist and thus can never be expressed. Writing can thus only ever be a gesture *towards* utopia, rather than achieving it. In Mannheim's (1936) classic study, a perfectly coherent and logical society can only lead to either absolute oppression or absolute boredom. The former is envisioned as dystopia (about which more in 9.4); the latter conjures images of victimless hedonism in a static and eventless pastoral idyll, hardly the stuff of narrative tension (or, indeed, narrative at all).

It is this basic contradiction between the attainment of a utopian objective (culminating in stasis) and the requirements of narrative action (kinesis) that resulted in the virtual disappearance from post-pulp science fiction of any true utopian universes. Though utopias were written from the Renaissance until the height of their popularity in the 1890s, science fiction in the twentieth century has largely been interested in failed, flawed or oppressive societies. Not until 'the utopian revival of the 1970s' (Moylan 1986: 56) did they re-emerge, and then in a different form altogether (see 9.3.2 below).

9.3.1 Typologies of Utopia

Scholes and Rabkin (1977: 173−4) trace utopian writing from Plato onwards, beginning with slave societies that are utopian only for the elite readership. The Renaissance utopias were based on a more egalitarian Christian humanism, with economic productivity or commonwealths replacing the slavery driving the utopia. The industrial revolution allowed machine technology to provide the economic conditions for utopia, solving the iniquitous moral problem, until twentieth century mass production and mechanisation made writers realise that machines themselves might enslave humans, and utopia became dystopia.

To this historical typology, Griffiths (1980: 106) adds a division into two motivations: utopias brought about by an external force, and those featuring an escape into the past. For example he cites Clarke's (1956) *Childhood's End*, in which the external force is animate: alien 'demons' arrive to herald the destruction of the Earth and the shift of humanity onto a new evolutionary plane. An example of an inanimate external force bringing about a utopian state is Wells's (1906) *In the Days of the Comet*, in which humanity is transformed by the gas in a cometary tail. Frank Herbert's (1968) *Dune* is an example of an escape to the past, ostensibly set on another planet but appearing very much like a return to a medieval utopia.

Where the utopian environment is motivated by a shift in time rather than place, the distinction made by Manuel and Manuel (1979) between 'eutopia' and 'euchronia' is justified, and utopias motivated by temporal parallelism rather than being set on an island or distant country or planet became more popular after 1850 (according to Moylan 1986: 6). In all of these cases, humans have no responsibility for the utopia: the change is either brought about by an external force or has been there all the time waiting to be discovered. In Williams's (1980: 203) scheme, these conservative types are subsumed and the typology of utopia extended. Utopias exist as paradises elsewhere (or 'elsewhen'), and as societies changed externally, as above, but Williams also adds utopias brought about by 'willed transformation' (by human effort) and techno-logical transformation. These last two types comprise central examples of science fictional *architexts*, especially when the human innovation in relation to the technological change is described directly.

All of the schemes for understanding utopias rest on the notion that the utopia is alternative to our world, involving some particular element that is responsible for the difference. These are marked as *points of differentiation* (see 7.4.1) in the text, and it is the cumulative effect of these that signal the appropriateness of an isomorphic mapping at the level of architext for the reader. The textual points of differentiation serve to indicate the points of contact and difference between our real-ity and the architext. In other words, the whole utopia (rather than just isolated symbolic elements within it) is mapped out metaphorically from the reader's reality and, crucially, this new idealised cognitive model of the utopia is then used to re-frame the reader's view of reality. The points of differentiation define the nature of the comparison. This is interanimation in cognitive metaphor, and the effect is that the utopian text functions as a constitutive isomorphism: reading utopia is the oppos-ite of escapism.

This is where Suvin (1979: 37–62) describes only half the story:

> Utopia is the verbal construction of a particular quasi-human community where sociopolitical institutions, norms and indi-vidual relationships are organized according to a more perfect principle than in the author's community, this construction being based on estrangement arising out of an alternative historical hypothesis.

> (Suvin 1979: 49)

The writerly-orientation in this formulation focuses on estrangement, but the isomorphic process negotiated by the reader serves to resolve the defamiliarising effect. That is, in the process of reading a utopian architext, the structuring of the alternative domain and its interanimation with reality results in a re-engagement between utopia and reality. Only in this way can the experience of reading utopia be seen as at all relevant. Well-crafted utopias are *constitutive architexts* in that they re-structure readers' perceptions of reality.

In chapters 2 and 7, I explored the linguistic and cognitive mechanisms by which alternative universes could be expressed in science fiction. By implication, I believe that the detail of the conceptual mapping is important for individual readers, and that all these texts are readable. Here I take issue with the mystical and ineffable notion of utopia:

> To write utopia is to indicate what cannot yet be said within present conceptual language or achieved in current political action. To write utopia is to perform the most utopian of actions possible within literary discourse. The form is itself more significant than any of its content.
>
> (Moylan 1986: 39)

Leaving aside the question of how the form can exist ethereally without content, this account badly underestimates the conceptualising power of cognitive metaphor, as a means of access to abstraction. Science fiction in general, and utopias in particular, are fundamentally concerned to dramatise and reify what is abstract and *almost* ineffable. If utopia proper fell out of favour through most of the twentieth century, it was for local political and historical reasons rather than any universal failure of the form. Moylan (1986) himself points out how utopia re-emerged when it was useful again as 'critical utopia', focusing on its isomorphic aspects:

> A central concern in the critical utopia is the awareness of the limitations of the utopian tradition, so that these texts reject utopia as blueprint while preserving it as dream. Furthermore, the novels dwell on the conflict between the originary world and the utopian society opposed to it so that the process of social change is more directly articulated. Finally, the novels focus on the continuing presence of difference and imperfection within utopian society itself and thus render more recognizable and dynamic alternatives.
>
> (Moylan 1986: 10–11)

9.3.2 Critical Utopias as Heterotopias

Moylan (1986: 55–195) explores four **critical utopias** of the 1970s: Joanna Russ's (1975a) *The Female Man*, Ursula Le Guin's (1975a) *The Dispossessed*, Marge Piercy's (1976) *Woman on the Edge of Time*, and Samuel Delany's (1976) *Triton*. Le Guin's novel is subtitled, 'An Ambiguous Utopia'; Delany's in response is an 'ambiguous heterotopia'. The term **heterotopia** is quoted by Delany (1976: 345) from Foucault (1970), in an appendix to *Triton*. All of these novels adapt a utopian setting in order to question the practicality of utopia itself, while also keeping alive the desire for utopia. It is the struggle *towards* utopia that is the motivating force behind **heterotopias**. They differ from traditional utopian texts in foregrounding the problematic issues of creating idealised societies, and the comparison between the science fictional ideal and the reader's reality is thematised in the novels. This is often effected through the narratological form itself, with characters and different worlds co-existing together through the text (Joanna, Jael, Janet and Jeannine in Russ (1975a); New York City and the future Mattapoisett in Piercy (1976)).

Where traditional utopian architexts can be seen as deep invisible forms of isomorphism (since the reader's reality is extra-textual and not explicitly on the surface of the text), heterotopian architexts combine reality and parallelism directly and explicitly. Though, as a result, they are more visible metaphoric forms, the narratological complexity of many such novels in practice makes the reader's task of interpretation anything but easy. Traditional utopias simply present a world to aspire to, better by implication than the reader's, but relatively straightforward to map real issues across, to be resolved fictionally, and then mapped back onto reality. The presence of a version of reality (or a counterpart of the reader's reality) in heterotopias intermingled with the alternative worlds means that this mapping is much more complex. Heterotopias make traditional utopias look more like easily mappable allegories (with a one-to-one mapping of attributes and relations and a high degree of clarity). Heterotopias problematise the process of reading architexts.

As an example of the more recent development of a **critical heterotopia**, Brown (1996) has discussed the works of Iain M. Banks (the science fictional persona of the mainstream novelist Iain Banks). In a series of novels (*Consider Phlebas* (1988), *The Player of Games* (1989), *Use of Weapons* (1992), *Excession* (1997)), a short story ('A Gift from the Culture' (1993: 8–28)), and a novella ('The State of the Art' (1993:

99–205)), Banks has created an architextual anarcho-communist techno-logical society known as 'the Culture'. As Brown (1996) points out, even Banks's other science fiction is defined by being 'non-Culture' novels; though *Feersum Endjinn* (1994) and especially *Against a Dark Background* (1995) take place in a universe that seems similar to the Culture universe in technology, physical laws, naming patterns and atmosphere, even if not explicitly mentioned.

The Culture is an advanced machine society, with artificial intelli-gences known as 'Minds' collectively administering the system. There is no 'government' as such: humans have been 'therapied' to remove their psychoses and there is near-unanimous agreement on rational policy decisions. There is room enough on the Culture's thousands of planets, ships and orbitals, and sufficient technology, for anyone to adopt any lifestyle they choose: living for centuries, changing sex or shape, terraforming their environment to suit whatever whims they have. What makes the Culture a heterotopia is that it is not really a system at all. As the detail of the Culture emerges across the architexts, it becomes apparent that its social organisation is a principle rather than a system. Politics, disagreements and wars still happen, but at a local level, toler-ated within the Culture.

Inevitably, even this heterotopia would produce a tedious narrative if it were left to be merely described, so the texts tend to take their narrative kinesis from some element of disruption: this often centres around the activities of the 'Special Circumstances' section of Contact, the part of the Culture that deals with non-Culture civilisations. Whether a global game on the planet Azad, war with the Idirans, or a super-advanced anomalous 'excession' from an alien civilisation that appears in the Culture's space, the Culture is defined by its delimitations. The last of these, in *Excession* (1997), marks out the Culture prototypically as a heterotopia. In previous texts it has been presented as the ultimate expression of the utopian state; here it is tested by something which is beyond the understanding even of the Minds, and it seems to be rejected as being too chaotic and uncivilised. Though this last novel focuses on the Minds as characters more than humans, their form of expression and idiosyncratic names ('Serious Callers Only', 'Shoot Them Later', 'Sleeper Service', 'Fate Amenable to Change'), and the final resolu-tion which gestures towards an even more advanced form of civilised existence, all serve to give the Culture a flavour that is recognisably human and understandable.

Though the names of the human characters appear alien (Stafl-Preonsa Fal Shilde 'Ngeestra dam Crose, for example), their motivations and behaviour are earthly and familiar. The heterotopian mixture of altern-ativity and base-reality is reinforced by the fact that it is ambiguous whether the universe of the Culture is either a parallel or a serial universe in relation to our base-reality. As Brown (1996: 71) points out, the Idiran-Culture war occurs between 1267 and 1367 AD, and the historical account given as an appendix (Banks 1988: 447) is 'extracted from *A Short History of the Idiran War* (English language/Christian calendar version, original text 2110 AD, unaltered)'. In 'The State of the Art' (Banks 1993: 99–205), a Culture Contact agent decides to stay on Earth in 1977. The Culture thus encompasses both our own time period and our own local positioning in the galaxy, and is presented as being 'out there' as well as involved in our reality. The traditional utopian separation of architextual universe and base-reality is thus dissolved.

Across all of Banks's architexts that configure the Culture, the reader builds up a frame for the universe as an idealised cognitive model, which is continually being mapped onto the base-reality throughout the nar-ratives. This strategy makes it difficult to separate out the pure science fictional alternative elements from the familiar experienced elements, and the complexities of the heterotopia thus serve to thematise the cognitive process itself in imagining the universe. Though the reader is not, of course, literally involved in the fictional world, Banks's nar-rative strategies engage the reader in the universe of the Culture, by making it difficult to distinguish the respective domains of knowledge (and their status) which are involved in making sense of the text. The accumulated detail of the Culture gradually makes it seem familiar to the reader, so that each subsequent novel is able to question its limits and test the notion of heterotopia itself.

Exploration

■ Apply the typologies of utopia to as many twentieth century utopian texts as you can find. Determinants for the types depend on, for example, whether the society is human-made or natural and accid-ental, whether it is directly created or whether it simply exists, whe-ther it is a utopia for all or only for some. Do there seem to be stylistic patterns which emerge across the types of utopia in this century? Are there more heterotopias than proper utopias? Clearly, to answer these questions thoroughly would be an enormous enterprise, but could you come to some preliminary conclusions on the basis of a few selected texts?

9.4 Dystopian Architexts

Dystopia is not the opposite of **utopia**. The contrary of utopia (no place) is our reality (this place); **dystopia** is a dis-placement of our reality. In cognitive linguistic terms, dystopia involves a conceptual *metonymy* rather than a metaphorical mapping. A metonymy is still an isomorphism, but it involves two categories within the same idealised cognitive model (surface examples of metonymy would be 'I've just read the new Iain M. Banks', or 'Mars attacks', where the metonyms stand for 'the book' and 'the Martian troops', respectively). Dystopias tend to be extensions of our base-reality, closely related to it or caricatures of it, rather than being disjunctive alternatives.

At a theoretical level, the metaphor/metonymy distinction depends on assumptions about basic-level categories and domains that are problematic for me. The questions of which ICMs (see 9.2.1) are discrete from each other and what is their conceptual content is far from being settled experimentally (if, given cultural and individual variation, it is resolvable at all), and without this resolution it seems to me highly debatable whether it is possible to say which domains are mentally real, or whether a category is part of a domain or constitutes a separate domain. ICMs are theoretical constructs in cognitive linguistics, with some experimental support; they should not be taken as fixed entities in their own right. It is possible that metonymy is in fact the same sort of isomorphic cognitive process as metaphor, but simply in an easily resolvable form, since the target and source domains are closely related and habitually connected. What we can say is that metonymy is an iso-morphic process between closely related parts of cognitive knowledge. (See Ungerer and Schmid 1996: 128–9; Croft 1993; Dirven 1993.)

Most dystopias are extrapolations of aspects of the present, and thus serve as political statements against certain ideologies or as warnings about current trends that need to be averted. The cognitive metonymy inherent in dystopias is thus an essential aspect of their poetics, in that the connection between base-reality and the dystopian world has to be close, clear and unambiguous to be successful. A more ambivalent meta-phoric strategy would allow too much reader-interpretation in which the central message might be lost. There is little question of missing the point of dystopias such as Zamiatin's (1972) *We*, Huxley's (1955) *Brave New World*, Orwell's (1948) *1984*, Pohl and Kornbluth's (1965) *The Space Merchants*, Harrison's (1967) *Make Room! Make Room!*, or Atwood's (1987) *The Handmaid's Tale* (featuring oppressive societies resulting from, respectively, a sort of mathematical communism, eugenics, Stalinism,

the hegemony of commercial advertising, overpopulation, and fundamentalist religious misogyny). In each of these, it is possible to produce
a non-dystopian reading by seeing the society from the perspective of
the controlling elite group: they are utopias if you are happy with com-
munality, are an Alpha, a Party member or prole, a PR man, a property
owner, or a male Commander. However, the focalisation of each of the
novels through one of the oppressed group means that such a reading
would be eccentric; the reader is stylistically discouraged from such
metaphoric identification.

The cognitive objective of dystopias is to restructure the reader's
ICM of base-reality by increasing the salience of certain disapproved
features. For example, the 'automatism' of state control over individual
free will in the first three of the dystopias mentioned above is the focal
point in those novels. This tendency towards state-control was clearly
evident in the early twentieth century societies (Russia and Britain)
from which the novels emerged, though, clearly too, *We, Brave New
World,* and *1984* are exaggerations from that base-reality. Nevertheless,
the whole ICM of 'contemporary society' includes specific features
such as a discussion of eugenics, for example, that is simply made more
important by the dystopian architext. Successful dystopias are those which
effect a permanent re-structuring of readers' ICMs of their own society. It seems evident that *1984* has been successful in this respect, with
terms such as 'Newspeak', 'Big Brother', 'room 101', 'doublethink' and
'thought police' entering the language in general. (This is a measurement of the success of the texts as dystopias only, rather than a judgement about their value as literature or narrative. *1984* is typical of many
dystopias in being politically effective while being stylistically more like
a tract or pamphlet.) In the next section I will briefly discuss an architext
which uses both surface metaphors and conceptual metonymies to present
an effective dystopian narrative.

9.4.1 Dystopian Metonymies in Bradbury's *Fahrenheit 451*

The surface texture of Bradbury's (1976b) *Fahrenheit 451* features many
striking and poetic metaphors, several of which were illustrated in
chapter 8. These have not only an original and impressionist local effect,
but they can be seen to prime the reader for more general isomorphic
interpretative strategies in reading the text. Alongside the points of
differentiation (see 7.4.1) that mark the text as science fictionally alternative, dystopias like Bradbury's contain metonymic *points of simulation*,
where the rich architextual world makes contact with the reader's

base-reality. In order that the dystopian society is identifiable with the reader's own society, the points of contact include all those particulars of the textual world that appear similar to the real world: the urban land-scape, families, people watching television, social evenings, advertising jingles, public transport, firemen, a police force, and so on. These are textual simulations of aspects of the real world (like 'counterparts', in possible worlds theory: see 7.2), and they are thus close metonymies.

However, it is important that these points of simulation in *Fahrenheit 451* are metonymies rather than identities, closely related but not the same concepts as in reality. 'Firemen' like the character Montag burn books in fire-proofed houses, creating fires rather than putting them out. Families, such as Montag and his wife, watch soap-operas on tele-vision, but the screen is the whole wall, the soaps are even more mindless and banal than in reality, and the viewer can play a part in the 'drama'. Advertising jingles are played on public transport as in reality, but in Montag's world they are incessant and intrusive. There are live televised police chases which involve the viewers as informants, but in the dystopia the chase is seen from the perspective of the hunted (Montag), and a Mechanical Hound is employed to track him down.

Such focalisation through a maverick individual is a common feature of dystopian narratives. It allows an ideological distance from the dystopia which enables it to be described as an object rather than a background setting. The focaliser (Montag, Winston Smith, D-503, or Offred, in the dystopias mentioned above) is often the apparent mouthpiece of the author, or is the representative of our society's view of the dystopia, representing the values of base-reality. However, this representation is itself metonymical: it is the simulated value-system of the implied reader, which real readers are stylistically encouraged to acquiesce in, regardless of whether it is their actual view. In this way the metonymy dramatises the re-structuring of the reader's ICM by enacting it in the reading process.

In order to demonstrate that the metonymy is simultaneously close but not identical to base-reality, many dystopias have an apologist-figure who explains the workings and motivations underlying the architextual society. In *Fahrenheit 451* this is the fire-chief, who at first identifies with Montag when he shares his impulse to take home some books (which are illegal), only to differentiate himself from Montag by lining up with the state's view that books make people unhappy and are socially dangerous. This strategy allows the dystopian society to be metonymically represented by an individual character, and the sub-versive view (simulating the values of base-reality) to be metonymically embodied in the focalised character Montag. The discontinuity between the subversive character and the values of the dystopia are dramatised in the narrative progression by Montag becoming increasingly marginalised: rejected by his work, his wife, and finally by society as a hunted criminal, he escapes the urban dystopia and encounters a rural counter-culture, where the book ends.

Fahrenheit 451 also develops narrative metonymies by which the reading experience is metonymically attached to the themes of the novel. Specifically (as in some other Bradbury texts), the narrative embodies an anti-technological aspect: the instruments of state control are the television, public transport, audio equipment, helicopters and a Mechanical Hound. These serve to reduce human individuality to a common denominator of 'viewer', 'listener', 'passenger'. Montag, making his escape on foot, is reduced by the hunting police Hound to his simple chemical composition, which embodies in the eyes of the state his only individuating characteristic, and is another metonymy. With science fiction metonymically identified with technological progress in the future, this anti-technological narrative angle serves to re-emphasise the agreement with the (non-science fictional) values of present day base-reality.

There are numerous such metonymical reversals in the text, dramatising the double-edged nature of metonymy itself as comprising similarity and difference. Where it is common to refer to books as their human authors ('the latest Iain M. Banks', 'read Orwell', 'Bradbury 1976b'), *Fahrenheit 451* ends by literalising this metonymy (as science fiction generally literalises metaphors) by presenting people as books. Montag escapes to a dissident rural community, led by 'Granger' (meaning 'farmer'), in which each individual has memorised a classic book, effectively becoming that text by interiorising it. There are contextual metonymies too: in base-reality 'Montag' is a brand of paper; Bradbury (1966) has recounted how he wrote this book about book-burning 'in an emotional blaze, in about nine days'; and my paperback edition of the novel has a cover illustration with flames licking at the curling corner of the front page.

451 degrees Fahrenheit is the temperature at which paper bursts into flames, a piece of scientific measurement that stands for the architext. At the end, Montag escapes from the urban dystopia, ironically filled with Bradbury's dense literate poetic metaphors, to a relatively pastoral utopia where literature survives, though with the conceptual content of books, rather than their material existence. At this point, all prose ends, as the narrative ends. The closure of the book itself is thus metonymically

representative of the gesture towards an inexpressible utopia. The end of dystopia is ultimately apocalyptic, either in a personal sense (the death of the character or their sublimation into a collective, or the termination of the role of 'reader' on finishing a novel) or in a communal sense (the whole society being destroyed). In *Fahrenheit 451* there is both. Montag disappears by being transformed into a text, and the illiterate society is destroyed in a nuclear apocalypse.

9.5 Apocalyptic Architexts

Where *utopias*, *dystopias*, and *heterotopias* are world-building, **apocalyptic architexts** dismantle the science fictional world. Since the lifespan of the Earth will eventually end in reality, science fiction which deals with apocalypse can be seen as an acceleration of the process, to a greater or lesser degree. Whether slow death or fast violent death, the demolition of the architextual world is usually foreseen in order to create a narrative with some tension.

There are two dimensions involved in apocalyptic narratives, which dictate the way that the demolition is perceived: point of view and causality. The spatial point of view can be from within the apocalypse or outside it. The former of these is more rare than the latter, since it involves a character being swept away along with the universe in which they are a part. Unless the narrative then switches perceptual viewpoint to contextualise the destruction, the narrative must end with the end of the focalised perception. Such narratives are most amenable to a first-person narration, or are strongly focalised through the narrating character's consciousness. A majority of the 400 'end of the world' stories listed in *The Encyclopedia of Science Fiction* (Clute and Nicholls 1993) have the apocalypse viewed from outside, either by an omniscient narrator or a human character who manages to escape the holocaust. Science fiction stories which feature a small 'ark-like' community of adventurers setting out to re-establish humanity among the stars are very common, and allow the end of the Earth to be narrated and reflected on in the past. A narration of apocalypse which is spatially detached or perceptually omniscient allows the rubble to be picked over and analysed, and allows the surviving characters to delineate the sense of loss involved.

The causes of the apocalypse can be divided into two types, along the same lines as the motivations towards utopia (in 9.3.1). The apocalypse

215

can be a result of an external agency, whether alien and wilfully hostile, or natural (such as a meteor, supernova, or disease); or the end of the world can be a result of human action. The role of technology in each of these types of apocalyptic text is not always predictable. A technological fix can often be tried against the external agency (fighting the aliens, deflecting or blowing up the meteor, for example), though the fix fails as often as it works. It is frequently the use of technology that is to blame for the human-made apocalypse (environmental damage, a scientific experiment too far, and so on), though even here are often 'bad' scientists who act irresponsibly and a 'good' scientist who foresees the danger and either tries to avert it, minimise it, collects a morally upright group to escape and survive it, or picks up the pieces afterwards.

Overlaying all apocalyptic architexts are the 'lucky escape' narratives, which also exploit a strategy of closure. In these, the spectre of apocalypse is raised and may even be recounted in speculative detail, only to be narrowly averted at the end, whether by accident or design. Wells's (1975) *The War of the Worlds*, written in 1898, is the archetypal external agency apocalypse with a lucky escape. With Martian tripods overrunning Europe and the end of the human race in prospect, there is no techno-logical fix, but the Martians all catch colds and die. In the film *Independence Day* (Emmerich 1997), the same scenario is given a twist which adds in the technological fix: the 'good' scientist creates a computer virus which is – miraculously – compatible with the aliens' system, causing their invasion fleet to crash. It is noticeable that the Hollywood insistence on an implausible and sickly-sweet 'happy ending' means that there are far more filmic 'lucky escape' narratives than in literature.

In those apocalypses which are caused by human action, the 'mad scientist' or evil politician of early science fiction has been replaced by a more collective responsibility for environmental disasters. It is remark-able how many British science fictional apocalypses focus on excep-tionally bad weather: lack of rain (Ballard's (1965) *The Drought*), flood (Ballard's (1983) *The Drowned World*), global warming (Elton's (1989) *Stark*); even the nuclear blast in Hines's (1990) *Threads* causes a nuclear winter. Many narratives point at the human love of technological advance without moral reflection, and so raise the familiar questions of early science fiction concerning determinism and free will. A classic which combines both is Walter Miller's (1970) *A Canticle for Liebowitz*, in which several nuclear apocalypses span many centuries as humanity destroys its own civilisation over and over again. The cycle is finally broken, for some, as the novel ends with the monks who look after the mystical technology escaping into space in an 'ark'. Perhaps such narratives should be known as 'arkitexts'?.

9.5.1 Greg Bear: Architect of Architexts

All apocalypses are transforming, even 'lucky escape' narratives, with their coda of a lesson learned by humanity. Those apocalyptic narratives which are truly architextual use the occasion for a dissection of human society: in the extreme crisis of impending holocaust, the architecture of morality, ethics, science and social organisation can be laid bare for inspection. Both world-building and world-destroying aspects of architextual writing are in evidence in the work of Greg Bear, who is marketed as being an heir to the 'hard' science and transcendental mysticism of Arthur C. Clarke.

In cognitive terms, transformative apocalypses offer a reconfiguration of readers' ICMs (see 9.2.1), in a variety of ways which are apparent in Bear's work. True apocalypses, with no escape clause, build up a complex world in some detail, in order to demolish it at the end. Most such apocalypses are set in the near future, so that the sense of imminent doom is increased. This means that the ICM of the fictional world in such narratives is usually at first very close to our own base-reality. This is the case with Bear's (1987) apocalypse *The Forge of God*. Mainly set between June 26th, 1996 and the end of March 1997, in a familiar simulated American landscape, a series of alien invasions marks the *point of differentiation* from our reality into the architextual world. The novel proceeds with realistic political wrangling and a search by a group of scientists for an explanation; this is the occasion for some comment on Earth society. The apocalypse begins with the realisation that an anti-matter 'bullet' or black hole has been fired at the core of the planet, and the Earth will be destroyed. The holocaust is recounted, first spatially from the inside through the eyes of a character in Yosemite park, then spatially from the outside using the perspective of a few of the lucky escapees in their 'ark' out in space. The ICM of Earth society (a simulation of almost every piece of knowledge and experience the reader possesses) is closed by the apocalypse. A brief coda, set on New Mars in 2397, begins to set up a new architextual world, in which the few survivors, nurtured by robot guardians from a benevolent alien race, join the galactic revenge quest to destroy the home of the 'planet-eaters'. (This coda becomes a full architext in its own right in Bear's (1992) sequel *Anvil of Stars*.)

Whereas apocalyptic demolition involves an ICM closure, Bear's (1985, 1989a, 1996) *Eon*, *Eternity*, and *Legacy*, all represent the same architextual universe and involve a re-framing of the ICM of current history. Again set in the near future, beginning on Christmas Eve, 2000, the sequence of novels does not destroy the world but creates an extra-polated future that has clear connections with Earth society in reality. The architext is very rich, with narrative action and character develop-ment set against carefully speculated science and an imagined social and political background. Such a universe is neither utopian (the world as it should be) nor dystopian (the world as it might terribly be, if not averted), but is more like a heterotopian architext in presenting realistic-ally a future that is complex and multi-layered.

Like Banks's Culture architexts, Bear's universe embeds our own base-reality within it as one of a series of many parallel worlds dis-covered in the course of the sequence. (The mechanism by which this is achieved is 'The Way', an infinite super-space corridor that connects different universes, originating in a hollowed-out asteroid with a cham-ber that goes on forever.) Furthermore, the relationship of our reality to the fictional universe is specified very carefully in terms of theoretical physics. Transformative architexts such as the universe of *Eon*, which combine the extrapolation and embedding of base-reality, can be seen as metonymic cognitive processes: the categories within the reader's 'base-reality' ICM are revised and re-categorised, but the fundamental structure remains.

The third form of transformative architext is more thoroughly meta-phoric, and it also features in Bear's work. In *Blood Music* (Bear 1988, a development of a short story, anthologised in Bear 1989b: 11–41), the architext transforms current human society transcendentally. Genetic experiments by Vergil Ulam on DNA molecules create 'noocytes' – cells that combine and attain intelligence. Out of all the cellular biolo-gical material of the Earth, humanity is absorbed into the 'noosphere', presented as a new level of evolutionary advance, a planet-wide unitary intelligence. Such a transformation (common to Stapledon's (1937) *Star Maker* and Clarke's (1956) *Childhood's End*) marks a discontinuity with our ICM of base-reality. The fictional architext is thus properly isomorphic. It is debatable whether such transcendence should be seen as apocalyptic, and terms such as utopia or dystopia seem equally irrelevant, since the values of base-reality have been utterly transformed by the narrative process as well. Moral judgements of 'goodness' or 'badness' are also transcended. The creation of a thoroughly new trans-cendent understanding of humanity's future treats the isomorphism as an opportunity of interpolating a new form of experience. This is con-stitutive isomorphism writ large. In such texts, the transformation can only be followed by the closure of the text, since transcendence depends on denying any further understanding. Where no further expression is possible, the architext ends.

Exploration

■ Compare the ends of the earth across science fiction texts that deal with it (such as those mentioned so far in this chapter). Consider specifically the point of view from which the narrative is told. Are there stylistic means of encoding the responsibility for the disaster, either explicitly or implicitly by suggestion? Is there any poetic justice in who survives, or is this based on the individual's political power, scientific knowledge, rationalism, or plain luck? You might try to answer these questions in relation to some of the very many disaster films featuring colliding worlds, alien invasion, meteor/comet strike, overpopulation, global flooding, global deserts, plagues, and so on.

9.6 Ergodic Architexts

So far in this chapter, I have discussed different ways in which science fiction manages the cognitive processes involved in configuring richly textured social architectures. Absolute utopia, absolute dystopia, total apocalypse and transcendent transformations are the ultimate expressions of these forms. However, there is one other means through which science fiction can effect a cognitive change in the way readers perceive reality, and this is to dramatise the creative process itself in the organisational form of the architext.

Science fiction has always been very closely tied to its readership (see chapter 4), and the development of 'fandom' alongside the literary genre has made the element of reader–writer interaction even more evident. With letters to the magazines, and the instant critical and commercial appraisal of the 'fanzines', science fiction readers have perhaps more influence over the direction of new publications than in any other genre. This influence, however, has until recently been limited by the logistic realities of text publishing, and traditionally the consumer of science fiction has still had to buy the completed product and process it as a finished text, in the conventional way. Recent innovations in electronic technology and publishing, however, have provided scope for involving the reader far more in the original construction of the architext.

Though electronic text-manipulation is a recent occurrence, reader-constructed fictional worlds have an old tradition. Borrowing from physics the term **ergodic** literature for such processes, Aarseth (1997) cites ancient systems such as the *I-Ching* or chess as examples of meaningful and coherent scenarios in which the reader has a significant if not crucial input. Ergodic texts are open and dynamic, requiring specific actions by the reader to generate the literary experience. I have emphasised repeatedly throughout this book the fact that the literary experience is essentially a matter of readerly reception and interpretation. Ingarden's (1973) inclusion of literature as a 'heteronymous' object, which only has existence beyond the physical book if it is perceived by an observing consciousness, is central to my understanding of literary meaning. Ergodic literature simply dramatises this process by placing it in the forefront of the text's organisation.

Within literature, readers have always had an ergodic role in the selection of texts to read. Choosing, in a bookshop or library, to follow *this* fictional world rather than *that* one is an important decision over which realities come to be mentally experienced. However, Aarseth's (1997) use of the term relates more specifically to readerly decisions within the boundaries of the text. There is a tradition (mainly in children's literature) of book-based ergodic literature. The many dozens of 'Fighting Fantasy Gamebooks' by Steve Jackson and Ian Livingstone require two dice and a pencil to negotiate the points of decision that send the reader back and forth across the hundreds of sections of the book (see, for example, Livingstone 1983, 1984, 1986; Jackson and Livingstone 1984, 1985, 1987). Typically, the book sets up a scenario, your character, and hints on play, and you roll the dice to determine your equipment, strengths, skills and level of luck. The book then provides a framework that you adventure through non-linearly. A second 'reading' of the book is highly unlikely to produce the same narrative. Even the question of authorship is not straightforward. The science fictional *Rebel Planet* for example, is 'concept copyrighted' Jackson and Livingstone (1985), though the text itself is written by Robin Waterfield, and the essential illustrations and maps are by Gary Mayes.

The books are marketed as 'part story, part game'. It is games that provide the original ergodic scenario, increasing in the complexity of the imagined world with the introduction of computer and role-play games. While chess produces a fairly simple architext with a lot of different narrative possibilities, recent interactive adventure games tend to develop a very rich architext. As Clute and Nicholls (1993: 468–71) point out, the relationship between game scenarios and science fiction is circular, with games copying science fiction scenarios and science fiction exploiting the market for games by novelising their worlds. Early computer adventure games were largely text-based; more recent products have high-speed graphics and a more mimetic interaction with the fictional world. The direction of development seems clearly towards virtuality and an indistinguishable identity of fictional world and user's environment, as the technology improves.

A current variant on such scenarios consists of shared-worlds games, in which a group of people participates, often in role-play, in a scenario. The internet has facilitated this development between remotely based participants. This experience is fundamentally different from other ergodic forms in that more than one reader is autonomous in relation to the given text. That is, the reading experience is closer to a base-reality scenario in that the reader does not have to project character motivations for the other participants. These collaborative texts have the framework of the architext established in the basic rules of the game, but details of characterisation and narrative are richly added as the game progresses.

Most scenario-based adventure games are set in fantasy worlds rather than science fiction, though there is often a science fictional element. The appeal of fast, realistic graphics encourages an emphasis on outward appearance and simple action that is similar to the mass of 'trashy' science fiction; it is difficult to imagine a computer game based on any of Banks's, Bradbury's or Bear's architexts that would be anything but superficial, or that would retain much of their propositional content. This is because such games have made an exclusive choice between action and idea. Greg Bear has discussed the possible consequences of a more integrated literary technology in a round-table discussion in Frongia and Allison (1992).

Bear sees the future of science fiction in hypertext, in which different levels of text, graphics, music and even taste and sensation could be combined and transmitted electronically, producing an 'enormous, three-dimensional, multimedia, shared-world experience' (Frongia and Allison 1992: 290). Bear describes this not only as potentially 'the death of individual artistry' but also as 'a radical expansion of the imagination' and 'a whole new art form' (Frongia and Allison 1992: 286, 285, 289). Clearly this sort of interaction in the creation of a fictional universe would bring the architext and the reader's base-reality into close proximity. Potentially this raises the possibility that whole new ways of reading literature might develop, revising fundamentally the definition and shape of literature and the literary experience itself.

9.7 Review

Cognitive linguistics is a powerful tool, still very much in the process of development, for 'understanding understanding' (in the phrase of Werth 1987). The study of language and mind, the nature of meaning and consciousness, is the central issue of our times. Understanding the literary experience is the concern of cognitive poetics, which is developing the capacity for accounting for readers' interpretations, unearthing the fundamental conceptual categories through which literature works, providing a means of relating cross-cultural perceptions, and allowing judgements to be made between different interpretations. There is much debate about the scope and potential of a cognitive approach to interpretation, but at least the discussion among these researchers has moved on from the indulgence and obscurity of some recent literary theory.

What can be said with confidence is that the fundamentally isomorphic nature of the experience of reading fictional literature is central to science fictional poetics. As demonstrated in this chapter, some science fiction goes further in dramatising this cognitive process itself, but all science fiction has the potential to be read this way. As it literalises metaphors, and dramatises understanding in configured universes, all science fiction presents some degree of architext, and requires the reader to enter into it in the process of reading it. All science fiction thus invites readers to exercise their isomorphic cognitive capacities, to share in the imaginative projection of the architext.

In the process, science fiction can accomplish a variety of things. Some science fiction can exploit the constitutive power of isomorphism to structure new scientific understanding (where 'scientific' here simply means systematically arranged knowledge). The rhetoric in which some science fiction is written can cognitively reanimate the familiar and everyday, by practising the reader's familiar ICMs (see 9.2.1) in mappings with alternative fictional universes. In these ways, some science fiction is able to unify the explanatory and expressive functions of conceptual metaphor in the presentation of an architext. Though there are variations in its specific stylistic rhetoric, in its general poetics science fiction is basically reader-oriented as a result. The architexts it presents are thus fully environmentally realised, rich, detailed universes, which readers (and other writers) can mentally complete and manipulate beyond the text in which they originate.

If conceptual metaphor is seen as being interanimating between source and target domains, then the combination of explanatory didacticism and expressive entertainment value in science fiction can be seen as a claim for the centrality of the genre in human communication. Readers understand the new in terms of the familiar, but the familiar is invested with a new meaning, perception and explanatory power in the experience. Innovative science fiction texts offer new mappings of the familiar world with fictional universes; as a genre, science fiction offers practice in different configurations of mappings. Regular mental exercise in a multiplicity of different mappings from base-reality has the cognitive effect of widening the prototype base of a reader: more real entities are perceived in a variety of ways. Science fiction thus has a real effect in the real world.

In this chapter, I have explored all too briefly how science fiction can take readers to different ends of the Earth. Even absolutes such as *utopia*, *dystopia* and *apocalypse* are shown within the science fiction genre to have degrees of interpretation and a variety of prototypes. The strongest statement of my argument here would claim that reading a variety of science fictional architexts makes you a better reader: better in the sense of being more cognitively adaptable than before, more engaged, more imaginative.

The chapter ends with some speculation about the future of science fiction and reading. Science fiction seems well-placed to take advantage of the new forms of media that could make traditional forms seem one-dimensional. However, on the basis of how oral cultures developed writing and reading, and negotiated the innovations of paper, the scribal system, printing, mass publishing and literacy, and electronically linked texts through the internet, such developments are likely to build on the existing cognitive capacities of readers. This means isomorphic configuration of fictional worlds. Whatever direction the literature of the future takes, science fiction seems likely to be central to it, and the modes of reading that centrally define the poetics of science fiction would seem to be a good preparation for that future.

Exploration

■ Take an example of each of the four types of architext: utopia, dystopia, apocalypse and ergodic narrative. For each, what are the points of simulation that connect it to our base-reality, and what are the points of differentiation that make it a fictional architext? Make a short list of these for each type. Are some points of differentiation essential to the architext and are some incidental? Are points of differentiation always the 'novums' that drive the science fictional world, or can they be incidental background detail? Do you think all science fiction depends for its definition on such points?

Speculations

■ Traditionally, utopias and satires have been political statements presented in such a form as not to incur the wrath of repressive regimes (often Church and Crown in Britain). The problem with this strategy is that it is preaching to the converted: only those able to 'decode' the allusions are able to read the piece *as* satirical. For others, they only read a fantasy. The danger, then, in fully worked-out rich architexts is that they are read as escapism not as political engagement. The crude remedy is to insert the connections with base-reality explicitly and polemically, but this runs the risk of destroying the artifice of the work in the interest of realising it as political tract. (This seems to me the case with *1984*, *Invasion of the Body Snatchers*, and *The Female Man* (Orwell 1948; Siegel 1956, Russ 1975a), none of which have survived the shifts in culture and politics very well as artistic texts, though they may well have been instrumental in bringing those shifts about.) Is successful architextual writing inevitably either exclusively elitist or simply read as escapism by the masses? Are clever self-reflexive heterotopias similarly dependent on highly trained and educated readers realising they are not just space-opera?

■ The trade-off between explanatory and expressive isomorphisms (Gentner 1982) promotes the separation of art and science. If science fiction is seen as a synthesis of science and art, then it is reasonable to expect to find both explanatory and expressive metaphoric forms in its corpus. This in turn would predict great unevenness in science fictional texture: shifting from richness to clarity and back in the course of a text. Certainly this can be found in some of the science fiction discussed in this book. The alternative, also in evidence, is a true dialectic progression out of the traditions of science fiction: the original pure sense of wonder and the engagement with science and technology have become an aesthetic of explanatory intricacy and elegance. If science fiction achieves this in the potential of its poetics, then perhaps a dialectical synthesis of science and art will have been produced by the literature of the future.

Further reading

The developing field of cognitive poetics contains more programmes and polemic than practice as yet, but the following present exemplary analyses with theoretical work: Johnson (1987), Lakoff and Turner (1989), Turner (1987, 1991, 1996), Gibbs (1994). On utopia and dystopia,

Moylan (1986) is a central study, and Philmus (1973) is interesting. Hatfield (1990) has written on Bear. The use of architexts within feminism is the subject of Barr (1987, 1992), Lefanu (1988), Longhurst (1989), Haraway (1991) and Armitt (1991).

There is a wealth of material on death, doom and apocalypse, such as Clarke (1992), Ketterer (1974), Wagar (1982), Rabkin, Greenberg and Olander (1983), Dowling (1987) and Davies (1990). New media are being explored and theorised by Colford (1996), Chernaik, Davis and Deegan (1993), Chernaik, Deegan and Gibson (1996) and Aarseth (1997).

REFERENCES

Note: science fiction literature and film are included together with critical material here, as I have always found it easier to retrieve references when they are not separated. It has become customary in research on science fiction to note the bibliographical labyrinth which often attaches to works. A novel might be a 'fixup' of a series of short stories, each of which might have a different date and place of publication. These might all have appeared under different titles, and there are usually also differences between British and American editions, not only in bibliographical detail but in content as well. Short stories, in particular, tend to be anthologised in various collections. Writers often use pseudonyms. Science fiction – apart from the staples of the genre – tends to have a short shelf-life, and there is a mass of material that comes into and out of print.

I have therefore followed the increasingly common and commonsense practice of citing the text that was most easily available to me. This is almost always the paperback, since I know of no one who buys hardback science fiction, except for journal reviewers who get them for free. So the date given is the edition I use. Where the information was available, I have also given the probable original date of publication in square brackets, the original title, and the original publisher if known.

Aarseth, E.J. (1997) *Cybertext: Perspectives on Ergodic Literature*, Baltimore: Johns Hopkins University Press.

Abbott, E. (1962) *Flatland: A Romance of Many Dimensions*, Oxford: Blackwell [1884].

Adams, D. (1979) *The Hitch-Hiker's Guide to the Galaxy*, London: Pan.

Adams, D. (1983) *The Meaning of Liff*, London: Pan.

Aldiss, B. (1970) *The Shape of Further Things: Speculations on Change*, London: Faber and Faber.

Aldiss, B. (1973) *The Moment of Eclipse*, London: Granada [1970, Faber & Faber].

Aldiss, B. (1990) *Barefoot in the Head*, London: Victor Gollancz [1969, Faber & Faber].

Aldiss, B. and Harrison, H. (eds) (1975) *Hell's Cartographers: Some Personal Histories of Science Fiction Writers*, London: Orbit.

Aldiss, B. and Wingrove, D. (1986) *Trillion Year Spree*, London: Paladin.

Allen, S. (ed) (1989) *Possible Worlds in Humanities, Arts and Sciences*, Berlin: de Gruyter.

Armitt, L. (ed) (1991) *Where No Man Has Gone Before: Women and Science Fiction*, London: Routledge.

Asher, R.E. and Simpson, J.M.Y. (eds) (1994) *The Encyclopedia of Language and Linguistics*, Oxford: Pergamon Press.

Ashley, M. (ed) (1974) *The History of the Science Fiction Magazine. Part 1: 1926–35*, London: New English Library.

Ashley, M. (ed) (1975) *The History of the Science Fiction Magazine. Part 2: 1936–1945*, London: New English Library.

Ashley, M. (ed) (1976) *The History of the Science Fiction Magazine. Part 3: 1946–1955*, London: New English Library.

Asimov, I. (1960) *Foundation*, London: Sphere.

Asimov, I. (1962) *Foundation and Empire*, London: Granada.

Asimov, I. (1964) *Second Foundation*, London: Granada.

Asimov, I. (1968) *I, Robot*, London: Granada [1950, Street & Smith].

Asimov, I. (ed) (1974) *Tomorrow's Children*, London: Futura.

Asimov, I. (ed) (1975) *Before the Golden Age Trilogy*, London: Futura.

Asimov, I. (1982) *Foundation's Edge*, London: Grafton.

Asimov, I. (1983) *The Robots of Dawn*, London: Grafton.

Asimov, I. (1985) *Robots and Empire*, London: Grafton.

Asimov, I. (1986) *Foundation and Earth*, London: Grafton.

Asimov, I. (1988) *Prelude to Foundation*, London: Grafton.

Asimov, I. (1990) *Azazel*, London: Bantam Books.

Atkins, E. (1996) 'The posthumanism of Philip K. Dick', *UCE Papers in Language and Literature*, 3, 19–29.

Atwood, M. (1987) *The Handmaid's Tale*, London: Virago [1986, Jonathan Cape].

Aubrey, C. (ed) (1982) *Nukespeak: The Media and the Bomb*, London: Comedia.

Baddeley, A.D. (1986) *Working Memory*, Oxford: Oxford University Press.

Baddeley, A.D. (1992) 'Working memory', *Science*, 225, 556–9.

Ballard, J.G. (1965) *The Drought*, London: Dent.

Ballard, J.G. (1983) *The Drowned World*, London: Dent [1962, Victor Gollancz].

Banks, I.M. (1988) *Consider Phlebas*, London: Orbit.

Banks, I.M. (1989) *The Player of Games*, London: Orbit.

Banks, I.M. (1992) *Use of Weapons*, London: Orbit.

Banks, I.M. (1993) *The State of the Art*, London: Orbit.

Banks, I.M. (1994) *Feersum Endjinn*, London: Orbit.

Banks, I.M. (1995) *Against a Dark Background*, London: Orbit.

Banks, I.M. (1997) *Excession*, London: Orbit.

Barnes, M.J.E. (1974) *Linguistics and Languages in Science Fiction-Fantasy*, New York: Arno.

Barr, M.S. (1987) *Alien to Femininity: Speculative Fiction and Feminist Theory*, Westport, Conn: Greenwood Press.

Barr, M.S. (1992) *Feminist Fabulation: Space/Postmodern Fiction*, Iowa City: University of Iowa Press.

Barron, N. (1987) *Anatomy of Wonder: A Critical Guide to Science Fiction* (Third edition), New Providence, NJ: R.R. Bowker.

Baugh, A. and Cable, T. (1978) *A History of the English Language* (Third edition), London: Routledge & Kegan Paul.

Bear, G. (1985) *Eon*, London: Grafton.

Bear, G. (1987) *The Forge of God*, London: Legend.

Bear, G. (1988) *Blood Music*, London: Legend.

Bear, G. (1989a) *Eternity*, London: Grafton.

Bear, G. (1989b) *Tangents*, London: Victor Gollancz.

Bear, G. (1991) *Queen of Angels*, London: Legend.

Bear, G. (1992) *Anvil of Stars*, London: Orbit.

Bear, G. (1994) *Moving Mars*, London: Orbit.

Bear, G. (1996) *Legacy*, London: Orbit.

Bear, G. (1998) *Foundation of Chaos*, London: Orbit.

Benford, G. (1998) *Foundation's Fear*, London: Orbit.

Bensen, D.R. (ed) (1963) *The Unknown*, New York: Pyramid Books.

Benson, G. and Stephensen-Payne, P. (1992) *John Brunner, Shockwave Writer: A Working Bibliography* (Third edition), Leeds: G. Benson.

Bergonzi, B. (1961) *The Early H.G. Wells*, Manchester: Manchester University Press.

Bex, T. (1995) 'Keats and the disappearing self: aspects of deixis in the Odes', in Green, K. (ed), 161–78.

Bex, T. (1996) *Variety in Written English*, London: Routledge.

Bixby, J. (1974) 'It's a *Good* Life', in Asimov, I. (ed), 355–74 [1953, Ballantyne Books].

Black, M. (1962) *Models and Metaphors*, Ithaca, NY: Cornell University Press.

Black, M. (1990) *Perplexities*, Ithaca, NY: Cornell University Press.

Blake, N. (ed) (1992) *The Cambridge History of the English Language*, Cambridge: Cambridge University Press.

Boardman, T. (ed) (1979) *Science Fiction Stories*, London: Octopus Books.

Bortolussi, M. and Dixon, P. (1996) 'The effects of formal training on literary reception', *Poetics*, 23, 6, 471–87.

Bova, B. (ed) (1989) *The Best of the Nebulas*, New York: Tor.

Boyd, R. (1993) 'Metaphor and theory change: what is "metaphor" a metaphor for?' in Ortony, A. (ed), 481–532.

Bradbury, R. (1966) 'At what temperature do books burn?' *The New York Times* (Sunday November 13, 1966), D11.

Bradbury, R. (1976a) *The October Country*, London: Grafton [1956, Rupert Hart-Davis Ltd.].

Bradbury, R. (1976b) *Fahrenheit 451*, London: Granada [1954, Rupert Hart-Davis Ltd.].

Bradbury, R. (1977a) *The Martian Chronicles*, London: Granada [1951, as *The Silver Locusts*, Rupert Hart-Davis Ltd.].

Bradbury, R. (1977b) *The Golden Apples of the Sun*, London: Granada [1953, Rupert Hart-Davis Ltd.].

Bradley, R. and Swartz, N. (1979) *Possible Worlds: An Introduction to Logic and its Philosophy*, Indiana: Hackett Publishing Co.

Bretnor, R. (ed) (1976) *The Craft of Science Fiction*, New York: Harper & Row.

Broderick, D. (1995) *Reading By Starlight: Postmodern Science Fiction*, London: Routledge.

Brooke-Rose, C. (1958) *A Grammar of Metaphor*, London: Mercury Books.

Brooke-Rose, C. (1981) *A Rhetoric of the Unreal: Studies in Narrative and Structure, Especially of the Fantastic*, Cambridge: Cambridge University Press.

Brown, C. (1996) 'Utopias and heterotopias: the "Culture" of Iain M. Banks', in Littlewood, D. and Stockwell, P. (eds), 57–74.

Brown, G. and Yule, G. (1983) *Discourse Analysis*, Cambridge: Cambridge University Press.

Brumfit, C. and Carter, R.A. (eds) (1986) *Literature and Language Teaching*, Oxford: Oxford University Press.

Brunner, J. (1988) *The Shockwave Rider*, London: Methuen [1975, Dent].

Bühler, K. (1982) 'The deictic field of language and deictic worlds', in Jarvella, R.J. and Klein, W. (eds), 9–30 [translated from *Sprachtheorie*, 1934].

Butler, A. (1996) 'Science fiction as postmodernism: the case of Philip K. Dick', in Littlewood, D. and Stockwell, P. (eds), 45–56.

Caldas-Coulthard, C. and Coulthard, M. (eds) (1996) *Texts and Practices: Readings in Critical Discourse Analysis*, London: Routledge.

Campbell, J.W. (1975) 'The brain stealers of Mars', in Asimov, I. (ed), 764–81 [1936, Beacon Magazines].

Carter, D. (1987) *Interpreting Anaphors in Natural Language Texts*, Chichester: Ellis Horwood.

Carter, P.A. (1977) *The Creation of Tomorrow: Fifty Years of Magazine Science Fiction*, New York: Columbia University Press.

Carter, R.A. (1984) 'Why have I started to talk to you like this? Narrative voices, discourse pragmatics and textual openings', in van Peer, W. and Renkema, J. (eds), 95–132.

Carter, R.A. and Nash, W. (1983) 'Language and literariness', *Prose Studies*, 6, 2, 123–41.

Carter, R.A. and Nash, W. (1990) *Seeing Through Language: A Guide to Styles of English Writing*, Oxford: Blackwell.

Carter, R.A. and Simpson, P. (eds) (1989) *Language, Discourse, and Literature: An Introduction to Discourse Stylistics*, London: Unwin Hyman/Routledge.

Caton, C.E. (ed) (1963) *Philosophy and Ordinary Language*, Urbana, Ill: University of Illinois Press.

Cawelti, J. (1976) *Adventure, Mystery, and Romance: Formula Stories as Art and Popular Culture*, Chicago: University of Chicago Press.

Chafe, W.L. (1987) 'Cognitive constraints on information flow', in Tomlin, R.S. (ed), 21–51.

Chafe, W.L. (1994) *Discourse, Consciousness and Time: The Flow and Displacement of Conscious Experience in Speaking and Writing*, Chicago: University of Chicago Press.

Chapman, E.L. (1984) *The Magic Labyrinth of Philip José Farmer*, San Bernardino: Borgo Press.

Charolles, M. (1983) 'Coherence as a principle in the interpretation of discourse', *Text*, 3, 1, 71–97.

Charolles, M. (1989) 'Coherence as a principle in the regulation of discursive production', in Heydrich, W., Neubauer, F., Petöfi, J.S. and Sözer, E. (eds), 3–15.

Chernaik, W., Davis, C. and Deegan, M. (eds) (1993) *The Politics of the Electronic Text*, Oxford: Office for Humanities Communication with the Centre for English Studies, University of London.

Chernaik, W., Deegan, M. and Gibson, W. (eds) (1996) *Beyond the Book: Theory, Culture and the Politics of Cyberspace*, Oxford: Office for Humanities Communication with the Centre for English Studies, University of London.

Chilton, P. (ed) (1985) *Language and the Nuclear Arms Debate: Nukespeak Today*, London: Pinter.

Chilton, P. (1986) 'Metaphor, euphemism, and the militarization of language'. Paper presented at the biannual meeting of the International Peace Research Association, Sussex University.

Cioffi, F. (1982) *Formula Fiction? An Anatomy of American Science Fiction, 1930–1940*, New York: Greenwood Press.

Clare, M. (1984) *Doris Lessing and Women's Appropriation of Science Fiction*, Birmingham: Centre for Contemporary Cultural Studies, University of Birmingham.

Clareson, T.D. (ed) (1971) *Science Fiction: The Other Side of Realism. Essays on Modern Fantasy and Science Fiction*, Bowling Green, Ohio: Bowling Green University Press.

Clarke, A.C. (1951) *The Sands of Mars*, London: Sidgwick & Jackson.

Clarke, A.C. (1956) *Childhood's End*, London: Pan [1954, Sidgwick & Jackson].

Clarke, A.C. (1968) *2001: A Space Odyssey*, London: Arrow.

Clarke, A.C. (1974) 'The Nine Billion Names of God', in *Of Time and Stars*, Harmondsworth: Penguin, 15–23 [1953, Ballantyne Books Inc.].

Clarke, A.C. (1982) *2010: Odyssey Two*, London: Granada.

Clarke, A.C. (1988) *2061: Odyssey Three*, London: Grafton.

Clarke, A.C. (1997) *3001: The Final Odyssey*, London: Voyager.

Clarke, I.F. (1992) *Voices Prophesying War, 1763–3749* (Second edition), Oxford: Oxford University Press.

Clute, J. and Nicholls, P. (1993) *The Encyclopedia of Science Fiction*, London: Orbit.

Colford, I.A. (1996) *Writing in the Electronic Environment: Electronic Text and the Future of Creativity and Knowledge*, London: Vine Press.

Cook, G. (1994) *Discourse and Literature*, Oxford: Oxford University Press.

Cooper, D.E (1986) *Metaphor*, Oxford: Blackwell.

Croft, W. (1993) 'The role of domains in the interpretation of metaphors and metonymies', *Cognitive Linguistics*, 4, 335–70.

Csicsery-Ronay, I. (1991) 'Cyberpunk and neuromanticism', in McCaffery, L. (ed), 182–93.

Csicsery-Ronay, I. (1992) 'Futuristic flu, or, the revenge of the future', in Slusser, G. and Shippey, T. (eds), 26–45.

Csicsery-Ronay, I. (1995a) 'Antimancer: cybernetics and art in Gibson's *Count Zero*', *Science Fiction Studies*, 22, 65, 63–86.

Csicsery-Ronay, I. (1995b) 'The sentimental futurist: cybernetics and art in William Gibson's *Neuromancer*', *Critique*, 33, 221–40.

Davies, M. and Ravelli, L.J. (eds) (1992) *Advances in Systemic Linguistics: Recent Theory and Practice*, London: Pinter.

Davies, P.J. (ed) (1990) *Science Fiction, Social Conflict and War*, Manchester: Manchester University Press.

De Beaugrande, R. (1980) *Text, Discourse and Process: Toward a Multi-Disciplinary Science of Texts*, Norwood, NJ: Ablex.

De Bolt, J. (ed) (1976) *The Happening Worlds of John Brunner: Critical Explorations in Science Fiction*, London: Kennikat Press.

De Camp, L.S. (1938) 'Language for time-travelers', *Astounding* (July 1938), 63–72.

Delany, S.R. (1966) *Babel-17*, New York: Ace Books.

Delany, S.R. (1968) *Nova*, New York: Bantam.

Delany, S.R. (1971) 'About five thousand one hundred and seventy five words', in Clareson, T.D. (ed), 130–45.

Delany, S.R. (1974) *Dhalgren*, New York: Bantam.

Delany, S.R. (1976) *Triton*, New York: Bantam.

Delany, S.R. (1977) *The Jewel-Hinged Jaw: Notes on the Language of Science Fiction*, Elizabethtown, NY: Dragon Press.

Delany, S.R. (1984) *Starboard Wine: More Notes on the Language of Science Fiction*, Pleasantville, NY: Dragon Press.

Delany, S.R. (1989) 'Neither the beginning nor the end of structuralism, post-structuralism, semiotics, or deconstruction for SF readers: an introduction', *The New York Review of Science Fiction* (in three parts), 6, pp. 1, 8–12; 7, pp. 14–18; 8, pp. 9–11.

Delany, S.R. (1990) 'Modernism, postmodernism, science fiction', *New York Review of Science Fiction*, 24, 1, 8–9

DeWitt, B. and Graham, N. (eds) (1973) *The Many-Worlds Interpretation of Quantum Mechanics*, Princeton, NJ: Princeton University Press.

Dick, P.K. (1965) *The Man in the High Castle*, Harmondsworth: Penguin.

Dick, P.K. (1972) *Do Androids Dream of Electric Sheep?* London: Grafton [1968, Rapp & Whiting Ltd.].

Dick, P.K. (1973) *Ubik*, London: Grafton [1970, Rapp & Whiting Ltd.].

Dick, P.K. (1974) *Flow My Tears, The Policeman Said*, London: Victor Gollancz.

Dirven, R. (1985) 'Metaphor as a basic means for extending the lexicon', in Paprotte, W. and Dirven, R. (eds), 85–119.

Dirven, R. (1993) 'Metonymy and metaphor: different mental strategies of conceptualization', *Leuvense Bijdragen*, 82, 1–28.

Diskin, L.F. (1980) *Theodore Sturgeon: A Primary and Secondary Bibliography*, Boston, Mass: G.K. Hall.

Doherty, G.D. (1964) 'The use of language in SF', *SF Horizons*, 1, 43–53.

Doležel, L. (1976) 'Narrative modalities', *Journal of Literary Semantics*, V, 1, 5–14.

Doležel, L. (1988) 'Mimesis and possible worlds', *Poetics Today*, 9, 3, 475–97.

Doležel, L. (1989) 'Possible worlds and literary fictions', in Allen, S. (ed), 223–42.

Dowling, D. (1987) *Fictions of Nuclear Disaster*, Basingstoke: Macmillan.

Downes, W. (1994) 'Register in literature', in Asher, R.E. and Simpson, J.M.Y. (eds), vol. 2, 3509–11.

Duchan, J.F.; Bruder, G.A. and Hewitt, L.E. (eds) (1995) *Deixis in Narrative: A Cognitive Science Perspective*, Hillsdale, NJ: Lawrence Erlbaum.

Eco, U. (1979) *The Role of the Reader: Explorations in the Semiotics of Texts*, Bloomington: Indiana University Press.

Eco, U. (1990) *The Limits of Interpretation*, Bloomington and Indianapolis: Indiana University Press.

Edwards, T.R.N. (1982) *Three Russian Writers and the Irrational: Zamyatin, Pil'nyak and Bulgakov*, Cambridge: Cambridge University Press.

Eliot, T.S. (1974) *Collected Poems: 1909–1962*, London: Faber.

Ellison, H. (1989) '"Repent, Harlequin", said the Ticktockman', in Bova, B. (ed), 62–71 [1965].

Elton, B. (1989) *Stark*, London: Sphere.

Emmerich, R. (dir) (1997) *Independence Day*, 20th Century Fox.

Emmott, C. (1989) *Reading Between the Lines: Building a Comprehensive Model of Participant Reference in Real Narrative*, unpublished PhD thesis, University of Birmingham.

Emmott, C. (1992) 'Splitting the referent: an introduction to narrative enactors', in Davies, M. and Ravelli, L.J. (eds), 221–8.

Emmott, C. (1995) 'Consciousness and context-building: narrative inferences and anaphoric theory', in Green, K. (ed), 81–97.

Emmott, C. (1997) *Narrative Comprehension: A Discourse Perspective*, Oxford: Clarendon Press.

Enkvist, N.E. (1989) 'From text to interpretability: a contribution to the discussion of basic terms in text linguistics', in Heydrich, W., Neubauer, F., Petöfi, J.S. and Sözer, E. (eds), 369–82.

Eysenck, M.W. and Keane, M.T. (1990) *Cognitive Psychology: A Student's Handbook*, London: Lawrence Erlbaum.

Fairclough, N. (1989) *Language and Power*, London: Longman.

Farmer, P.J. (1974) *To Your Scattered Bodies Go*, London: Granada [1971].

Fillmore, C. (1975) *Santa Cruz Lectures on Deixis, 1971*, ms, Indiana University Linguistics Club.

Fillmore, C. (1982) 'Towards a descriptive framework for spatial deixis', in Jarvella, R.J. and Klein, W. (eds), 31–59.

Fish, S. (1980) *Is There a Text in This Class? The Authority of Interpretive Communities*, Cambridge, Mass: Harvard University Press.

Fishburn, K. (1985) *The Unexpected Universe of Doris Lessing*, Westport, Conn: Greenwood Press.

Fleischman, S. (1982) *The Future in Thought and Language: Diachronic Evidence from Romance*, Cambridge: Cambridge University Press.

Fleischman, S. (1990) *Tense and Narrativity: From Medieval Performance to Modern Fiction*, London: Routledge.

Forceville, C. (1995) '(A)symmetry in metaphor: the importance of extended context', *Poetics Today*, 16, 4, 677–708.

Foucault, M. (1970) *The Order of Things*, New York: Pantheon [*Les Mots et les Choses*, 1968, Vintage].

Fowler, R. (1986) *Linguistic Criticism*, Oxford: Oxford University Press.

Franklin, H.B. (1980) *Robert A. Heinlein: America as Science Fiction*, Oxford: Oxford University Press.

Frayn, M. (1981) *A Very Private Life*, Glasgow: Fontana.

Freund, E. (1987) *The Return of the Reader: Reader-Response Criticism*, London: Methuen.

Friend, B. (1973) 'Strange bedfellows: science fiction, linguistics, and education', *English Journal*, 62, 998–1003.

Frongia, T. and Allison, A. (1992) '"We're on the eve of 2000": writers and critics speak out on cyberpunk, HyperCard, and the (new?) nature of narrative', in Slusser, G. and Shippey, T. (eds), 279–92.

Gentner, D. (1982) 'Are scientific analogies metaphors?' in Miall, D. (ed), 106–32.

Gerrig, R.J. (1993) *Experiencing Narrative Worlds: On the Psychological Activities of Reading*, New Haven: Yale University Press.

Gibbs, R.W. (1994) *The Poetics of Mind: Figurative Thought, Language, and Understanding*, Cambridge: Cambridge University Press.

Gibson, W. (1984) *Neuromancer*, London: Victor Gollancz.

Gibson, W. (1986) *Count Zero*, London: Victor Gollancz.

Gibson, W. (1988) *Mona Lisa Overdive*, London: Victor Gollancz.

Gibson, W. (1993) *Virtual Light*, London: Viking.

Gibson, W. (1996) *Idoru*, London: Viking.

Gibson, W. and Sterling, B. (1990) *The Difference Engine*, London: Victor Gollancz.

Givón, T. (1989) *Mind, Code and Context: Essays in Pragmatics*, Hillsdale, NJ: Lawrence Erlbaum.

Goatly, A. (1997) *The Language of Metaphors*, London: Routledge.

Green, K. (1992) 'Deixis and the poetic persona', *Language and Literature*, 1, 2, 121–34.

Green, K. (ed) (1995a) *New Essays in Deixis: Discourse, Narrative, Literature*, Amsterdam: Rodopi.

Green, K. (1995b) 'Deixis: a revaluation of concepts and categories', in Green, K. (ed), 9–25.

Greenberg, J.H. (ed) (1963) *Universals of Language* (Second edition), Cambridge, Mass: MIT Press.

Greenberg, M.H. and Olander, J.D. (eds) (1980) *Ray Bradbury*, New York: Taplinger.

Greenberg, M.H.; Waugh, C.G. and Waugh, J-L. (eds) (1992) *The Giant Book of Science Fiction Stories*, London: Magpie Books.

Greene, G. (1994) *Doris Lessing: The Poetics of Change*, Ann Arbor: University of Michigan Press.

Greenland, C. (1983) *The Entropy Exhibition: Michael Moorcock and the British 'New Wave' in Science Fiction*, London: Routledge & Kegan Paul.

Griffiths, J. (1980) *Three Tomorrows: American, British and Soviet Science Fiction*, London: Macmillan.

Hacker, B.C. and Chamberlain, G.B. (1981) 'Pasts that might have been: an annotated bibliography of alternate history', *Extrapolation*, 22, 4, 334–78.

Halliday, M.A.K. (1978) *Language as Social Semiotic*, London: Edward Arnold.

Halliday, M.A.K. and Hasan, R. (1976) *Cohesion in English*, London: Longman.

Hanson, C. (1989) *Re-reading the Short Story*, Basingstoke: Macmillan.

Haraway, D.J. (1991) *Simians, Cyborgs, and Women: The Reinvention of Nature*, New York: Routledge.

Harrison, H. (1967) *Make Room! Make Room!* Harmondsworth: Penguin.

Hatfield, L. (1990) 'The galaxy within: paradox and synecdoche as heuristic tropes in Greg Bear's science fiction', *Extrapolation*, 31, 3, 240–57.

Haynes, J. (1989) *Introducing Stylistics*, London: Unwin Hyman/Routledge.

Heinlein, R. (1959a) *The Menace from Earth*, New York: Signet.

Heinlein, R. (1959b) *6 x H*, New York: Pyramid Books.

Heinlein, R. (1965) *Stranger in a Strange Land*, London: Grafton.

Herbert, F. (1968) *Dune*, New York: Ace Books.

Heydrich, W., Neubauer, F., Petöfi, J.S. and Sözer, E. (eds) (1989) *Connexity and Coherence: Analysis of Text and Discourse*, Berlin: de Gruyter.

Hines, B. (1990) *Threads, and Other Sheffield Plays* (edited by M. Mangan), Sheffield: Sheffield Academic Press.

Hirst, G. (1981) *Anaphora in Natural Language Understanding: A Survey*, Berlin: Springer-Verlag.

Hoban, R. (1982) *Riddley Walker*, London: Picador [1980, Jonathan Cape].

Hockett, C.F. (1955) 'How to learn Martian', *Astounding* (May 1955), 97–106.

Hockett, C.F. (1963) 'The problem of universals in language', in Greenberg, J.H. (ed), 1–29.

Hoey, M. (1983) *On the Surface of Discourse*, London: Allen & Unwin.

Hoey, M. (1991) *Patterns of Lexis in Text*, Oxford: Oxford University Press.

Hofmann, T.R. (1993) *Realms of Meaning*, London: Longman.

Hollinger, V. (1991) 'Cybernetic deconstructions: cyberpunk and post-modernism', in McCaffery, L. (ed), 203–18.

Holub, R.C. (1984) *Reception Theory: A Critical Introduction*, London: Methuen.

Hook, G. (1983) 'The nuclearization of language', *Journal of Peace Research*, 21, 3, 259–75.

Hudson, R. (1995) *Word Meaning*, London: Routledge.

Hunter, W.F. (ed) (1996) *The Short Story: Structure and Statement*, Exeter: Elm Bank.

Huntington, J. (1989) *Rationalizing Genius: Ideological Strategies in the Classic American Science Fiction Short Story*, London: Academic Press.

Huxley, A. (1955) *Brave New World*, Harmondsworth: Penguin [1932, Chatto & Windus].

Ingarden, R. (1973) *The Literary Work of Art*, Evanston, Ill: University of Illinois Press.

Iser, W. (1978) *The Act of Reading: A Theory of Aesthetic Response*, Baltimore: John Hopkins University Press.

Jackson, H. (1988) *Words and Their Meaning*, London: Longman.

Jackson, H. and Stockwell, P. (1996) *An Introduction to the Nature and Functions of Language*, Cheltenham: Stanley Thornes.

Jackson, S. and Livingstone, I. (1984) *Talisman of Death*, London: Puffin.

Jackson, S. and Livingstone, I. (1985) *Rebel Planet*, London: Puffin.

Jackson, S. and Livingstone, I. (1987) *Beneath Nightmare Castle*, London: Puffin.

Jakubowski, M. and Edwards, M. (eds) (1983) *The Complete Book of Science Fiction and Fantasy Lists*, St. Albans: Granada.

Jakubowski, M. and James, E. (eds) (1992) *The Profession of Science Fiction: SF Writers on Their Craft and Ideas*, Basingstoke: Macmillan.

James, E. (1994) *Science Fiction in the Twentieth Century*, Oxford: Oxford University Press.

Jameson, F. (1984) 'Post-modernism; or the cultural logic of late capitalism', *New Left Review*, 146, 53–92.

Jameson, F. (1991) *Post-modernism; or the Cultural Logic of Late Capitalism*, London/New York: Verso.

Jameson, M. (1963) 'Doubled and redoubled', in Bensen, D.R. (ed), 119–36 [1941, Street & Smith].

Jarvella, R.J. and Klein, W. (eds) (1982) *Speech, Place and Action: Studies in Deixis and Related Topics*, Chichester: John Wiley.

Jeffries, L. (1993) *The Language of Twentieth Century Poetry*, Basingstoke: Macmillan.

Johnson, M. (1987) *The Body in the Mind: The Bodily Basis of Meaning, Imagination, and Reason*, Chicago: Chicago University Press.

Jones, M. (1996) 'J.G. Ballard: neurographer', in Littlewood, D. and Stockwell, P. (eds), 127–45.

Jones, P. (1995) 'Philosophical and theoretical issues in the study of deixis: a critique of the standard account,' in Green, K. (ed), 27–48.

Juno, A. (ed) (1984) *J.G. Ballard*, San Francisco: V/Search Publications.

Katamba, F. (1994) *English Words*, London: Routledge.

Kaplan, C. and Rose, E.C. (eds) (1988) *Doris Lessing: The Alchemy of Survival*, Ohio: Ohio University Press.

Kaylor, N.H. (ed) (1997) *Creative and Critical Approaches to the Short Story*, Lampeter: Edwin Mellen.

Kern, G. (ed) (1988) *Zamyatin's* We: *A Collection of Critical Essays*, Ann Arbor: Ardis.

Ketterer, D. (1974) *New Worlds for Old: The Apocalyptic Imagination, Science Fiction and American Literature*, Bloomington: Indiana University Press.

Kornbluth, C.M. (1953) *A Mile Beyond the Moon*, Garden City, NY: Doubleday.

Kövecses, Z. (1986) *Metaphors of Anger, Pride and Love*, Amsterdam: Benjamins.

Kövecses, Z. (1988) *The Language of Love*, Lewisburgh: Associated University Press.

Kripke, S. (1972) *Naming and Necessity*, Cambridge, Mass: Harvard University Press.

Krueger, J.R. (1966) 'Names and nomenclatures in science-fiction', *Names*, 14, 203–14.

Krueger, J.R. (1968) 'Language and techniques of communication as theme or tool in science-fiction', *Linguistics*, 39, 68–86.

Kubrick, S. (dir) (1968) *2001: A Space Odyssey*, Metro-Goldwyn-Mayer.

Kuiper, K. and Allan, W.S. (1996) *An Introduction to English Language*, Basingstoke: Macmillan.

Lakoff, G. (1987) *Women, Fire and Dangerous Things: What Categories Reveal about the Mind*, Chicago: University of Chicago Press.

Lakoff, G. and Johnson, M. (1980) *Metaphors We Live By*, Chicago: University of Chicago Press.

Lakoff, G. and Turner, M. (1989) *More Than Cool Reason: A Field Guide to Poetic Metaphor*, Chicago: University of Chicago Press.

Leech, G.N. and Short, M.H. (1981) *Style in Fiction*, London: Longman.

Lefanu, S. (1988) *In the Chinks of the World Machine: Feminism and Science Fiction*, London: Women's Press.

Le Guin, U.K. (1975a) *The Dispossessed*, London: Grafton.

Le Guin, U.K. (1975b) 'The Day Before the Revolution', in *The Wind's Twelve Quarters*, London: Victor Gollancz, 285–303.

Le Guin, U.K. (1981) *The Left Hand of Darkness*, London: Grafton.

Le Guin, U.K. (1982) *The Language of the Night: Essays on Fantasy and Science Fiction*, (edited by S. Wood), New York: Berkley.

Le Guin, U.K. (1983) *The Compass Rose*, London: Victor Gollancz.

Le Guin, U.K. (1989) *Dancing at the Edge of the World: Thoughts on Words, Women, Places*, London: Gollancz.

Leinster, M. (1979) 'First contact', in Boardman, T. (ed), 7–39 [1945, Street & Smith].

Leith, D. (1983) *A Social History of English*, London: Routledge.

Lessing, D. (1975) 'Preface to *The Golden Notebook*', in *A Small Personal Voice: Essays, Reviews, Interviews* (edited by P. Schlueter), New York: Vintage Books, 23–43.

Lessing, D. (1981a) *Shikasta*, London: Grafton [1979, Jonathan Cape].

Lessing, D. (1981b) *The Marriages Between Zones Three, Four, and Five*, London: Grafton [1980, Jonathan Cape].

Lessing, D. (1983) *The Making of the Representative for Planet 8*, London: Grafton.

Levack, D.J.H. (1981) *PKD: A Philip K. Dick Bibliography*, San Francisco: Underwood/Miller.

Levinson, S.C. (1983) *Pragmatics*, Cambridge: Cambridge University Press.

Lewis, D. (1973) *Counterfactuals*, Cambridge: Cambridge University Press.

Lewis, D. (1986) *On the Plurality of Worlds*, Oxford: Blackwell.

Lindskold, J.M. (1993) *Roger Zelazny*, New York/Oxford: Maxwell Macmillan International.

Littlewood, D. and Stockwell, P.J. (eds) (1996) *Impossibility Fiction: Alternativity – Extrapolation – Speculation*, Amsterdam: Rodopi.

Livingstone, I. (1983) *City of Thieves*, London: Puffin.

Livingstone, I. (1984) *Deathtrap Dungeon*, London: Puffin.

Livingstone, I. (1986) *Trial of Champions*, London: Puffin.

Longhurst, D. (ed) (1989) *Gender, Genre and Narrative Pleasure*, London: Unwin Hyman.

Lovejoy, A.O. (1930) *The Revolt Against Dualism: An Inquiry Concerning the Existence of Ideas*, London: Allen & Unwin.

Lucas G. (dir) (1977) *Star Wars: A New Beginning*, Lucasfilms/20th Century Fox.

Lyons, J. (1977) *Semantics, Vols. I and II*, Cambridge: Cambridge University Press.

McCaffery, L. (ed) (1991) *Storming the Reality Studio: A Casebook of Cyberpunk and Postmodern Science Fiction*, Durham/London: Duke University Press.

McCarthy, M. (1991) *Discourse Analysis for Language Teachers*, Cambridge: Cambridge University Press.

McCarthy, M. and Carter, R.A. (1994) *Language as Discourse: Perspectives for Language Teaching*, London: Longman.

McConnell, F. (1981) *The Science Fiction of H.G. Wells*, New York: Oxford University Press.

McCrum, R., Cran, W. and MacNeil, R. (1992) *The Story of English* (Revised edition), London: Faber/BBC Books.

McHale, B. (1987) *Postmodernist Fiction*, London: Methuen.

McHale, B. (1991) 'POSTcyberMODERNpunkISM', in McCaffery, L. (ed), 308–23.

Mackenzie, N. and Mackenzie, J. (1973) *The Time Traveller*, London: Weidenfeld & Nicolson.

Maitre, D. (1983) *Literature and Possible Worlds*, London: Middlesex University Press.

Malzberg, B. (1982) *The Engines of the Night: Science Fiction in the Eighties*, Garden City, NY: Doubleday.

Mannheim, K. (1936) *Ideology and Utopia: An Introduction to the Sociology of Knowledge*, New York: Harcourt.

Manuel, F.E. and Manuel, F.P. (1979) *Utopian Thought in the Western World*, Cambridge, Mass: Belknap Press.

Martindale, C. and Dailey, A. (1995) 'I.A. Richards revisited: do people agree in their interpretations of literature?', *Poetics*, 23, 4, 299–314.

May, C.E. (1995) *The Short Story: The Reality of Artifice*, New York/Oxford: Maxwell Macmillan International.

Menger, L. (1981) *Theodore Sturgeon*, New York: Frederick Ungar.

Meyers, W.E. (1980) *Aliens and Linguists: Language Study and Science Fiction*, Athens: University of Georgia Press.

Miall, D. (ed) (1982) *Metaphor: Problems and Perspectives*, Brighton: Harvester Press.

Miller, G.A. (1956) 'The magic number seven, plus or minus two: some limits on our capacity for processing information', *Psychological Review*, 63, 81–93.

Miller, W.M. (1970) *A Canticle for Liebowitz*, London: Corgi [1960].

Milroy, J. and Milroy, L. (1991) *Authority in Language*, London: Routledge.

Milroy, L. (1987) *Language and Social Networks* (Second edition), Oxford: Blackwell.

Monk, P. (1985) 'The syntax of future shock: structure and the center of consciousness in John Brunner's *The Shockwave Rider*', *Extrapolation*, 26, 3, 220–30.

More, T. (1910) *Utopia*, London: Dent [1516 in Latin; translated by R. Robinson, 1561].

Moskowitz, S. (ed) (1970) *Futures to Infinity*, New York: Pyramid Books.

Moskowitz, S. (1974) *Science Fiction by Gaslight: A History and Anthology of Science Fiction in the Popular Magazines, 1891–1911* (Second edition), Westport, Conn: Hyperion.

Moylan, T. (1986) *Demand the Impossible: Science Fiction and the Utopian Imagination*, London: Methuen.

Nair, R.B.; Carter, R.A. and Toolan, M. (1988) 'Clines of metaphoricity, and creative metaphors as situated risk-taking', *Journal of Literary Semantics*, XVII, 1, 20–40.

Nicholls, P. (ed) (1978) *Explorations of the Marvellous: The Science and the Fiction in Science Fiction*, London: Fontana [1976, as *Science Fiction at Large*, Gollancz].

Nicholls, P. (ed) (1982) *The Science in Science Fiction*, London: Michael Joseph.

Niven, L. (1973) *Ringworld*, London: Orbit [1972, Victor Gollancz].

Niven, L. (1976) 'The words in science fiction', in Bretnor, R. (ed), 178–94.

Nolan, W.F. (ed) (1970) *A Wilderness of Stars*, London: Victor Gollancz.

Noon, J. (1993) *Vurt*, London: Pan.

Olander, J.D. and Greenberg, M.H. (eds) (1978) *Robert A. Heinlein*, Edinburgh: P. Harris.

Ortony, A. (ed) (1993) *Metaphor and Thought* (Second edition), Cambridge: Cambridge University Press.

Orwell, G. (1948) *1984*, London: Secker & Warburg.

Panshin, A. (1968) *Heinlein in Dimension*, Chicago: Advent.

Paprotte, W. and Dirven, R. (eds) (1985) *The Ubiquity of Metaphor*, Amsterdam: John Benjamins.

Parrinder, P. (1995) *Shadows of the Future: H.G. Wells, Science Fiction and Prophecy*, Liverpool: Liverpool University Press.

Philmus, R.M. (1973) 'The language of utopia', *Studies in the Literary Imagination*, 6, 2, 62–78.

Piercy, M. (1976) *Woman on the Edge of Time*, New York: Knopf.

Pohl, F. (1989) 'Astounding story', *American Heritage*, 40, 6, 42–54.

Pohl, F. and Kornbluth, C.M. (1965) *The Space Merchants*, Harmondsworth: Penguin [1953].

Pringle, D. (1979) *Earth is the Alien Planet: J.G. Ballard's Four-Dimensional Nightmare*, San Bernardino: Borgo Press.

Putnam, H. (1990) *Realism with a Human Face*, Cambridge, Mass.: Harvard University Press.

Pyles, T. (1971) *The Origins and Development of the English Language*, New York: Harcourt Brace Jovanovich.

Rabkin, E.; Greenberg, M.H. and Olander, J. (eds) (1983) *The End of the World*, Carbondale, Ill: Southern Illinois University Press.

Ramis, H. (dir) (1993) *Groundhog Day*, Columbia Pictures.

Rauh, G. (ed) (1983a) *Essays on Deixis*, Tübingen: Gunter Narr Verlag.

Rauh, G. (1983b) 'Tense as deictic categories. An analysis of English and German tenses,' in Rauh, G. (ed), 229–75.

Rescher, N. (1975) *A Theory of Possibility*, Pittsburgh: Pittsburgh University Press.

Richards, I.A. (1924) *Principles of Literary Criticism*, London: Routledge & Kegan Paul.

Ricoeur, P. (1977) *The Rule of Metaphor: Multidisciplinary Studies of the Creation of Meaning in Language* (trans. Czerny, R.), Toronto: University of Toronto Press.

Rimmon-Kenan, S. (1983) *Narrative Fiction: Contemporary Poetics*, London: Methuen.

Ripps, H.A. (dir) (1990) *12:01 PM*, Chanticleer Films.

Rogers, A. (1964) *A Requiem for Astounding*, Chicago: Advent.

Rogers, I.A. (1968) 'The time plays of J.B. Priestley', *Extrapolation*, 10, 9–16.

Ronen, R. (1994) *Possible Worlds in Literary Theory*, Cambridge: Cambridge University Press.

Rorty, R. (1982) *Consequences of Pragmatism (Essays 1972–1980)*, Minneapolis: University of Minnesota Press.

Rosch, E. and Lloyd, B.B. (eds) (1978) *Cognition and Categorization*, Hillsdale, NJ: Lawrence Erlbaum.

Rowe, M.M. (1994) *Doris Lessing*, Basingstoke: Macmillan.

Rubenstein, R. (1975) 'Outer space, inner space: Doris Lessing's metaphor of science fiction', *World Literature Written in English*, 14, 1, 187–97.

Rubenstein, R. (1979) *The Novelistic Vision of Doris Lessing: Breaking the Forms of Consciousness*, Urbana, Ill: University of Illinois Press.

Russ, J. (1973) 'Speculations: the subjunctivity of science fiction', *Extrapolation*, 15, 1, 51–9.

Russ, J. (1975a) *The Female Man*, New York: Bantam.

Russ, J. (1975b) 'Towards an aesthetic of science fiction', *Science Fiction Studies*, 2, 2, 112–19.

Russell, B. (1957) 'Mr. Strawson on referring', *Mind*, 66, 385–9.

Ryan, M.L. (1991a) *Possible Worlds: Artificial Intelligence and Narrative Theory*, Bloomington and Indianapolis: Indiana University Press.

Ryan, M.L. (1991b) 'Possible worlds and accessibility relations: a semantics typology of fiction', *Poetics Today*, 12, 3, 553–76.

Ryder, M.E. (1998) 'I met myself (me?) coming and going: co(?)-referential noun phrases and point of view in time travel stories'. Paper presented at 18th Poetics and Linguistics Association conference, University of Berne, April 1998.

Sagan, C. (1981) *Cosmos*, London: Macdonald.

Sage, L. (1983) *Doris Lessing*, London: Methuen.

Samuelson, D.N. (1980) 'Note: SF and poetry', *Science Fiction Studies*, 7, 1, 112.

Samuelson, D.N. (1994) 'Necessary constraints: Samuel R. Delany on science fiction', *Foundation*, 60, 21–41.

Sanders, J.L. (1980) *Roger Zelazny: A Primary and Secondary Bibliography*, Boston, Mass: G.K. Hall.

Sapir, E. (1949) *The Selected Writings of Edward Sapir* (edited by D.G. Mandelbaum), Berkeley: University of California Press.

Scholes, R. and Rabkin, E.S. (1977) *Science Fiction: History, Science, Vision*, Oxford: Oxford University Press.

Schrödinger, E. (1935) *Science, Theory and Man*, London: Allen & Unwin.

Schrödinger, E. (1978) *Collected Papers on Wave Mechanics*, New York: Chelsea Publishing [1928].

Schwetman, J.W. (1985) 'Russell Hoban's *Riddley Walker* and the Language of the Future', *Extrapolation*, 26, 3, 212–19.

Sell, R.D. and Verdonk, P. (eds) (1994) *Literature and the New Interdisciplinarity: Poetics, Linguistics, History*, Amsterdam: Rodopi.

Semino, E. (1997) *Language and World Creation in Poems and Other Texts*, London: Addison Wesley Longman.

Seuren, P.A.M. (1985) *Discourse Semantics*, Oxford: Blackwell.

Shaw, P. and Stockwell, P. (eds) (1991) *Subjectivity and Literature from the Romantics to the Present Day: Creating the Self*, London: Pinter.

Shelley, M. (1998) *Frankenstein, or, The Modern Prometheus* (ed David Stevens), Cambridge: Cambridge University Press [1816].

Shippey, T. (ed) (1991) *Fictional Space: Essays on Contemporary Science Fiction*, Oxford: Basil Blackwell.

Sholder, J. (dir) (1993) *12:01*, Chanticleer Films/New Line Cinema.

Short, M.H. (1989) *Reading, Analysing and Teaching Literature*, London: Longman.

Short, M.H. (1996) *Exploring the Language of Poems, Plays and Prose*, Harlow: Addison Wesley Longman.

Short, M.H. and Candlin, C. (1986) 'Teaching study skills for English literature', in Brumfit, C. and Carter, R.A. (eds), 89–109.

Shute, N. (1966) *On the Beach*, London: Pan [1957, William Heinemann].

Siegel, D. (dir) (1956) *Invasion of the Body Snatchers*, Allied Artists.

Simpson, P. (1993) *Language, Ideology and Point of View*, London: Routledge.

Simpson, P. (1997) *Language Through Literature: An Introduction*, London: Routledge.

Slusser, G. (1977a) *Robert A. Heinlein: Stranger in His Own Land* (Second edition), San Bernardino: Borgo Press.

Slusser, G. (1977b) *The Bradbury Chronicles*, San Bernardino: Borgo Press.

Slusser, G. and Shippey, T. (eds) (1992) *Fiction 2000: Cyberpunk and the Future of Narrative*, Athens: University of Georgia Press.

Smith, E.E. and Jonides, J. (1997) 'Working memory: a view from neuroimaging', *Cognitive Psychology*, 33, 1, 5–42.

Smith, J. (1976) *Neville Shute*, Boston, Mass: Twayne.

Sonnenfeld, B. (dir) (1997) *Men In Black*, Columbia Pictures.

Stapledon, O. (1937) *Star Maker*, London: Methuen.

Stapledon, O. (1972) *Last and First Men* and *Last Men in London*, Harmondsworth: Penguin [1930, Methuen].

Stephens, J. and Waterhouse, R. (1990) *Literature, Language and Change*, London: Routledge.

Stephensen-Payne, P. (1990) *Philip José Farmer, Good-Natured Ground Breaker: A Working Bibliography*, Leeds: P. Stephensen-Payne.

Sterling, B. (ed) (1988) *Mirrorshades: The Cyberpunk Anthology*, London: Paladin.

Stockwell, P. (1990) 'Scripts, frames and nuclear discourse in the Washington superpower summit, December 1987', *Liverpool Papers in Language and Discourse*, 2, 18–39.

Stockwell, P. (1991) 'Language, knowledge, and the stylistics of science fiction', in Shaw, P. and Stockwell, P. (eds), 101–12.

Stockwell, P. (1994a) 'How to create universes with words: referentiality and science fictionality', *Journal of Literary Semantics*, XXIII, 3, 159–87.

Stockwell, P. (1994b) 'To be or not to be a phagocyte: procedures of reading metaphors', in Sell, R.D. and Verdonk, P. (eds), 65–78.

Stockwell, P. (1999) 'The inflexibility of invariance', *Language and Literature*, 8, 2, 125–42.

Strang, B. (1972) *A History of English*, London: Methuen.

Strawson, P.F. (1963) 'On referring', in Caton, C.E. (ed), 162–93.

Sturgeon, T. (1963) 'Yesterday was Monday', in Bensen, D.R. (ed), 43–61 [1941, Street & Smith].

Suvin, D. (1979) *Metamorphoses of Science Fiction: On the Poetics and History of a Literary Genre*, New Haven: Yale University Press.

Suvin, D. (1990) 'Locus, horizon, and orientation: the concept of possible worlds as a key to utopian studies', *Utopian Studies*, 1, 2, 69–83.

Suvin, D. (1991) 'On Gibson and cyberpunk SF', in McCaffery, L. (ed), 349–65.

Swift, J. (1967) *Travels into Several Remote Nations of the World, in Four Parts, by Lemuel Gulliver*, Harmondsworth: Penguin [1726, Benjamin Motte].

Szilard, L. (1961) *The Voice of the Dolphins and Other Stories*, New York: Simon & Schuster.

Tabbi, J. (1995) *Postmodern Sublime: Technology and American Writing from Mailer to Cyberpunk*, Ithaca: Cornell University Press.

Tallis, R. (1988) *Not Saussure: A Critique of Post-Saussurean Literary Theory*, Basingstoke: Macmillan.

Talmy, L. (1980) *The Representation of Space by Language*, ms. Cognitive Science Program, University of California at San Diego.

Taylor, J. (1990) 'From pulpstyle to innerspace: the stylistics of American New-Wave SF', *Style*, 24, 4, 611–27.

Toffler, A. (1970) *Future Shock*, London: Bodley Head.

Tomlin, R.S. (ed) (1987) *Coherence and Grounding in Discourse*, Amsterdam: John Benjamins.

Tompkins, J. (ed) (1980) *Reader-Response Criticism: From Formalism to Post-Structuralism*, Baltimore: Johns Hopkins University Press.

Toolan, M. (1998) *Language in Literature: An Introduction to Stylistics*, London: Arnold.

Touponce, W.F. (1984) *Ray Bradbury and the Poetics of Reverie: Fantasy, Science Fiction and the Reader*, Ann Arbor: UMI Research Press.

Tracy, R. (1983) 'Cognitive processes and the acquisition of deixis,' in Rauh, G. (ed) (1983a), 99–148.

Truffaut, F. (dir) (1966) *Fahrenheit 451*, Rank/Anglo Enterprise/Vineyard.

Turner, M. (1987) *Death is the Mother of Beauty: Mind, Metaphor, Criticism*, Chicago: Chicago University Press.

Turner, M. (1991) *Reading Minds: The Study of English in the Age of Cognitive Science*, Princeton: Princeton University Press.

Turner, M. (1996) *The Literary Mind*, Chicago: Chicago University Press.

Umland, S.R. (ed) (1995) *Philip K. Dick: Contemporary Critical Interpretations*, Westport, Conn: Greenwood Press.

Ungerer, F. and Schmid, H-J. (1996) *An Introduction to Cognitive Linguistics*, London: Longman.

Van Dijk, T.A. and Kintsch, W. (1983) *Strategies of Discourse Comprehension*, New York: Academic Press.

Van Peer, W. and Renkema, J. (eds) (1984) *Pragmatics and Stylistics*, Leuven: Acco.

Verdonk, P. and Weber, J.J. (eds) (1995) *Twentieth-Century Fiction: From Text to Context*, London: Routledge.

Vonnegut, K. (1970) *Slaughterhouse Five*, London: Jonathan Cape.

Wagar, W.W. (1982) *Terminal Visions: The Literature of Last Things*, Bloomington: Indiana University Press.

Wakelin, M. (1988) *The Archaeology of English*, London: Batsford.

Warrick, P.S. (1980) *The Cybernetic Imagination in Science Fiction*, Cambridge, Mass: MIT Press.

Warrick, P.S. (1987) *Mind in Motion: The Fiction of Philip K. Dick*, Carbondale, Ill: Illinois University Press.

Watson, I. (1975) 'Towards an alien linguistics', *Vector 71* (Journal of the British Science Fiction Association), 2, 3, 14–23.

Weber, J.J. (ed) (1996) *The Stylistics Reader*, London: Arnold.

Weir, P. (dir) (1998) *The Truman Show*, Paramount Pictures.

Wells, H.G. (1901) *The First Men in the Moon*, London: Odhams Press.

Wells, H.G. (1906) *In The Days of the Comet*, London: Odhams Press.

Wells, H.G. (1914) *The World Set Free*, London: Odhams Press.

Wells, H.G. (1953) *The Time Machine*, London: Pan [1895].

Wells, H.G. (1975) *The War of the Worlds*, London: Pan [1898].

Wells, H.G. (1993) *The Shape of Things to Come*, London: Everyman [1933, Hutchinson].

Werth, P. (1987) 'Understanding understanding', *Journal of Literary Semantics*, XVI, 129–53.

Werth, P. (1994) 'Extended metaphor: a text world account', *Language and Literature*, 3, 2, 79–103.

Werth, P. (1995a) 'How to build a world (in a lot less than six days, and using only what's in your head)', in Green, K. (ed), 49–80.

REFERENCES

Werth, P. (1995b) '"World enough and time": deictic space and the interpretation of prose', in Verdonk, P. and Weber, J.J. (eds), 181–205.

Werth, P. (1999) *Text Worlds: Representing Conceptual Space in Discourse*, London: Longman.

West, G. (1930) *H.G. Wells*, London: Gerald Howe.

Whorf, B.L. (1957) *Language, Thought, and Reality: Selected Writings of Benjamin Lee Whorf* (edited by J.B. Carroll), Cambridge, Mass: MIT Technology Press.

Wilcox, F.L (dir) (1956) *Forbidden Planet*, Metro-Goldwyn-Mayer.

Williams, R. (1980) *Problems in Materialism and Culture*, London: Verso.

Wilson, D. (1975) *Presuppositions and Non-Truth-Conditional Semantics*, London: Academic Press.

Wollheim, D.A. and Carr, T. (eds) (1965) *The World's Best Science Fiction: 1965*, New York: Science Fiction Book Club.

Wolmark, J. (1994) *Aliens and Others: Science Fiction, Feminism and Postmodernism*, Iowa City: University of Iowa Press.

Zamiatin, Y. (1972) *We*, London: Penguin [1924, Dutton].

Zelazny, R. (1971) *The Doors of his Face, the Lamps of his Mouth, and Other Stories*, London: Faber & Faber.

INDEX